FILM	YEAR	DIRECTOR	STAR
The Four Feathers	1938	Zoltan Korda	Ralph Rich... C Aubrey Smith
Goodbye Mr Chips	1939	Sam Wood	Robert Do...
The Thief Of Bagdad	1939	Powell/Whelan Berger	Sabu, Co...
The Lion Has Wings	1939	Powell & Hurst	Ralph R...
The Spy in Black	1939	Michael Powell	Conrad...
Contraband	1939	Michael Powell	Conrad...

DENHAM STUDIO 1946-1950

FILM	YEAR	DIRECTOR	STAR
Odd Man Out	1946	Carol Reed	James Mason, Robert Newton, Kathleen Ryan, Cyril Cussack
Great Expectations	1946	David Lean	John Mills, Alec Guinness, Finlay Currie, Jean Simmons
Fame is The Spur	1947	Roy Boulting	Michael Redgrave, Rosamund John, Bernard Miles
Sleeping Car to Trieste	1948	John Paddy Carstairs	Jean Kent, David Tomlinson, Albert Lieven, Alan Wheatley
Hamlet	1948	Laurence Olivier	Laurence Olivier, Jean Simmoms, Basil Sidney, Terence Morgan
History of Mr Polly	1949	Anthony Pellisier	John Mills, Sally Ann Howes, Megs Jenkins, Finlay Currie
The Chiltern Hundreds	1949	John Paddy Carstairs	Cecil Parker, A E Mathews, David Tomlinson, Marjorie Fielding
The Perfect Woman	1949	Bernard Knowles	Patricia Roc, Nigel Patrick, Stanley Holloway, Miles Malleson
The Rocking Horse Winner	1950	Anthony Pellieser	John Mills, Valerie Hobson, John Howard Davies, Ronald Squire
Morning Departure	1950	Roy Baker	John Mills, Richard Attenborough, Lana Morris, Nigel Patrick

PINEWOOD STUDIOS 1950-1959

FILM	YEAR	DIRECTOR	STAR
Waterfront	1950	Michael Anderson	Robert Newton, Richard Burton, Kathleen Harrison
The Verger)		Ken Annakin	James Hayter, Kathleen Harrison
Mr Knowall) Trio	1950	Ken Annakin	Nigel Patrick, Anne Crawford
Sanatorium)		Ken Annakin	Michael Rennie, Jean Simmonds
So Long at the Fair	1950	Terrence Fisher	Jean Simmons, Dirk Bogarde, David Tomlinson, Honor Blackman
Hotel Sahara	1951	Ken Annakin	Peter Ustinov, Yvonne de Carlo, David Tomlinson, Albert Lieven
Appointment With Venus	1951	Ralph Thomas	David Niven, Glynis Johns, Kenneth More
Clouded Yellow	1951	Ralph Thomas	Trevor Howard, Jean Simmons, Barry Jones, Kenneth More
Night Without Stars	1951	Anthony Pellieser	David Farrar, Nadia Grey
Penny Princess	1952	Val Guest	Dirk Bogarde, Yolande Donlan, A E Mathews
Red Peppers)			Kay Walsh, Ted Ray
Fumed Oak) Meet Me Tonight	1952	Anthony Pellieser	Stanley Holloway, Betty Ann Davies
Ways And Means)			Valerie Hobson, Nigel Patrick
Genevieve	1952	Henry Cornelius	John Gregson, Dinah Sheridan, Kenneth More, Kay Kendall
Made in Heaven	1952	John Paddy Caratairs	David Tomlinson, Petula Clark, A E Mathews
Malta Story	1952	Brian Desmond Hurst	Alec Guinness, Jack Hawkins, Anthony Steel, Muriel Pavlow, Renee Asherton
A Day to Remember	1953	Ralph Thomas	Stanley Holloway, Joan Rice, Donald Sinden
You Know What Sailors Are	1953	Ken Annakin	Sarah Lawson, Michael Horden, Donald Sinden, Dora Bryan, Bill Kerr
Personal Affair	1953	Anthony Pellieser	Gene Tierney, Leo Genn, Glynis Johns, Pamela Brown
Doctor in The House	1953	Ralph Thomas	Dirk Bogarde, Kenneth More, James Robertson Justice, Donald Sinden, Kay Kendall, Donald Housten, Muriel Pavlow
Young Lovers	1954	Anthony Asquith	Odile Versois, David Knight, David Kosoff
One Good Turn	1954	John Paddy Carstairs	Norman Wisdom, Joan Rice, Thore Hird
Above Us The Waves	1954	Ralph Thomas	John Mills, John Gregson, Donald Sinden, Michael Medwin
Doctor At Sea	1955	Ralph Thomas	Dirk Bogarde, Bridget Bardot, James Robertson Justice
An Alligator Named Daisy	1955	J Lee Thompson	Donald Sinden, Diana Dors, Jean Carson,
Lost	1955	Guy Green	David Farrah, Julia Arnell, Joan Rice

cont. on back endpaper

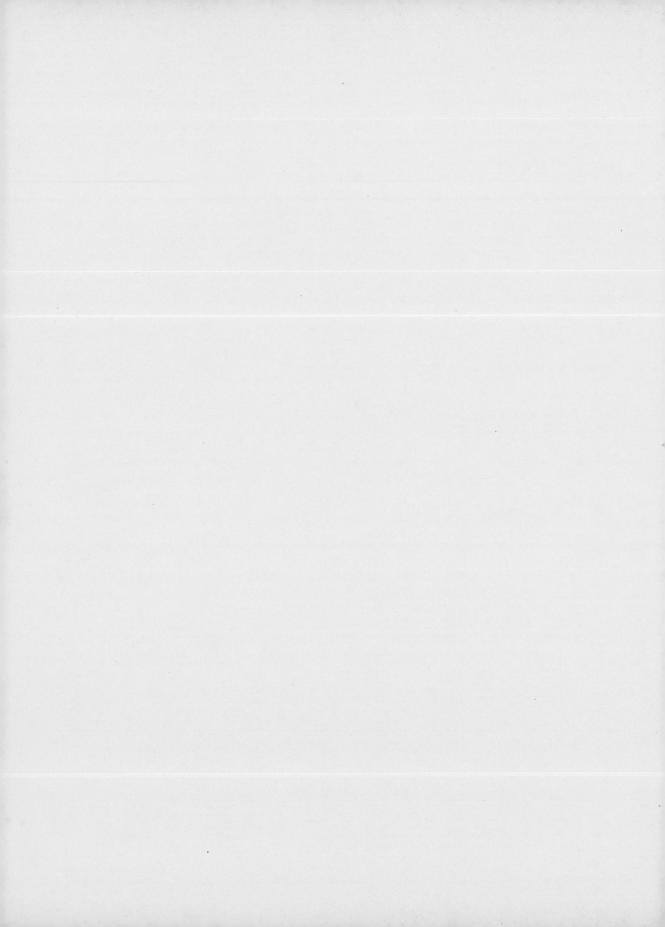

FLICKERING SHADOWS

A Lifetime in Film

To Sir John. (Johnnie)
with Grateful Thanks.

Mitch.

John Mitchell

Forewords by Sir John Mills CBE
and Ken Russell

First published in Great Britain 1997 by
Harold Martin & Redman Ltd.
The Wells House, Holywell Road, Malvern Wells,
Worcestershire WR14 4LH

British Library Cataloguing in Publication Data

A catalogue record for this book is available
from the British Library

ISBN 1 901394 01 8

Typeset and Designed by Harold Martin & Redman Ltd
Printed and Bound in Great Britain

Cover Photo:
The film crew on the set of *The Rocking Horse Winner*,
a John Mills Production starring John Mills and Valerie Hobson.

Contents

Author's Note

As someone who has worked in the film industry for a very long time I think it appropriate that the title of this book should be credited to the late Roger Jones, an original member of 'Location Caterers' who fed film crews everywhere in the world. At the end of a meal break, during which he had catered to the requirements of, literally, hundreds, he would survey the crowd, sigh and say, 'It's only flickering shadows on a silver screen.' It is people like Roger who helped film people like me keep our feet firmly on the ground.

Acknowledgements

I wish to express my thanks to the following for their support and encouragement:

Sir John Mills CBE   EON Productions

Lord Brabourne   Rank Organisation

Betty Box OBE   Warfield Productions

Ken Russell

Stills Photographers

Lord Snowdon   *Photographs from the*

Wilf Newton   *collections of Keith Pamplin,*

W. Daniels   *John Mitchell and the British*

Bob Penn   *Film Institute.*

George Whittear

Larry Ellis

Frank Connor

My particular thanks go to John Rowe for his insistence that I should complete the manuscript, for putting it on computer and his meticulous researching.

Crew Members

Ron Butcher   Austin Partridge

Jack de Conink   John Pitt

Danny Daniel   Trevor Rutherford

Jack Goodwin   Frank Slogett

Gus Lloyd   Basil Fenton Smith

Dudley Messenger   Charles Van De Goor

Keith Pamplin

Forewords

When John Mitchell wrote to tell me he was writing this book, not only was I delighted to hear from an old friend after many years, I was also thrilled to know that he was recording for posterity all those early years and the trials and tribulations of our business!

Flickering Shadows is for all those who ever longed to 'get into films', and for those who, like me, continue to be enthralled by the magic of the silver screen. John's informative style draws the reader into that fascinating world of film-making, film actors and that dedicated band of men and women who make up a film crew.

I am sure I can be accused of bias but, in my opinion, this book is not to be missed.

SIR JOHN MILLS, CBE

Generally, I hate soundmen. They're a pain in the neck. After your very best take they invariably say, 'Sorry, Gov, we'll have to go again.' 'Whats up?' you ask. 'Plane, train, automobile,' they'll answer, or anything else that comes to mind. They'll always have one excuse or another to cover the fact they screwed up. And whenever you are going for a take and it's all go, go, go, the sound department is always the one you are waiting for to say 'ready'. How many times have I said to the assistant director, 'Ready to go?' and heard him reply with a mixture of resignation and contempt, 'Still waiting for sound, Guv!' What is it with these guys?

I guess I've been spoiled, though, because for my first big feature film I was fortunate enough to have John Mitchell on sound. Apart from being master of his craft, he also had the art of being completely invisible. You never saw him and you never heard him either. But if ever you did seek him out – well out of everybody's way – he was always ready with a pixie smile to sort out your problems – an oasis of calm in a studio full of chaos. What better vantage point to observe the rise and full of the British Film industry?

KEN RUSSELL

Chapter One

THE KID AND THE MOVIES

My earliest memory of flickering shadows dates from 1921, when my mother took me to see Charlie Chaplin in *The Kid*. I was four years old and was living with my parents in Morley in Yorkshire.

I can vividly remember trying to work out how it was all happening. They could not be real people in front of me because they were so large and didn't talk, but at the same time they moved and opened their mouths. I supposed I couldn't hear them because a nice lady was busy playing lovely music on a piano all the time. And what was the function of the bright beam of light that poured from a little window high up on the wall behind us? I was fascinated by the dust motes rising up and dancing through it over my head to be swallowed up by the giant figure of Chaplin. That shaft of light was like a beacon and set the seal for me on a lifelong fascination with moving pictures. Many years later I found a kindred spirit in illustrious company; the very same dancing dust and smoke particles had captured young David Lean's imagination during early visits to his local cinema in Croydon.

Only six months after my mother had taken me to *The Kid* she died of rheumatic fever while we were on holiday in Kent. One of my last memories of her was me taking an embroidered and coloured card of *Little Boy Blue* up to her room, to help her get better. But even my skill with needle and wool could not turn the tide of her illness.

On the day of her funeral I was taken by tram into Maidstone to stay with a friend of my Aunt Gwen's, who was one of my father's sisters. No one had told me about my mother, but somehow even at that tender age I knew what had happened to her. What I could not understand was being left with a strange spinster lady, who gave me a shuttlecock and battledore and sent me out to the garden on my own; how on earth was I supposed to play with no one to return it?

My father left me with my Aunt Gwen, while he tried to sort out his life. Despite his grief, or maybe because of it, he took a decision that ensured our continuing happiness and spared us both so much of the sadness and sense of

Charlie Chaplin with Jackie Coogan in The Kid, *1920.*

loss my mother's death might otherwise have brought. Since her childhood my mother had had a close friendship with the lady I had always known as Auntie Maud. They were like sisters and when my father asked Auntie Maud to marry him, and she accepted, I was given a second mother in every living sense.

They set up home in Whitley Bay, not far from Newcastle, where I joined them some six months later. The rigours of life beside the North Sea soon palled and we moved inland to Jesmond, a suburb of Newcastle, where we set up home again and I went to my fourth school.

In the Depression of the twenties the north of England suffered more than most areas. Treats for children were in very short supply, though I was among the privileged group of children who had fathers in work; mine was a civil servant, working first for Customs & Excise and later, when we moved to Leeds, for the Ministry of Pensions. At school my playmates had fathers who had not worked for years and brothers who had never worked. One awful day a boy in my class was proudly showing off a tuppenny comic which his father had managed to buy him when I snatched it from his hand and in so doing tore it in half. The boy was in tears and our teacher tried earnestly to repair the damage. Next day my father came to school with a replacement, which I had to pay for with my week's tuppence pocket money.

Our move to Leeds introduced me to the Majestic Cinema, to which I was permitted infrequent visits to see films that my parents considered suitable. *The Great Fire of London* really stands out in my memory. It was long before the days of colour but the fire scenes were enhanced by a red filter placed in front of the projector lens; not only was the image on the screen in fiery red, the entire auditorium was bathed in a glow that made it appear that the cinema itself was on fire. For a small boy it was a very exciting experience.

The Majestic had an organ at the side of the auditorium. The organist accompanied all the films, creating sound effects to heighten the illusion: steam trains puffing and clattering across the screen; peals of thunder; horses' hoofs clip clopping through wild west streets.

Seeing Douglas Fairbanks Snr in *Robin Hood* was another landmark for me, with his jumping for the drawbridge as it carried him over the moat. I was also thrilled by *The Black Pirate* (probably the first Technicolor two-strip film), where he daringly plunges his dagger into the mainsail to slice down to the deck below, one of the film's many dramatic thrills.

From Newcastle we moved to Acton in West London, where my cinema going continued, highlighted by Saturday evening at the Globe in Acton High Street. This was peak time and people would wait patiently for the second 'house'. There were no continuous performances, so the patron was made to feel a valued client from the welcome of a magnificently uniformed commissionaire, who not only kept the orderly queues for the ninepenny seats, the one and threes and one and ninepennies in the front circle; he also exercised firm control over unsociable behaviour.

The Globe boasted a full orchestra as well as an organ; audiences expected a programme of a main and second feature, with stage show and newsreel – true value for money, free of boring advertisements and filled instead with wonderful trailers of forthcoming events.

On Saturday afternoon at the Crown Cinema seats were fourpence downstairs and sixpence in the circle. There were no tickets, just a hexagonal slab of metal which came clattering down a chute from the cashier, to be retrieved by the usherette who showed you to a seat pin-pointed by her wavering torch beam.

Sound had arrived by the time I was twelve. We weren't totally sold on the idea, though my life for one would have been rather different without it!

Several attempts by my mother to settle me into a school in my early teens finally saw me sitting the entrance examination at The City of London School at Blackfriars. The results were far from successful; the formidable headmaster, F R Dale, was not at all sure that he wanted me as a pupil. My maths was abysmal, I had no Latin and my French was pathetic. However, my mother finally persuaded him to take me into the classical 2b, for the not-so-bright boys, on the condition that I went to a crammer to improve my French.

My father tracked down a Monsieur De Bevaire who taught French at Battersea Polytechnic. He agreed to give me lessons six days a week during the summer holidays. This certainly gave me a wonderful grounding which stood me in good stead during my film career.

Wednesday afternoon at the City of London School was given over to sports. I have never been able to hit, catch or throw a ball, so I soon learned to dodge that chore to spend my afternoons at the newly built Savoy Cinema in East Acton. Only one problem stood in my way, where to find the sixpence

The 3rd Acton Club troop at summer camp. I am 6th in from the left.

for admission? At the start of term my father would purchase a book of tickets at one and threepence each for my lunch in the school dining-room. The meals were truly magnificent: joint of the day carved from under a counter-balanced plated dome, by a white coated chef in a tall hat. I found that a chap called Brass was happy to buy my daily ticket for one shilling. Already he showed signs of being a cut above the rest of us, even in his dress, for though we all wore a uniform of black jacket, striped trousers and white shirt with starched collar and tie, his was embellished with a brocade waistcoat across which stretched a gold watch chain and fob.

The next move was to buy from a pal called Dubery the sandwiches his mother had lovingly prepared for his lunch for the sum of sixpence. Dubery was an excellent sketch artist, a dab hand at drawing aeroplanes, particularly the front-line fighters of the day, Hawker Fury's and Gladiators. His drawings sold for tuppence each so that he earned sufficient to stave off his hunger in the tuck shop. I then had my admission to the Savoy afternoon matinee where I would settle down to an enjoyable show of two feature films with an excellent stage show thrown in, for me a much more enjoyable pastime than playing rugger, made even sweeter with a bag full of fig toffee and Dubery's sand-wiches.

At this time, the school film projector was the only piece of film equipment with which I was familiar; but then I discovered a wide selection of books on the subject at the library in Acton. One in particular was on sound recording, and this mysterious world intrigued me further.

It was no easier before the war than it is now for school leavers to find jobs; and I was not an exception. I had decided that I would not reach academic heights, certainly not university. Through the Public Schools Headmaster Conference I applied to be put on their appointments list. My first interview was at the Amalgamated Dental Company, where, surrounded by dentists' chairs, pincers and false teeth, I was relieved to find I was not chosen from my fellow applicants. Next was an interview with Shanks, the famous manufacturer of sanitary ware. Again I found with much relief I was not destined to spend my life bogged down in toilets.

My school had a very good system whereby old Citizens, as former pupils were known, made themselves available to talk to and advise boys about their particular profession. My form master listened to my request for him to see if there was anyone who was connected with films. A Mr Masterson was contacted, Managing Director of the American Western Electric Company in the UK, which,

Scouts' summer camp.

with the Radio Corporation of America, had a near monopoly in sound recording and reproduction equipment. An appointment was made for me, but although he was most helpful in answering questions, he was not over enthusiastic about my working in the film production business. I had already decided that making them had to be more exciting than just seeing them in a cinema, but he stressed the unstable state of British film production. During our talk he wheedled out of me that my other main interest was aircraft.

Masterson then asked to meet my father over lunch to tell him he had dissuaded me from films, but that he could give me an introduction to a friend who was principal of the aviation school at the famous De Havilland works at Stag Lane, Hendon. As I was too young for admittance to the school, he recommended I should try for a place at the Regent Street Polytechnic, in the School of Engineering; then he would interview me again to assess my suitability for a place at De Havillands.

My day was made complete with a tour of the factory where the famous De Havilland Tiger Moth and Rapide aeroplanes were being made and assembled. It was a far cry from the hi-tech computerised method of today's aircraft manufacturers. Fuselages and wings were made entirely of wood, mainly spruce, with fabric stretched over the framework to be treated with a spirit based dope which was brushed on, then allowed to dry and stretch the fabric drum-tight. In the assembly shop was a very special version of a Rapide passenger biplane, normally fitted out to carry up to six people. This one had large fuel tanks in place of seats in the main section of the fuselage; it was being prepared for the ill-fated attempt by Amy Johnson and her husband Jim Mollison to fly the Atlantic non-stop east to west.

That view of De Havillands made me sufficiently determined to make the aircraft industry my goal by enrolling at the Polytechnic. There I quickly settled into the curriculum, particularly enjoying the practical work in the workshop, the draughtsmanship, but still not the mathematics. I really had put aside my desire to work in films; my whole interest turned towards aircraft, especially as De Havilland had started to build an enormous plant at Hatfield where they were working on the first Comet. (Propellor driven, it went on to win the England-Australia air-race).

Then, by sheer chance, I bumped into an ex-school pal named Eric May. He was working in the film projection department at Ealing Studios, where his uncle was chief projectionist. As my interest was so obviously aroused by what he told me about his job he offered to get permission for me to visit the studios.

True to his word, the following weekend, he asked me to meet him at the main gate of Associated Talking Pictures Studio at Ealing Green. We passed the ever-watchful eye of Robbie, an ex-Guards Sergeant Major and commissionaire at the main gate, to enter the atmosphere of a real live studio. On our left was the canteen with the glamorous name of 'The Inn'; costumed extras were queuing outside for tea-break; their faces coloured in a strange bright orange make-up that I was to learn was needed for the black and white panchromatic film used in film cameras at that time. Across the street were the various departments: carpenters' shop, paint shop, plasterers' and property department, where the sets were prefabricated ready for assembly on the studio stage. Alongside the shooting stage were dressing-rooms, make-up and hairdressing departments, together with the cutting-rooms where editors worked away piecing together miles of film.

Across the corridor were heavy sound-proofed double doors leading through a sound trap that could be isolated by solenoid locks from the studio itself when the shooting light was on. After a few minutes the light changed to green and the solenoid clunked off, allowing the door to be pushed open. For the first time I heard 'two bells', the signal that it is clear for people to leave or

Associated Talking Pictures, Ealing Green.

enter the set, and stepped inside.

My first impression was one of bewilderment for it was fairly dark, and we were hemmed in behind high wooden structures leaving only a gap to walk through against the heavily padded rockwool insulated walls of the studio. Above, I could see a criss-cross of girders from which hung wooden cradles suspended by chains on which large black lamps were perched – these, I was to learn, were 'spot rails', the girders were the 'gantry'.

Eric whispered to me to be quiet as we stumbled along in the shadows and suddenly came into a brightly-lit town square full of people for the Gracie Fields film *Love Life and Laughter*. Everywhere were lamps and strange pieces of equipment behind which people were perched – at last I was actually experiencing the thrill of being on a film set. Everyone turned to look at the visitor, making my very self-concious, a feeling that I still have when stepping on to a strange set. Most directors do not like strangers; it is the accepted etiquette to ask permission of the first assistant director to come on. But from that moment I knew that films were in my blood for good. The thrill of anticipation and fascination has never left me.

I was allowed to stay and watch some real filming that day. Actors and their surroundings stood out against the lights as all around everyone else merged into shadows: the director beside his camera and crew, and the continuity girl perched on her stool, script, notebook and stop-watch at the ready. The electricians were waiting for the lighting cameraman's instruction to 'Put another wire on the 2K' or, 'Come down on the dimmer a touch', with at times 'Make it Chinese (or) English.' The chargehand property man stood ready to move a piece of set dressing, such as a vase or ornament to suit the camera, or to pour out a fresh glass of wine or cup of tea for the next take. Everyone on the studio 'floor' had his or her particular job to do when required. So often a first-time visitor will ask why there are so many people standing around, apparently with nothing to do. The answer is just that film making is very much a matter of time 'means money'; to have all the various specialists standing by to perform their roles without delay makes good economic sense – dabbing perspiration or tidying a hairstyle by make-up, or the painter dulling down a shiny door which is causing a 'flare' to the camera. Precious minutes can be saved if these people are to hand, which is why they are known as 'standbys'.

My visit came to an end, and I had seen more than enough to whet my appetite, but how to get through those gates past Robbie as a worker? It was

back to the drawing board and engineering school for me.

A few months later I had a call from Eric to tell me that he was leaving Ealing Studios to join John Logie Baird, the inventor of the Baird television system. To my delight Eric asked me if I would like his job at Ealing, working under his uncle. There was just one snag: his uncle would not be averse to receiving a small cash inducement for taking me on. I put it to my parents, who, long-suffering as they were, both agreed that if it was the life I would really like they would not stand in my way. Making aeroplanes was a respectable job, whilst somehow to be 'in films' was not quite nice; my poor mother had visions of her son being subjected to the attentions of loose women.

However, silver did cross the palm of Eric's uncle. I survived an interview with Bill Lott, the Studio Manager (father of Barbara Lott, the actress who played Ronnie Corbett's mother in TV's *Sorry*). In those days there was no formal apprenticeship, but Ealing did give its young intake a very good

On the set of Love
Life and Laughter.

grounding, at the same time requiring them to put in many hours of work for the princely sum of one pound per week, Monday to Saturday. (There was an extra five shillings if you worked on Sunday, and one and threepence supper money for working after eight o'clock.) I was in seventh heaven and waited impatiently for the two weeks to pass before Eric left for his new job in the new-fangled business called television.

The day finally came, and with it a decision from my father that I should make the journey from our home in Acton to the studios at Ealing Green on foot; he said it would be good for me! I could have journeyed by tram or ridden my bicycle, but had no thought of arguing with my father; besides, he walked to work in Westminster himself – a lengthy journey across the Royal Parks – and did so winter and summer for ten years.

So off to work in films I went with the added challenge of a three-mile walk there and back!

The main theatre and re-recording room, Associated Talking Pictures, Ealing Green.

Chapter Two

Ealing Studios

That first morning, 9 December 1933, I set out from home just after seven. Starting time was eight o'clock, but I did not want to be late on my first morning at work; and having previously made a test walk, I knew that this would give me ten minutes in hand.

I passed through the main gate under Robbie's watchful eye and made my way along a catwalk at the rear of the studio building to the main theatre projection room. There I clambered up a circular iron staircase to be confronted with a bank of projectors and sound reproducers that were already having their daily check-out. Arc lamps were trimmed with new carbons which were being burned in to form the perfect crater necessary to give a bright light with the minimum of flicker on the theatre screen. The sound heads had loops of film running, on which were recorded varying frequencies to allow the machines to be balanced equally to give identical results in the theatre below.

With an 'Excuse me, sir,' I made the fellow at the projector jump, and in answer to my request for Mr May, he laughed, telling me to call him Charlie and that 'Jags' May was not yet in. This was my first lesson; Christian names were the order of the day in the film world, except of course when speaking to people like the director or producer.

If I had any delusions of grandeur on my first day in films they were soon shattered by Charlie, who called me away from my fascinated inspection of the projectors to tell me that Jags liked to have a cup of tea with a slice of bread and dripping from the 'Inn' each morning on his arrival, and not to forget to ask for plenty of beef jelly on the bread, 'Oh, you may as well bring me the same,' he added. That brought me down to earth with a bang.

When Jags did arrive he swallowed the tea, ate his bread and dripping, and said that he would pay me later but that I was to join him in the 'BP' booth. Not wanting to show my ignorance of the fact I didn't know what 'BP' stood for, I followed him back along a catwalk, down some iron stairs and into a room built into the wall of the studio, or 'stage', a hangar-like building in which the filming took place. Inside was an enormous Ross projector pointing

Exterior and interior shots of the Majestic Cinema where I spent much of my youth.

its Zeiss lens through a porthole into the stage. The projector was very steady and was used to show moving scenes of roads and other backgrounds previously filmed on location. The picture was shown onto a large translucent screen set up in the stage. On the other side was placed a horse buggy in which Fay Compton and her companion Esmé Church would sit to play their next scene from the script of *Autumn Crocus*. With a property man shaking the buggy to give a semblance of motion, they and the moving projected background were re-photographed to create the illusion of them riding along a road in the Austrian Tyrol. Overhead, suspended on a long telescopic arm, was the microphone which picked up their speech. This, I learned, was Back Projection – BP.

Jags soon had me hard at work sorting out the numbered rolls of film which tallied with the scene numbers in the script, these having been prepared in advance in the cutting-rooms.

Ealing Studios were run by Basil Dean. He was a London theatrical producer famous for his success in the West End and feared for his irascible temper. The moment Mr Dean swept past Robbie's main gate in his Lancia limousine, everyone was alerted by Westy, the head telephonist. I was soon to find out that if his first call was the main theatre to view either the previous day's rushes or edited scenes, we had to have the arc lamps 'struck up', so that the projectionist could start the film rolling on the single buzzer signal given from below as Mr Dean lowered himself into his chair. One long buzz signalled 'Stop the projector' – looking through the porthole, one would see Basil Dean stride from the theatre on his way to strike terror in the next victim on his list.

On that first day we had successfully completed a number of scenes against the background of alpine scenery, with the next one running on the projector and I was busy rewinding the used rolls through black velvet, my hands protected by white fabric gloves to avoid any scratching of the film's emulsion. Suddenly the buzzer signalled 'stop' – Jags switched off the projector, swinging the dowser down over the high intensity arc lamp. The door of the booth crashed open to reveal a very irate man, eyes staring from behind thick-lensed glasses, who screamed in a distinctive high-pitched voice that I was to get to know alarmingly well. A scratch had appeared on the projected image on the screen, which Basil Dean said Jags May had caused. It was a ridiculous accusation resulting in a heated argument. Jags had obviously had similar run-ins before with the managing director and this one ended with him telling Dean to 'stick his job.' For a moment there was quiet, then Basil Dean stepped back to scream 'You're fired.' In those days his word was law, there was no recourse to a union shop steward to appeal for reinstatement, so poor old May collected his cards and coppers and left the studio, not only never to return, but never to work in a film studio again.

So ended my first day in the film industry. In retrospect I might never have had a career in films if Jags May had been fired a week earlier, for without my meeting him through Eric I would have had no introduction. I have often wondered how an alternative career in aviation would have turned out – would I have been involved in the building of Concorde or the Harrier Jump Jet – who knows?

By the following day a replacement chief projectionist had been found, which taught me the valuable lesson that no one is indispensable, however important their function. Percy Moss, the new chief, was an extrovert character, whose brash manner showed no fear of Basil Dean. We ploughed through the many rolls of back-projection plates of the Austrian scenery with no further problems. This was not the case in the studio, where two ponies were pulling the buggy, trotting on a treadmill in front of the screen. Suddenly the treadmill jammed, the ponies plunged forward and broke through the translucent screen just like a circus act jumping through a paper hoop. Basil Dean threw up his hands in despair, storming off the set, and delegating the task of replacing the screen and putting things right to his first assistant, a tall, willowy young man by the name of Carol Reed. Like David Lean, his film career had its workaday beginnings. They both became world famous directors knighted by the Queen for services to the film industry.

My next job was in the small projection room where editors viewed their 'rough cuts' – assemblies of sequences made up from hundreds of small sections of picture and sound film which they spliced together. Until the final process that produces the 'married' print that is run in cinemas, picture and sound are always separate, giving more flexibility of handling during editing. That's what makes the familiar clapper-board indispensable to film editors – from it, they synchronise the two.

Many times I had an unexpected visitor in my little theatre – Gracie Fields, whose dressing room was just down the corridor. She would look round the door with a, 'Hallo luv, can I come in?' This was heady stuff for a lad not quite seventeen – in the mid-1930s she was the most famous and highest paid British film star, earning £30,000 per film!

That small cutting-room theatre might well have caused an early end to my career when I was running a short 'rough cut' sequence for the Austrian film editor of *Autumn Crocus*. With the projector laced up and running, I noticed through the porthole a tiny spot of light in the centre of the screen, which slowly increased in size and colour. Turning to the machine, I saw that the film had jammed in the projector gate. The safety shutter had not closed as I switched off, and a fire spread up to the top spool box, whose doors were open. This common practice was against all the rules. Suddenly Stern, the Austrian editor, crashed through the door, with a large fire extinguisher belching foam that he sprayed all over the projector and me. When the flames had been extinguished I was faced with reporting to the chief projectionist. The incident could have been much more serious, for in those days cine film was made from celluloid nitrate and was highly inflammable. The studio manager, Bill Lott, had me up before him but did not fire me on the spot, which was normal practice for such a misdemeanour; instead I was given the task of stripping down the projector mechanism, cleaning the lens and spool boxes, not to mention the projector room walls and floor. So I learnt a salutary lesson – always to treat film with the greatest respect and never to run a projector with spool box doors open.

It was not long before I could see the limitations of being a projectionist – the real hub of the film business was what went on on the sound stage. I spent every available moment, using any excuse and opportunity to creep through the heavy padded sound trap doors and onto the stage, where I would stand in the shadow of the film set to watch a film being made.

In those early days at Ealing Studios the sound recording equipment was housed in sound-proofed booths mounted on huge castors which enabled them to be pushed from set to set and sited wherever the sound recordist could watch the actors through double-glazed windows. The sound booth was divided by a partition. In the smaller section was housed the actual sound recording machine; in the more spacious section were the amplifiers and mixing panel presided over by an ex-BBC sound engineer, Bungy Williams. I had apparently caught the eye of Bungy, who asked me what my ambitions were; whether I would like to join the sound department if a vacancy occurred. I had supposed the camera department would offer the most obviously glamorous jobs, although my choice would have been the cutting-rooms, if I had been given the opportunity.

However, in those days when there always seemed to be a crisis in the film industry, jobs were scarce and it would have been stupid to turn down such an offer. Not long afterwards, an opportunity did arise; I became a junior recordist and began my induction into the very involved process of putting sound onto film. My first task was to learn about dark room practice; how to load and unload exposed and unexposed film into magazines in total darkness. The golden rule was dinned into me; never to switch on a light until the film was either safely in its black bag in a taped film can, or in a magazine with the lid securely screwed on. Just one comment was made in this respect; if a mistake was made in accidentally exposing the film, 'Just don't bother to come in tomorrow' – it was the 'sack' and they meant it.

Soon the unfamiliar became an everyday matter of procedure. I settled into my new job, rewarded with an increase in salary from one pound to thirty shilling per week.

The next two years kept me very busy; a period which was a peak for British films. The first film I worked on in that airless sound booth was *The Shakespeare Murder Mystery*, for Fox British Productions, an offshoot of the American Fox Company. This was the product of a piece of British government legislation that required foreign films shown in this country (which in effect meant American) to finance an equivalent footage of a British-made product from their cinema profits. On paper this appeared to be a very good way to foster our British film industry. In practice it resulted in the making of very cheap films that became known as 'quota quickies.' What had not been appreciated was that the law called only for a footage requirement, with no proviso on minimum cost. Full length productions were made in ten days on a minimum budget, with cheap actors, poor scripts, minimal sets and the lowest rates that technicians could be persuaded to accept.

The Shakespeare Murder Mystery was directed by Al Parker, who had been responsible for the Douglas Fairbanks Snr film *The Black Pirate*. Al was a man of fiery temperament who was not averse to kneeling in front of an actor not giving the performance expected of him, hands clenched together, head upturned to heaven, saying, 'Jiste all Chrity, give me strength.' I remember well one Saturday afternoon when Al did just this with Anna Lee; a beautiful young, inexperienced actress, who had to cry real tears in front of the camera. Not one tear drop would trickle down her cheek until Al sent for an onion from the canteen which was peeled by the propman and held under her eyes by the director. By this time the poor girl was terrified, tears gushed down her face as she sobbed her heart out, so much so that shooting on her had to be stopped for the day.

'Quota quickies' did some good in offering a proving ground for many a

director or technician whose first chance to gain experience would stand them in good stead for the future. One ten-day production that was not an American 'quota quickie' was financed by Hinds, the high street jeweller. It was in fact the first 'Hammer' production, the forerunner of the famous post-war horror movies. The film was called *The Public Life of Henry The Ninth* and starred Leonard Henry, who was a well-known variety and radio comic. The whole film was shot in two weeks, and the Hammer logo with Bombardier Billy Wells (later the famous Rank man with the gong) was filmed one lunch hour. For Hammer the former heavy-weight boxer was filmed beating out a horseshoe on an anvil. The background music for the film was recorded on a Saturday, with the film being dubbed and re-recorded on the Sunday, taking twenty-four hours of non-stop work. Total production time to delivery was three weeks in spite of which it was a very successful box office draw with cinema patrons.

By now Carol Reed had been given his first assignment as director, with a

Cast and crew of The Public Life of Henry the Ninth – *the first Hammer Production, 1934. I am sitting on the floor in the middle of the picture.*

film starring Hughie Green, who was then touring the music halls as 'Hughie Green and his Gang.' Playing opposite him in *Midshipman Easy* was Margaret Lockwood. My most notable memory is of the film set of the square-rigged man o'war, rather like the *Bounty* I was to work on fifty years later, which was built some forty feet up on tubular scaffolding high above the roof tops of Ealing Green to give un-hindered sky-line to the camera. Carol Reed followed this with a production of *Laburnum Grove*, the successful J B Priestly play, this time with a star-studded cast of Edmund Gwenn, Cedric Hardwicke, Victoria Hopper and Katie Johnson. After this came *The Lonely Road* starring Clive Brooke.

Two very prestigious films were also made during that period at Ealing by an Italian, Count Ludovico Toeplitz. The first was *Loves of a Dictator* with Clive Brooke and Madeleine Carroll, which included a brilliant performance by the then unknown actor Emlyn Williams. The trade paper *Variety* described *Loves of a Dictator* in 1936 as 'one of the most lavish costume pictures that has yet to come out of England'. It was supposed to have cost 500,000 dollars. Certainly the sets were enormous and lavish, with a huge exterior flight of steps which filled the whole of the Ealing back lot.

The second film was *The Beloved Vagabond* with Maurice Chevalier in the lead, filmed with a dual language cast to provide a French and English version. This was a laborious method of producing multi-language films before the technique of post-synchronising dialogue, which involved re-voicing by careful writing of dialogue in the new language to match the lip movements, hence the term 'lip synchronisation.' Directed by Curtis Bernhardt and photographed by Franz Planer, it was an interesting film to work on, particularly from a sound point of view. After completing a scene with the English-speaking cast, we would replace those actors who were not bilingual and go through the whole process a second time. Maurice Chevalier, in his role as a French artist, also had to sing, which presented another poser for sound. In those days he did not like to sing to playback, which meant that we had the absurd situation of having an orchestra hidden out of sight with only the conductor able to see the singer by peeping round the corner of the set. Meanwhile, Chevalier would be chased by a microphone on a boom as he moved about, presenting terrible problems in maintaining any consistent balance of voice and orchestra. However, a result was achieved, which seemed quite good when the film was recently shown on television.

The enormous success that Basil Dean had had with the Gracie Fields film

Sally in Our Alley, followed by *Love Life and Laughter* and *Sing As We Go,* set him looking for another star with the same popularity and his eye fell on George Formby, who was little known to cinema audiences before 1935, but a firm favourite with the summer masses who flocked to Blackpool during the Wakes weeks, to watch him raise the roof at the Hippodrome. George had made a few very small budget films at the studio in Manchester owned by Frank Randle (himself a former variety comedian) who had put Arthur Lucan and Kitty McShane onto the cinema screen in *Old Mother Riley.*

George's wife Beryl had a reputation in marked contrast to George's easy-going manner. She had been the champion clog dancer of Lancashire before leaving the stage to marry George. Now acting as his agent and manager, she negotiated a contract that put him into the top salary bracket. Beryl vetted all of his scripts, making sure that his love scenes were not too amorous. His leading lady had to be approved by her, making certain that she was neither too pretty nor too young.

A script for a film called *No Limit* was written for the George Formby gormless character by Walter Greenwood, set against a background of the famous TT Races in the Isle of Man. It was to be directed by Monty Banks, an

George Formby in No Limit.

American Italian who later married Gracie Fields. Monty had come into films via the Hal Roach comedies and his experience of making slapstick comedies in the States made him the ideal person, in Basil Dean's eyes, to take George in hand in his first big film.

The production was planned for June of 1935 to tie in with the races and provide footage of the crowds and riders from camera positions set up around the course over the three race days. I had never been away on location before so it was a great thrill to be told that I was allocated to the production as recordist, which meant that I would run the recording machine under the watchful eye of Val Valentine, the head of Ealing Sound Department.

The studio was very busy and the permanently employed staff were all working on other productions, so the other two members of the crew had to be recruited from elsewhere. The maintenance engineer came from HMV Records, never having seen film recording equipment. Our boom operator had been a barn storming pilot who gave five-shilling flights to people foolhardy enough to trust themselves in his Gypsy Moth biplane. By this time I had been in films for eighteen months, which made me a veteran along with Valentine.

We set off in convoy, destination Liverpool, where the Isle of Man steam

packet company's cargo carrier *Peveril* made regular crossings to Manx. Our *Above: George Formby*
stopover was at the Stork Hotel in Liverpool, in those days a good commercial *Left: Beryl Formby*
house (and one that I was to use many times during my war years in the
Navy).

Next morning we drove to the docks, where after weighing our sturdy
left-hand-drive American REO Speedwagon trucks, they were hoisted on board.
Peveril was due to sail on the evening tide, so the rest of the day was our own.
Val had not deigned to come with us, having slept in, after a heavy night spent
sampling local Liverpool beer. He had the float, some eighty pounds, out of
which bills were to be paid. An hour before sailing we joined the ship and
selected our bunks in the saloon. It was my first experience of the sea which I
was looking forward to with mixed feelings – would I be sick or would I find
my sea legs?

As it came near to departure time there was still no sign of Val; not that
there was much we could do but keep hoping for him to show up in time.

Then we saw his shambling figure staggering along the dockside, clutching in his arms a large Winchester bottle of red liquid. Clambering up the gangway he tottered towards me, leered at me muttering 'Mitch, you bitch,' then staggered to the saloon, where he eyed us all as he put his hand into his hip pocket. Suddenly he was sober, crying out 'Christ, I've lost it.' His pocket had been picked and not one single note of that float remained. It was my first contact with an alcoholic but my education was soon to be expanded.

Leaving the dockside and steaming down the Mersey was a thrill I was to experience many times in my life. The Skipper and his mate were great characters. Apart from Val sleeping off his drunken stupor, we all lingered late into the night on the bridge having hit the swell of the Irish Sea as we cleared the mouth of the river. Happily I was not sick, probably because everything was new and exciting. Even turning-in on my bunk and feeling the rolling motion of the ship was OK and I was soon fast asleep.

We steamed into Douglas harbour and waited for the trucks to be swung ashore before driving off to our hotel headquarters. A very chastened Val had quite a bit of explaining to do when he met the production manager, who asked for his expenses' details and bills.

The filming got under way with scenes in which George and Florence Desmond played a most unlikely couple. They had some typically comic sequences, interspersed with songs from George and ukulele, some with Flo Desmond.

I had developed a stye on each eye which Beryl Formby noticed and insisted on treating for me. Every morning she used to inspect them, bathe them with lotion and complete the treatment by rubbing each one with her gold wedding ring. It was a remedy that I had never heard of, but there was no doubting its effectiveness, for in a few days both styes had vanished completely. Certainly this side of Beryl's character was one that was never mentioned in contrast to her fearsome reputation when it came to negotiating deals for George.

The Isle of Man was bursting at the seams with thousands of TT Motor Cycle fans. An even greater excitement for me was to find that our hotel housed the formidable Italian Guzzi motor cycle team headed by the legendary rider, Teni. They had taken over a block of lock-up garages where the bikes, in Italian racing red, were kept under strict security, for even in those days there was intense interest shown by rival teams such as the British Nortons, whose rider Stanley Woods was world champion. Practice laps of the road circuit, which was only available for a couple of hours in the first light of dawn, were closely watched by 'spies' from the other camps who took up positions at known problem corners and sections of the course, noting times and riding techniques for comparison with their own teams.

We had been given permission by the race authorities to shoot scenes during the lead up to the actual races, so that George Formby could appear on the starting grid with his absurd Shuttleworth motor cycle, made in his mother's backyard in Wigan. The waiting crowds in the grandstands loved it and co-operated in mock starts right through to the final scene where George, who had run out of petrol at Governors Bridge, pushed his weird contraption in a state of total exhaustion, egged on by Florence Desmond and the pit crew, to collapse at the chequered flag.

My first location work was a revelation to me. I learned a great deal, probably much more than I might have done if poor old Val had not so often been suffering from too much drink from the previous night. I often found him slumped in his chair in the sound truck, when I opened up in the morning to carry out the line-up tests of the recorder. Our equipment was powered from large rechargeable batteries which also supplied power to run the picture camera. These were charged overnight ready for the next day's shooting; without their power we were unable to produce the three-phase supply. On one of Val's bad nights he had made his way to the truck, fearful of being left behind for an early call and had accidentally knocked the switch of the battery charger to the 'off' position. By the time this was noticed it was too late to do anything about it. I spent the day praying that our half-charged batteries would hold out, or that we would finish early, but fate was against us. Monty Banks decided to take advantage of a sunny evening to film a scene on Onchan Head with George, Flo and a donkey. It was a longish scene ending with George mounting the stubborn moke and followed by Flo smacking its rear to get it moving. By the time we were ready to shoot, our batteries were very low and the generator was running slow which meant that the camera would also run at far less than its twenty-four frames per second. The same was true of the sound recorder. The consequences were too awful to contemplate: on the screen the action would be speeded up when projected at the normal rate and the voices would rise in pitch to match it. There was nothing we could do – Val was already well into his second bottle of scotch. I just hoped that the speed would not be too much below normal.

In those days there was a delay while the 'rushes' were processed in the laboratories in London, then synchronised in the studio cutting-rooms, before being sent back to the location ready for running in a local cinema for director and crew. I spent days in agony waiting for the arrival of these particular scenes because I was quite sure that there would be trouble when they were shown. The lights dimmed and that day's work started to unwind on the screen. To begin with everything was fine. The first shots in the donkey scene were OK too. There was no sign of their being other than correct speed – maybe I had exaggerated the problem. We came to George mounting his steed. At first it was quite normal but gradually began to gather speed until he was frantically kicking the donkey with Flo smacking away like someone demented. I shrank into my seat terrified that there would be an almighty row when the lights went up. Suddenly the whole crew started to roar with laughter and carried on even when the lights had been turned on; loudest of them all was Monty Banks. Very little in the way of an inquest was held, but it was another lesson learnt for me – never take chances, always speak up, even if it causes annoyance at the time, for one will never be thanked days later at rushes, for a disaster on the screen.

No Limit was a huge success and George Formby was transformed overnight from a music hall entertainer to film star, making many films at Ealing. He long remained a firm favourite with his ukulele and toothy grin.

Soon after *No Limit* was completed I was assigned to a new production by a British production company, Phoenix Films, which had been formed by a young production manager turned producer called Hugh Percival, and an illustrious London stage director, Reginald Denham. Their first film was a who-dunnit, set at the BBC in their new headquarters in Lansdown Place; the title was *Death at Broadcasting House*. It was a film with a very modest budget, scripted by Val Gielgud, brother of John Gielgud, and starring Ian Hunter, Donald Wolfit and the then unknown Jack Hawkins. They filmed it at the Wembley studios of British Fox, and it was quite a success.

Their second production, *The Silent Passenger*, a Dorothy L. Sayers story, was filmed at Ealing after they had secured release through Associated Film Distributors owned by Associated Talking Pictures. Hugh Percival was a tall, dark, bespectacled man who wore a ginger harris tweed suit with patch pockets, a brown shirt and tie, and heavy brown bespoke boots which were polished to a mirror-like gloss. He smoked an enormous Dunhill briar pipe, and peered at you over a bushy black moustache. I met up with Hugh following the war working on *Our Man in Havana*, for which he was the producer, and *The*

Prince and the Showgirl, which he supervised as production executive. Never, ever did I see him dressed in anything else – same suit, same colour Harris tweed, same boots, glasses and pipe. Curiosity got the better of me whilst we were working on *The Prince and the Showgirl* in 1956 – I just had to ask him if they were the originals from 1934. He fixed me with his quizzical look, puffed a cloud of smoke from the Dunhill pipe and said, 'Take five for the suit, take six for the shoes.'

I worked on one more Phoenix film production, *Calling the Tune*, which told the lifestory of the gramophone. For a soundman it was a very interesting project, harking back to the early days of acoustic recording when the famous Charlie Penrose used to sing his 'laughing policeman' song into what looked like a large megaphone to which a sapphire needle was fixed on a membrane at the narrow end. This vibrated to cut a groove of varying depth on a rotating cylinder of wax. I always remember my father telling me of his elder brother buying one of these cylindrical machines from Gamages by mail order. If you bought twelve cylinder records you were given the spring clockwork player free!

Many celebrities had parts in *Calling the Tune*. George Robey did one of his acts, updated to suit the times with, I remember, a little song that described the then new Belisha beacons as 'Globular Appendages.' Sir Cedric and Lady Hardwicke performed a scene from Shakespeare and we had a recording session with Henry Wood conducting the London Symphony Orchestra playing the music from *The Flying Dutchman*.

During my time at Ealing the name of Alexander Korda became increasingly influential in the British film industry. Korda had come to this country in 1932, having made films in Berlin and Paris. With him he brought a script for a film entitled *The Private Lives of Henry VIII*. He rented studio space at British and Dominion Studios and cast Charles Laughton in the lead. The film cost £60,000 and grossed half-a-million dollars in its first year. It made Charles Laughton a world-famous star; it made Alexander a greatly sought-after film-maker; and it made the Prudential Insurance Company realise that a lot of money could be made from investing in films. Such was their enthusiasm that they approached Korda with the offer to build him a studio where he could continue to make his films.

It was always understood that Korda envisaged a 'one film' studio where he could indulge in his dream to make films about the British Empire. This was not to be the case, for the Prudential saw that films were making enormous

*Denham
Studios.*

profits in America. Their plan was to build an exceptional studio, in effect a British Hollywood, in which to make films for American filmgoers in particular. For this purpose 130 acres were purchased at Denham in Buckinghamshire, where in 1934 the foundations were laid for seven sound stages, some as big as any in California. They were serviced by a corridor nearly a quarter of a mile long, down which were the dressing-rooms, make-up rooms, offices, theatres, sound and camera departments, carpenters and plasterers shops, plus a power house that could have serviced a small town.

There was also an enormous exterior 'back lot' where Korda filmed many of the scenes for *Things to Come* during the construction period of the studios. One thing the architects did forget was to provide the editors with their cutting-rooms. They were finally situated in the converted stables of the original mansion house of Denham Place, which Korda used as offices.

In 1935, everyone in the film industry was talking about the operation at Denham, not least myself. I had driven out several times to watch its progress, marvelling at the scale of the project. By now I was a boom operator at Ealing Studios; and with an eye to the future, I thought it would be a good move if I could join Korda's London Film Productions, where the latest sound equipment was being installed. Fate again favoured me. Western Electric were the equipment suppliers; their General Manager was the Mr Masterson who had dissuaded me at my school from joining the film business. I wrote to him saying that I was now in my third year in 'sound' at Ealing Studios, and asked if he could arrange an interview with A W Watkins, Korda's director of sound. This he was kind enough to do and I met 'Watty' who offered me a job as boom operator. So, in May 1936 I gave in my notice to Ealing to join Korda's new 'empire' at Denham.

London Film Productions Sound Truck.

Chapter Three

PRE-WAR DENHAM

My first complete film on joining Denham was also the first to be made in England using the three-strip Technicolor process. This brought true colour to the screen using technical wizardry that involved a specially designed camera, through which ran three films, each sensitive to either red, green or blue. A whole range of carbon arc lamps were designed and manned by a large team of electricians and very strict rules of procedure, that had never been required with black and white cinematography, were adhered to. For this first British production, the exposed negatives were sent to the Technicolor laboratories in Hollywood for processing, while a UK plant was being built near what is now Heathrow airport. In spite of pushing budgets through the ceiling, audience figures showed that colour had big pulling power.

The film was called *Wings of the Morning* and starred Henry Fonda who had made a great hit in an earlier Technicolor film, *The Trail of the Lonesome Pine*, in which the magnificent scenery of the American west had been displayed to its full glory.

The Technicolor three-strip camera showing its mechanism.

Wings of the Morning had a horse racing background for which the soft colours of the English countryside were ideal. Two-thirds was filmed out of doors, much of it in the grounds of nearby Denham Court. A large number of scenes were shot with real gypsies in an encampment complete with traditional cluster of horse-drawn caravans, wood fires, children scurrying about and lurchers lying sound asleep or getting under everyone's feet.

Henry Fonda and Annabela in Wings of the Morning.

With the pressure of the budget, our irascible producer Robert T Kane was calling for longer and longer hours as the film progressed. In those days there was no overtime pay. We were employed for a six-day week, which meant he could work us outside at Denham Court during the daylight hours and then return to the studio sound stage, where an identical encampment had been created for night-time shooting. For a working day that often lasted from seven in the morning to ten or eleven at night I took home £6 a week.

The crew weren't alone in feeling the strain. On one occasion in the studio the director, Harold Schuster, was arranging a set-up with Ray Rennahan, the famous Technicolor cameraman, when he became aware of a tall gypsy hanging around the camera and getting in the way. With stubble on his chin, a scar on his cheek and an insane leer, the poor fellow was obviously mentally retarded. But his loose-limbed shuffle, with his head on one side, and constant interruptions finally made Schuster snap. The production manager was sent for to deal with the problem and the unwanted 'extra' was paid off with a fiver – five times the normal daily rate for an extra in 1936.

Order was restored and shooting continued until we heard strange animal noises from high up in the gantry among the huge carbon arc lamps. Leaning over the safety rail was our gypsy friend making babbling noises and grinning down at us. Schuster stopped work and refused to continue until the idiot was removed. Security men climbed up to tussle with him and managed to bring him down to the stage floor, where he broke away and made a rush at the director. There, confronting him, he tore off his hat, peeled off a false nose and wig to reveal Henry Fonda!

Schuster took it well and Henry agreed to go quietly on condition that his £5 note was signed by the director and crew. Maybe it was his subtle way of

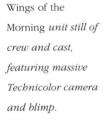

Wings of the Morning unit still of crew and cast, *featuring massive Technicolor camera and blimp.*

protesting to Robert T Kane for the hours he was making us all work.

Technicolor featured too in the first film I worked on with Herbert Wilcox and Anna Neagle, *Victoria The Great,* though it was only used in the final scenes showing the celebrations surrounding Queen Victoria's Diamond Jubilee. This may have been due in part to the trouble Herbert had in raising money to make the film. His approach to RKO in Hollywood for finance produced the initial reply, 'Not with Neagle playing the Queen.' They finally bowed to his insistence, 'No Anna – no film', by offering fifty percent of the budget, leaving Herbert to scour the City for the other half, which he gathered in dribs and drabs during the filming.

Herbert Wilcox and Anna Neagle were one of the first famous British film couples I worked with. Before the First World War Herbert had been a professional billiard player in Brighton. When the war started he had joined the army and later transferred to the Royal Flying Corps, which Anna Neagle proudly commemorated by always wearing a magnificent diamond-encrusted wings brooch that Herbert had given her.

Anna had started her career in the chorus line. I was never sure how Herbert had got into films but like most directors in the 1930s he dressed and behaved in the most gentlemanly of manners. We all wore collars and ties then and Herbert set the tone by always appearing immaculately turned out in a blue pin-striped suit, white shirt, gold cuff-links and subdued patterned tie, topped with a blue overcoat with velvet collar, his hair sleek and well-brilliantined, not a strand out of place.

Anna was equally smart and even on set the couple never lost the graciousness they carried with them. If Anna made a slip, or missed her marks for the camera, Herbert would always say reassuringly, 'Not your fault, Anna dear.'

Victoria The Great provided the audience with the queen's story from her earliest years to her Diamond Jubilee. It dealt with her courtship and marriage to Prince Albert and an attempt on Victoria's life which was thwarted by Albert's bravery. For Anna and Anton Walbrook, who played the Prince Consort, it provided a great opportunity to establish themselves as stars of film dramas.

In Anna's case this was no small task, for the script required her to span Victoria's life from the age of eighteen, when she was woken one morning by the Duke of Wellington (played by C Aubrey Smith) to be told that she was queen, to the elderly lady most of us recognise from photographs. She always had a wonderful complexion and with her hair worn down below her shoulders in the first scene she looked every inch the young queen. As she matured, particularly after the death of Albert, the make-up department had to start ageing her and by the time she was playing the queen near the end of her life this was taking hours. Even producing wrinkles was a laborious process in which cotton wool was twisted into the three- or four-inch lengths to be stuck onto the skin with colodion and then built up with make-up.

The film was made on a shoestring with great skill. The sets were a masterpiece of ingenuity which, with the clever use of furniture, drapes and ornaments, masked its low budget.

When it was released it proved to be a great success, not only in Britain but in America too. RKO came back to Herbert Wilcox straightaway asking for another Queen Victoria film, this time to be made entirely in colour and at their expense. Herbert was always a wily old bird and already had the script they wanted entitled *Sixty Glorious Years*. He was also master of public relations and managed to get an audience with King George V who gave permission for us to film at Buckingham Palace, Windsor Castle and Balmoral. This was unheard of. In fact on the rare occasions that newsreel crews had been allowed in to shoot the royal family just getting into their car in the palace courtyard, they all had had to wear morning dress!

At Buckingham Palace we filmed in the quadrangle. At Windsor we filmed extensively in the castle precincts, the gardens and mews. Then we moved north to film at Balmoral.

Once again Herbert's sense for publicity came to the fore. He had two additional coaches added to the night train to Aberdeen for our exclusive use. He also contacted the press in Scotland and the BBC, well in advance of arrival, with the result that when we pulled into Aberdeen station at eight o'clock in the morning there was a crowd of several thousand that would do credit today to stars like Madonna, waiting to catch a glimpse of Anna. As the train gently pulled to a stop, she came to the door of her carriage wearing a magnificent mink coat, gave her by now familiar regal wave and announced, 'Please don't let my poor people be crushed', in an equally regal voice.

These royal locations gave us all we needed for exterior scenes but for the interior ones we had to rely on studio sets, meticulously, though not expensively, constructed to match the interiors of the royal palaces. Some of the long rooms were built in perspective, whilst others with very high ceilings were built to a height of twenty-five feet or so, above which a very clever artist at Denham called Papa Day created what were known as 'glass-shots'. He used to paint on

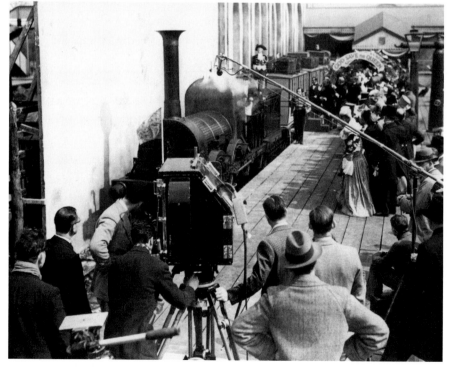

On the set of Victoria The Great. *To the right of the top picture I am operating the microphone boom.*

Filming Sixty
Glorious Years – *we
were the first film
unit to be allowed to
shoot inside the
grounds of Windsor
Castle.*

glass the continuation of the walls and ceiling, complete with all the details of vaulting and even chandeliers. The camera filmed the actors playing the scene in the set. A black matte was fixed in front of the lens to cover the area above the set. Later, Papa Day would set up his glass painting to fill exactly the matted area and the finished result, with vaulted ceiling, chandeliers and actors became one complete frame by optical printing.

Sixty Glorious Years was an enormous financial success, which assured the Wilcox/Neagle team of never having to beg for finance again, even though Herbert's fortunes declined after the Second World War while his wife's continued to rise.

I worked for them again in 1957, this time with Anna as producer and Herbert director. The star of this film, *These Dangerous Years*, was their great friend Frankie Vaughan. The story-line was centred on the boys' clubs on which Frankie devoted so much of his work for charity.

Twenty years on post-war changes in protocol produced an easier going atmosphere on the film set; I found I could call Mr Wilcox, Herbert. But in other respects of working with them the intervening years disappeared. Prior to filming, senior members of the crew were asked to assemble in the boardroom at Pinewood Studios. It was a magnificent panelled library that had been salvaged from the *Mauretania*, when the liner was broken up, and reassembled in the old house at the studios.

Anna Neagle and Herbert Wilcox – one of Britain's most famous film partnerships.

We waited patiently, some no doubt puzzling over the slight curve in the walls and the doors, maybe forgetting that the lines of a ship were rarely straight athwartships. Then the door opened and Anna appeared still swathed in her full-length mink, followed by Herbert immaculate as I remembered him from before the war. He introduced us one by one, saying in my case, 'You remember John, don't you Anna?'

'Of course I do,' she replied, still in regal tones. 'You were such a young boy then.'

As shooting progressed I came to recognise other subtle changes that had taken place. Herbert had a portable dressing-room on the set where he would go while a scene was being lit. Sometimes he would invite us to join him with the comment, 'Come in, I want you to meet a Mr Walker' – Mr Walker, it turned out, resided in a bottle sporting a red or black label.

Herbert, one of the most persuasive men I have ever met, had lost nothing of his supreme showmanship. One of the sequences of *These Dangerous Years* featured a boxing match. Herbert, typically, had invited a number of celebrities to watch the day's filming. They included Bessie Braddock, Billy Butlin and a good many other well known faces. What they didn't know was that they were all to sit in ringside seats while the boxing was filmed. Behind them Herbert seated two rows of extras; the rest of the audience consisting of life-size paintings, some of which could be juggled by propmen out of sight.

After filming I told Herbert that I took my hat off to him for conning so many people of repute. His reply was that he gave them a slap-up lunch with plenty to drink and that they were as good as gold for the rest of the afternoon.

Denham Studios had closed by the time of *These Dangerous Years*, but when I left Ealing to work there in 1936 everyone in the film industry was talking about Alexander Korda's new empire.

Unit still for Under the Red Robe, *photographed by world famous Hollywood cameraman James Wong Howe and directed by Victor Suestrom. I am kneeling in the front row.*

Although Korda was a great Anglophile with a passion for films about the British Empire, he'd always had the idea up his sleeve of making an epic from Robert Graves's classic of the Roman Empire *I, Claudius*, seeing it as a further vehicle for Charles Laughton. Graves was only too happy to sell the film rights; he was living in Majorca at the time and apparently was having trouble paying his mortgage. When Korda asked him to write the film script he was very pleased to take that on as well. After directing Laughton as Henry VIII and later Rembrandt, Korda had decided not to go through the ordeal again. In any case he was more than busy as the head of production of London Films, overseeing

the many films in production at Denham.

I, Claudius was going to made on a lavish scale. Josef Von Sternberg, the Austrian film director, who had successfully worked with Marlene Dietrich in *The Blue Angel, Shanghai Express* and *Morocco,* was asked to direct it.

Meanwhile, Korda, who was always very good to fellow Hungarians, commissioned a second script from a writer named Lajos Biro and sent this to Robert Graves for his comments. They were quite hilarious, for Biro not only spoke English with a strong accent, he wrote what Graves described as 'fractured English'. In spite of this Graves realised that his own script had little chance of being used, but didn't block the film because he needed the money.

Enormous sets were built on the largest stages at Denham and everything was in motion for a major film production when Von Sternberg arrived and Korda's dream of *I, Claudius* began to turn into a nightmare. Von Sternberg read the script and demanded extensive re-writes. He looked at the sets and called for a lot of changes. He insisted that he was not having Merle Oberon in the film, but lost out on that because she happened to be Mrs Alexander Korda. About the only casting he did approve of was that of Emlyn Williams as Claudius's scheming cousin and Flora Robson in the role of Claudius's mother. As for Charles Laughton, it was clear even before shooting began that there was no love lost between director and star.

On the first day of shooting we, the technicians, had an eight o'clock call, and a shooting call for eight-thirty. We were due to start filming in the Senate. Everyone was pretty apprehensive; by now we had seen Von Sternberg roaming around the studios.

Eventually this funny little man with a goatee beard strode on the set, legs encased in riding boots and breeches, topped by a flamboyant blouse-like shirt, a form of turban on his head, a riding crop in one hand. He marched to a tall Dickensian-style desk he had had made, sat down upon a high stool, his secretary beside him, and addressed cast and crew through a microphone. If confirmation were needed Josef Von Sternberg was a bully of the first order, this was it. His harangue completed, the camera at last turned on *I, Claudius.* It was not to be uneventful, for Joe interfered with everything.

The cameraman was Georges Perinal, the famous French cinematographer with whom Korda had worked so much in the past. He would light the set only to have Von Sternberg change it. Then he would push the camera operator to one side and start operating the camera. He picked on small-part actors mercilessly. Bruce Winston, a flabby mountain of a man, cast as a senator, was

On the set of the ill-fated I, Claudius. *Director Josef Von Sternberg, Merle Oberon and Charles Laughton.*

reduced to a quivering mass with Von Sternberg's sarcasm, much to everyone else's disgust and embarrassment.

Laughton too was having trouble. He was not the easiest of people; moody and introverted. He would shamble onto the sound stage with his leg twisted to reproduce Claudius's limp and we would then watch him disappear down the full length of the enormous building until he eventually reappeared to announce 'I'm ready'. Then we would rehearse a scene, maybe between him and Emlyn Williams, with Von Sternberg interfering, until a decision was made to shoot. The camera would run, the clapper board go in, Von Sternberg calling 'action'. Laughton would start the scene, perhaps fluff, or stop, saying, 'That was the worst cockney accent I've ever heard.' Meanwhile, Emlyn would remain calm, speaking his lines and giving a performance that was quite brilliant. The camera would roll again, this time for Laughton to stop, exclaiming, 'Joe – I can't get into the man. I just can't.' After a couple of weeks of this the atmosphere was becoming very fraught and it was decided to give Laughton a rest.

While the star was away Von Sternberg turned his attention to the scenes with the vestal virgins. He called for the casting director and the wardrobe designer to ask how many virgins had been hired. The answer was six, for that was the number in classical times. Von Sternberg wanted sixty and the casting director was packed off to London to find fifty-four more virgins by eight o'clock the following morning. The costume designer wasn't spared. Von Sternberg took it into his head that the virgins were to be naked, clad only in layers of tulle. Sixty suitably decorous costumes had to be hastily run up overnight for shooting the next day.

By now we were already seriously behind schedule, with Laughton's return awaited with some foreboding. However, when he appeared on set several days later it was to announce triumphantly to Von Sternberg, 'I've got the man!' In his hand he was carrying a gramophone record which from then onwards he listened to every morning in his dressing-room before being called on set. This was the recording of Edward VIII's recent abdication speech.

Shooting continued until an unexpected turn of events changed things dramatically. Merle Oberon, who was being driven to London for a costume fitting, was involved in a collision with another vehicle. She was flung against a side window, her face lacerated by the broken glass. In hospital the doctor, who at first had refused to believe she was who she had said she was, pronounced a lengthy stay while plastic surgery restored her celebrated beauty. As the contract stated that she alone could appear in the film, the Prudential Insurance Company, who were backing *I Claudius,* got together with Korda and decided to cease production. Cynics said that Merle's driver was in fact Alexander Korda in chauffeur's uniform and cap! Whatever the truth, it was as much a relief to Charles Laughton as Korda and the men from the Pru, that *I, Claudius* became 'the epic that never was'.

Some time during the 1960s the BBC found a pile of film cans in a vault, all that remained of the doomed project. There was enough film to edit several scenes, which confirmed what many of us had thought, that Laughton's

Return of the Scarlet
Pimpernel, *1937.*

performance as Claudius, at its best, could have been sensational; we already
knew the power of the performances given by Emlyn Williams and Flora Robson.
Dirk Bogarde, who narrated the documentary the BBC made about the film,
The Epic That Never Was, went as far as saying that a speech of Laughton's
made to the Senate was one of the most powerful and moving ever spoken on
film.

Chapter Four

THE FOUR FEATHERS

A year after *I Claudius*, Alexander Korda returned to more familiar and safer ground when he set to work on bringing to the screen A E W Mason's great historical adventure, based on Kitchener's campaigns that followed the murder of General Gordon in Khartoum, *The Four Feathers*. Korda assembled a fine cast led by Ralph Richardson, John Clements and June Duprez, backed by Henry Oscar, Jack Allen, Donald Gray and John Laurie.

We started studio work in the May of 1938 on a beautiful set of the old general's house and garden. This was followed by a sequence at the general's dinner-table where he re-enacts a favourite battle using fruit as the army units, dipping a finger in his claret and drawing it across the table to depict 'The Thin Red Line'.

The actor originally cast to play the general proved to be totally inadequate after the first day and Zoltan Korda, the director and Alexander Korda's brother, decided to stop filming and re-cast. By chance C Aubrey Smith happened to be in London after finishing filming his part as Duke of Wellington in *Sixty Glorious Years*. Alex persuaded him to take over as the general in *The Four Feathers*, on the promise that all his scenes would be finished in six days to allow him to keep an appointment in Hollywood to rejoin his cricket team of British actors (he had recently introduced the game to California). In the finished film he appears in the first and last scenes and a good many in between: Korda was able to keep his promise.

We continued with scenes of John Clements, playing Harry Faversham the disgraced hero, as he watched his regiment leave for the Sudan after resigning his commission, his revolver clenched in his hand ready to blow out his brains. These were shot on a tiny set with a sloping mansard roof, which gave me great problems in positioning the microphone. I wasn't helped by Georges Perinal behind the camera, who had little time for sound problems. Hidden in a cupboard, I had to pop out on a word cue. The first time I did this a microphone shadow fell on the wall behind, prompting Zolly, the owner of a violent temper to shout, 'You are sacked!' Very fortunately for me, sound director Watty Watkins appeared on set, calmed Zolly and I was re-instated.

We then moved to the famous Denham Studio lot where a steep bank had been constructed beside the River Colne, on which the set of Omdurman town had been built as the setting for many scenes which would slot in with our later work in the Sudan. We had hundreds of Asian and Afro-Caribbean extras, mostly recruited from the London Docks. Zolly loved them – not that this prevented him from shouting and screaming at them in his thick Hungarian accent, finally giving in by calling his first assistant director, Geoff Boothby, to say, 'Geoff, you tell them what I want. I do not know myself.'

As preparations were being finalised for our location dates in Sudan, which had been put on hold because of the Munich crisis, I was told my place was being taken by another boom operator because I was considered too young. I was more than disappointed; after all, I had just celebrated my twenty-first birthday. Luckily my replacement failed his medical, I passed mine with flying colours and the ticket to the Sudan was mine.

While the director and cast flew out to Khartoum on the regular Imperial Airways flying boat service, the film crew set sail on the P & O liner *Mooltan*; not that this was any great hardship as we travelled first-class and wore black tie every evening after our first night at sea.

Considering the scale of the scenes we were going to be filming in the desert our full unit was very small by today's standards, comprising: two camera crews of four; one sound crew of three; two make-up men; two property men; one continuity girl; one first and second assistant director; a production manager; a buyer and contact man in Khartoum; and Zoltan Korda himself.

The sound equipment, carefully cushioned and packed, and weighing about half a ton, had been sent on ahead by sea. Before leaving we had been issued with tropical kit from a theatrical costumier which must have dated from Kitchener's time. Over-large topees were handed out with the dire warning that they were to be worn as soon as we emerged from our tents. Anyone who disobeyed would die of sunstroke, or go blind. A similar concern for our health no doubt led to the issuing of 'pads, cholera, protection for use of.' Knee length shorts and shirts as rough as sandpaper completed our kitting-out. Most of this was substituted with more suitable attire when we reached Port Said and paid a visit to the legendary Simon Artz store that sold almost anything. For five bob I bought a light-weight Bombay Bowler sun helmet. For the same amount street touts offered a variety of unsavoury diversions from their sisters to antics with a donkey. Hurrying from these, we caught the afternoon train for Cairo and our first glimpse of Egypt.

A few hours winding through the city's hordes in a horse-drawn carriage was all we had time for before boarding the night train for Aswan, where we transferred to a stern-wheeler, wood-burning steamer for an unforgettable journey up the Nile to Wadi Halfa. By afternoon we were abreast the mighty crouching figures of the four gods sitting at the entrance of the Temple of Abu Simbel; in 1938 they were still in their original location just above the high-water line of the river bank.

Our journey up river to Wadi Halfa took just over two days, passing between the Cataracts which form a barrier to large vessels. Once more we packed our bags in the oven-like heat, ready to disembark and join another train. A more motley crew would have been hard to find, as my photograph of us on the riverbank with our luggage shows. In the middle is Robert Krasker, the first unit camera operator, who was later to become famous as director of photography of such classics as *Henry V, Brief Encounter* and *The Third Man*. Bob was wearing his London-issue pig-sticking topee, a lounge suit, collar and tie, with his Harris tweed overcoat over his arm in a temperature well in excess of 100 degrees Fahrenheit. Bizarre as Bob's appearance was, he was in good company when we met up with the director on location.

Camera operator Bob Krasker (in the centre of the picture facing camera) suitably attired for temperatures of 100 plus degrees.

Zolly presented a most remarkable sight. He suffered from a skin complaint that flared up in sunlight. To combat painful eruptions on his hands and face he wore a large red fabric mask, tied with tapes that stretched over his ears to be secured by a bow at the back of his neck. His head was protected by a very large brimmed sun helmet. He always wore shirts with long sleeves tightly buttoned at the cuff over white fabric gloves and never appeared in anything briefer than full-length trousers. To add to his woes he also had chronic dyspepsia that he countered by chewing tablets. These caused a rim of white froth around his lips, so that in his frequent outbursts of rage it was hard to tell whether he was foaming at the mouth in a fit of temper, or overflowing from his medication.

The final train journey took us further south towards Khartoum. The carriages were divided into two-berth compartments, with louvered shutters over the windows and just a fan suspended from the ceiling to give some movement to the stifling air.

Our meals were served in the restaurant car by bare-footed servants in long robes like night-shirts, who carried large trays with the various courses that had been prepared by squatting cooks in the coal-fire galley. The cutlery was heavily plated and the food served on equally heavy plates. The food was not to be outdone. On our journey through the broiling desert we were treated to a good, solid steak and kidney pudding or roast lamb plus all the trimmings, with baked jam roll and custard to round off the meal.

At seven o'clock the following morning the train shuddered to a stop on its narrow gauge rails, just long enough for us to be hustled off with our luggage, before it let out a couple of toots and chugged off across the sand towards Khartoum, some ninety miles further down the line. There hadn't been much explanation of what to expect next. So it came as a relief when a cloud of dust appeared on the horizon and crept towards us to reveal a convoy of trucks. They drew alongside our group and we quickly realised our fate was firmly in the hands of the British Army. Piling into the trucks for the final leg of our journey, we bounced and rattled over desert, finally cresting an escarpment to see an enormous tented encampment that had been pitched by the garrison troops of the East Surreys. Here was our home for three months which conveniently doubled as Lord Kitchener's headquarters when filming required. Each tent had been kitted out with four metal-framed beds. There was little else apart from a table and the mosquito nets under which we were soon to become adept at tucking ourselves in.

We were addressed by a sergeant-major in immaculate starched khaki shirt and shorts with creases like knife edges. We were, he said, under army discipline, never to go outside the tent without wearing a helmet and never to wear short-sleeve shirts after sunset. Water for washing had to be brought from the Nile in tankers and, for the four of us per day, was rationed to four inches in a collapsible canvas bath. Drinking water had to be purified in camp and was an even more precious commodity. The sergeant-major told us that we were to eat in the Sergeants' Mess. The director, more senior technicians and actors were to use the Officers' Mess. Their superior status also brought them a tent to themselves, complete with orderly. 'Other ranks', we were informed, were not even allowed in our lines, nor near either of the messes.

As well as the East Surreys, there was a large contingent of Sudan Defence Force Mounted Infantry, who were to provide our cavalry in the film, together with hundreds of camels and riders to form the followers of the mad Mahdi. A third element was made of several hundred members of the Hadendowa tribe, 'Fuzzy Wuzzies' as they were known in Kitchener's day. They had been brought several hundred miles in railway goods wagons from their home in the Red Sea Hills. For many it was their first ride in a train and certainly the furthest

Hadendowa and their interpreter.

they had travelled from home.

The logistics for this huge undertaking had been masterminded by a Frenchman, Charles David, who some years later married the Canadian film star Deanna Durbin. He had been greatly assisted by the army and air force who turned the whole thing into an exercise, ferrying ninety miles out into the desert every piece of film gear together with tents, beds, catering equipment, hundreds of hampers filled with period uniforms and native clothing and stockpiles of weapons. Behind it all, of course, lay Alexander Korda's not insignificant influence with the Colonial Office and army, which must have made him the envy of every other film producer on location abroad before the war.

The actual river gunboat that Kitchener had brought all the way up the Nile from Alexandria (too late to save Gordon) was moored in Khartoum as headquarters for the sailing club. This was borrowed for the film and towed downstream to our riverside location a mile or so from the main camp, where her hauling past the cataracts was to be re-enacted.

The first few days after our arrival were spent unpacking and preparing our equipment, making tests and setting up dark-rooms, black velvet enclosures housed inside the army tents provided. To make sure they would be absolutely light-proof they were only used at night and were sited on the fringe of the camp with the strict rule that vehicles using headlights were to keep well clear.

Me with tent mates.

We cross the Nile to a location.

Our home, doubling as Kitchener's HQ.

One big problem was how to stop the photographic picture and sound films becoming affected by the heat, which was likely to desensitise the delicate emulsion. To prevent the potentially disastrous consequences large cases were made, zinc lined, in which loaded magazines and cans of film would be stored in racks over slabs of ice. This called for a daily delivery from the Khartoum Ice Factory of huge blocks of ice in damp sacks, which arrived by convoy for us to break up to replenish the cool boxes. There were strict instructions that the ice was for cooling only; it was far too precious to be used in drinks. Some weeks later I did bend the rule slightly, during a particularly hot and dusty day that had started with an early morning call at five o'clock. Back in camp to reload some film, I half-filled a dustbin with ice and jumped in. Unyielding, freezing slabs never felt as good before or since.

Quite a few of the crew did not take kindly to the rigours of army discipline. Certainly the very basic nature of our new life had come as a shock. Living out of a suitcase quickly tested our patience. Even carefully folded clothes consigned to the case under our beds soon became coated with fine dust that penetrated the slightest gap, despite all our attempts to seal the lid.

The biggest shock for most of us was undoubtedly the first morning. We were woken by the braying of the bugler's reveille, followed by a mad scramble to the latrines and wash-house. Situated some way from the sleeping tents was an enclosure made of six-foot poles across which hessian had been stretched to screen off rows of 'toilets, dry, army for the use of'. No attempt had been made to screen off each unit; so that first morning's experience of communing with nature in the company of twenty or so other chaps sitting side by side was, for most, an embarrassing start to the day.

Our desert reveille came at dawn. By daylight we were well on our way to locations often several miles out into the desert from camp. On occasions we had to wade across the river at the shallows to shoot scenes on an island with the sun-blinded Ralph Richardson and John Clements.

Day after day we worked our way through the script. On one occasion we set the scene for the British troops forward encampment, which was barricaded behind a square zareba, hastily built from chopped down thorn bushes to offer some protection from the Fuzzy Wuzzies who might attempt to break through to slash the men to pieces with their razor-sharp swords. On *The Four Feathers* these were not the usual property department weapons, but the real thing, which our Hadendowa friends spent hours sharpening, sitting on their haunches in their camp at the end of the day.

The scene in question involved a small company of troops (our friends, the East Surreys) who had been sent out to give advance warning of an expected attack on Kitchener's main force from the mad Khalif of Omdurman. The scene was supposed to take place at night but as we had no arc lamps it was filmed during the day with blue night filters in front of the camera lens.

On the first rehearsal the Fuzzy Wuzzies just leapt over the thorn barriers to slash away at the soldiers, though it was made clear through interpreters that they were to stop short of actually butchering them. The army didn't appreciate the enthusiasm with which they entered into their film roles and prepared for the next take by dropping small chips of stone down the muzzles of their rifles, from which they fired blanks.

When the attack was repeated, the ranks of riflemen opened fire, peppering the Hadendowa and stopping them in their tracks, their bare chests bleeding from the stone missiles. An army corporal with a Red Cross armlet was soon on the scene, an enormous jar of iodine under his arm, a great wad of cotton wool in his hand, going along the ranks of the bloodied Hedandowa much to their apparent delight; being wounded in battle brought great prestige. Getting them to 'die' in front of the camera was less straightforward. It took considerable negotiation on the part of their chief, who spoke a little English, before some of them agreed to be shot or bayoneted; their loss of face being compensated by a suitably attractive bonus.

This skirmish was a prelude for the famous scene in which the Khalif's troops, hundreds of men on foot, with horsemen and camel riders massing across the plain, charged the ranks of British troops and their cannon. It had taken days to plan this scene, with our three cameras set up on high rostrums perched on huge piles of smooth rocks known as jebels. There were no walkie-talkies in those days, so messages to the attacking force had to be carried across the plain by horsemen. The British troops awaited their signal from a large white flag lowered at a point close to the cameras. Once the charge was started nothing could stop its relentless approach. It had to be right first time – and it was. I have often wondered how the assistant directors of today would have approached the task without that indispensable tool of their trade, the modern hand-held radio.

We did have one communication link back in camp, in the form of an RAF corporal. He had been seconded to the army and had set up aerial masts and a transmitter which was our sole radio contact with the outside world.

Corporal G H York RAF was something of an enigma in the strict hierarchy of service life. As a corporal he was entitled to better accommodation and messing facilities than army 'other ranks'. But with the intense rivalry between the services that existed then, he was refused the hospitality of the Sergeants' Mess. He did, however, persuade the major in command that he should be

Ready for the Battle for Omdurman.

My lifelong friend Yorkey.

allowed to set up his own tent and radio base on a hillock some distance from camp, (a) to get better radio reception and (b) to be as far away from the army as possible. The one concession he was allowed was a daily issue of beer and cigarettes from Charles David.

Yorkey and I became friendly, possibly because we both had a Yorkshire background and also because I was somewhat annoyed at what I mistook to be his mistreatment; although I quickly realised he had got just what he wanted in his little encampment on the hillock. I used to go up to his tent for a chat in the evening, sometimes to be interrupted by Ralph Richardson, who would stroll across from the camp to ask Yorkey to pass through a message for his wife at home for onward transmission by Cable & Wireless in Cairo.

Yorkey soon endeared himself in another way. He worked out a routine whereby he would raid our ice store in the camp, collect bottles of beer, wrap them in a blanket and bring them out to his particular pals, the sound crew sitting it out under the scorching heat of the desert sun. The sight of that lonesome army truck coming nearer in an enveloping cloud of dust was for ever welcoming and helped to make us firm friends.

Yorkey's encampment became the subject of conversation among the film crew when we had just finished shooting a scene in which Kitchener had been reviewing his troops. We had taken a break for lunch when one of the unit commented, 'You realise that one of the masts flying an RAF ensign was in shot during that last sequence!'

With only about three weeks left to work out of the camp, Johnny Cook, our senior soundman, contracted the dreaded tummy complaint known by various lurid names around the world. Each day poor old Johnny would make his way out to the location, well supplied with toilet rolls but suffering every jolt in the truck until he had to call for halt alongside a convenient rock. His condition became so bad that he was put in the sick bay on doctor's orders. This left the sound crew reduced to two technicians, ably supported by a couple of privates from the East Surreys who had attached themselves to us and were proving invaluable, helping to carry equipment, set it up and run the cables to microphone and camera.

We struggled on for a couple of days until our maintenance man, Jerry, failed to show up to load batteries and film into the truck. I hurried to his tent to find him under his mosquito net with a raging temperature. Jerry was obviously in no state for work, so after a quick call to the doctor, I collected

The sound crew and our ton of recording equipment: Johnny Cook (mixer), Jerry Brunker (maintenance), me (boom operator), together with two East Surrey Regiment privates (our helpers and humpers).

Blackie and Ron, our two soldier helpers, and set off for the day's shooting with faint heart and facing the tasks of sound mixing, recording and placing the microphone for the scenes in front of the camera. Ron, who had been a most observant and enquiring helper, came to the rescue, for it was several days before Johnny joined us and over a week before Jerry was able to work again, very weak and a good stone lighter.

Zolly asked me one day during Jerry's absence, 'Mitch, how much do they pay you?' When I told him it was seven pounds a week, he just nodded but didn't suggest any form of bonus for the time I kept things going while my two crew members were off sick. It was not without a little irony that I remembered being rejected at Denham for work in Sudan on the grounds that I was 'too young'.

Before we left our camp, scenes had to be filmed of the aftermath of the battle, with the surrounding desert strewn with bodies, horses and camels. Zolly, who was striving for realism, had goats killed, dressed them in uniforms and laid out to await the vultures. The bodies, together with those of the horses and camels, which had somehow been procured, quite humanely we were assured, were put in position for the cameras and allowed to putrefy. Vultures are canny. They will never approach a carcass directly but will wheel around overhead, making passes to have a good look, before finally making their first assault. This is all very well when it happens, but days can pass before these hideous birds begin to gorge.

Zolly insisted that the crew should move out to the location very early each morning and settle into hides and holes in the desert to await the vultures. Day after day passed. The animal carcasses swelled with putrefied gases, the stench became unbearable. So much for the glamour of film work. Our patience was almost exhausted by the time the vultures did turn up, began their routine and finally dropped down for the feast. When they had finished all that remained, stark on the rocky ground, were bare animal bones, tattered uniforms and a weary film crew.

While we were thus occupied, the fortunate actors had been sent back to Khartoum to enjoy the luxury of a hotel set in lush gardens overlooking the Nile. We joined them on the paddle steamer for the final scenes to be shot on location. Setting up camera and sound departments was carried out with great relief – we had all of us had more than enough of tents and the desert. Our RAF corporal installed himself in a wired-off cage on the upper deck, raised an aerial and was once again in business. Down below was the luxury of a cabin free from dust. There was unlimited water for washing; bliss, even if it came straight out of the river the colour of chocolate. We said goodbye too to army grub and tucked into meals prepared and served by Sudan Railway staff who crewed the steamer.

Upstream in Khartoum we disembarked, the gunboat returned to the sailing club and we set about packing our equipment for the journey home. Imperceptibly time had caught up with us and we began to realise that our work on the film was all but over.

I was deputed to dispose of all our heavy batteries that had been loaded onto a cart drawn by two diminutive donkeys. We set off to the Greek merchant who was going to buy them, our route taking us past the Grand Hotel. On the way back I got the driver to drop me off outside its entrance, where I was met at the top of the steps by an indignant under-manager who told me curtly that the British did not ride with natives in donkey carts. My tuition in colonial etiquette was soon to be extended.

My pal Yorkey had returned to his RAF barracks and was back to his normal routine. We met up in the evenings for a drink and chat, having been informed that apart from officers, other ranks of all services were restricted to three streets. This didn't particularly worry either of us, until one evening I took him back to the Grand for a meal. All hell broke out when the management realised that my guest was an RAF corporal. Yorkey left quietly enough, in spite of my protestations. I believe that incident cemented our lifetime friendship that exists to this day. At least he was better treated by the film company. Before we left Khartoum, Zolly presented him with a 16mm Bolex cine camera with a suitably inscribed plaque thanking him for keeping open our lines of communication.

On the train journey from Khartoum to Port Sudan, we halted at a place called Shendi where I had arranged to say farewell to another friend. This was a young officer cadet from the Sudan Defence Force who had been bivouacked by the river bank to be near water for their horses. His name was Achmed Bashir Tombal; in fact he was the senior cadet in the SDF. The son of a chief of an area towards the Somali border, Achmed was a tall, very handsome chap, tribal knife cuts slashed across each cheek, always dressed in immaculate native-style starched uniform surmounted by a form of turban.

I first got to know him from my love of riding, which prompted me to ask him about his horse. From that came an invitation to borrow a mount whenever filming allowed. We had very little free time, but as the weeks dragged on it

Achmed.

became clear that seven days of non-stop work could not be kept up and it was decided to allow us a rest day every two weeks. This gave me the opportunity to ride, which pleased Achmed because there were always horses needing to be exercised. Our friendship was relaxed and we got on well together. He invited me to visit his family, but our bosses back at Denham ruled this out. However, before I left the Sudan for good we arranged to meet up at Shendi.

I had coveted a pair of the open sandal-like boots worn by the SDF; cool to wear, they were tough enough to withstand rough desert treatment. A telegram to Shendi giving the date that we would pass through on the train alerted Achmed and he was waiting by the track as we came to a stop. Under his arm was a parcel with my sandals, wrapped in a copy of the Shendi daily paper. I had previously asked Achmed if there was anything that I could send him from England in return. He was shortly due to be commissioned as a second lieutenant and would assume a British army officer's uniform with feet clad in brown regulation boots. To my surprise he produced a shoe catalogue from Lennards in the Edgware Road; he had earmarked the boots he wanted. We took an outline of both his feet from which Lennards had to make a special pair of size fourteen boots to fit him. At £5 the cost to me was not small, but I sent them off to Achmed with the hope that in his ensuing army career they would serve him well.

In the next few years I used to wonder what had happened to my friend

– the Sudanese forces were well to the fore in the western desert campaign, it was really too much to hope that as a young officer he had survived. Forty years later I got my answer. It came in Kenya where I was working on the television adaptation of *The Flame Trees of Thika*. One of the characters was a Somali servant, named in the script as Ahmed. As soundman I had queried this with, Roy Baker, the director, pointing out that anyone from Somalia or the Sudan would be called Achmed, with the guttural sounding 'c', as opposed to the softer sounding Ahmed found in the Middle East.

My comment did not impress Roy Baker. But I was convinced I was right and brought up the subject at supper that night. Eating with us was Hilary Hook, a retired colonel living in Kenya who took tourists on wildlife safaris. Hearing my mention of Achmed Bashir Tombal, he called across, asking how I knew him. I explained that we had met forty years earlier. In return he told me that Achmed had not only survived the war but had risen to the rank of brigadier and was now a senior member of the Sudan government!

A few years earlier at home in the Cotswolds I had had another chance meeting associated with *The Four Feathers*. At a drinks party in the village I got into conversation with another brigadier, who had retired to Oakridge from the British Army. When I mentioned my work in films he chimed in that he had been concerned years before with a film called *The Four Feathers*, while serving with the East Surrey regiment. It turned out that he had been the major acting as our camp commandant, even appearing in the film, as his wife reminded me. Complete with period uniform and false moustache he had portrayed Kitchener.

Our travels in the Sudan ended in 1938 beside the Red Sea where we left the train in Port Sudan to await the arrival of a Bibby Line passenger cargo ship from Rangoon that was to take us to Marseilles. We docked two days before Christmas, in freezing weather. It was so cold the train's wheels froze on the rails and held us up for hours before we could start for Paris and the sleeper berths had been booked on the night train to London.

On Christmas Eve 1938 we stepped onto the platform at Victoria where the officers of His Majesty's Customs and Excise were waiting to pounce. Not that we had much to declare. Apart from the odd sword and dagger, a clutch of photographs and a lifetime of memories this was the end of *The Four Feathers*. I knew I would never forget it and I have always been pleased that the desert battles we sweated and strained to film have been borrowed and used in a good many later films. Sir Alexander Korda remade *Storm Over The Nile* starring Anthony Steele and Laurence Harvey; and a much later version was filmed inland near Almeira with Robert Powell and Beau Bridges.

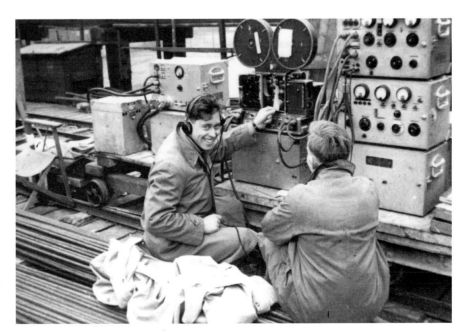

On location on Waterloo Bridge, 1938, for the filming of A Window in London.

Chapter Five

NOT A SHOT FIRED IN ANGER

That Sunday morning in September 1939, when news came through that war had been declared, I was washing my car at the rear of the flat in Ealing owned by my parents. The declaration was followed in minutes by the first air raid sirens of the war.

Quite soon afterwards the first raid by RAF Wellington bombers was made on Wilhelmshaven and the Kiel canal. This prompted Alexander Korda to put the whole of Denham Studios' facilities to the task of making a full feature-length propaganda documentary boosting the pride and effort Britain was putting into winning the war. We were all involved in the production of *The Lion has Wings*, starring Merle Oberon, Ralph Richardson, June Duprez, Robert Douglas and many others. Full co-operation was given by the Air Ministry, even to the point of their supplying a written-off Wellington Bomber fuselage in which simulated flight scenes were filmed in the studio.

We were also still completing the final stages of the classic *The Thief of Bagdad*, apart from a hiatus caused by the hurried return home of the American contingent headed by the director and the cameraman, who was in such a hurry that he handed a magnificent camel hair overcoat to my assistant. All the remaining scenes were shot on the wide sands at Pendine, near Tenby in South Wales. Somehow war seemed very unreal with life carrying on much as it had always been until one day on the sea shore we heard that the aircraft carrier *Courageous* had been torpedoed and sunk in the Channel by a German U-Boat, with large loss of life. I remember staring out to sea as if it was possible to see the stricken ship before it slipped below the surface.

With my age group coming up for registration for the armed forces (I had missed the first wave of conscription in 1938 by being one year too old), I realised that I would get my call-up papers sooner or later with no choice of which service I would be posted to. *The Lion has Wings* triggered off a renewed interest in aeroplanes which prompted me to apply for entry into the RAF for training as a Sergeant Pilot. But half the youth of the nation had the same idea and my application was refused with regret.

In Naval uniform, 1940s.

If it was not to be the RAF, why not try the Navy? Having heard that my experience in sound might be of interest to the anti-submarine branch, I wrote off to the Admiralty and much to my surprise received a reply by return calling me to attend a selection board at an address in Grosvenor Square. I was confronted across a baize covered trestle table by a Rear Admiral, two RN Captains and two Commanders. My first reaction was to wonder why they were not on their ships, but I was soon concentrating on their questions: school background, qualifications, but my mention of my present occupation brought an 'Oh films' from the admiral as if such a job was certainly not a recommendation for the Senior Service.

In despair one of the 'four ring' Captains had a sudden inspiration, 'By the way, can you use a megger?' (this being a hand-operated high voltage generator wound manually to measure resistance in a circuit). I could and I really saw a gleam of hope for me and a naval career, when to my amazement the other captain began to ask me about *The Four Feathers*, which he had obviously seen and, fortunately for me, appeared to have enjoyed. The rest of the interview was spent recounting my experiences in the Sudan and ended with me being offered a commission in the special branch of the RNVR as a temporary acting Sub-Lieutenant. I was to undertake a course at the Anti-Submarine School at HMS *Osprey*, Portland, but, and it proved to be a big but, the interviewee before me had filled the last place on the course, leaving me with that well known phrase so often heard in the entertainment world – 'Don't call us, we'll call you.'

I returned next day to continue work on Michael Powell's production of *Contraband* starring Conrad Veidt, which gave me my first insight of how war could change attitudes. Veidt, a refugee from Nazi Germany, who was a charming man as well as a wonderful actor much liked by British audiences, had ordered some refreshments from the studio restaurant. They were brought on the set by a young waiter who dumped the tray beside Conrad's chair with a muttered, 'Bloody German bastard.' Veidt rose to his full height, fixed the young man with his piercing eyes and he quietly said, 'Thank you very much,' as the film crew watched in embarrassment.

After weeks of anticipation an Admiralty envelope arrived ordering me to report to Portland on 9 January. I gave notice of my call-up at London Film Productions to Watty, himself a former naval officer, and left the sound department at Denham for my new and hopefully short-lived role in anti-submarine warfare. What I had not bargained on was that not far over the horizon fate had also cast me as a married man.

It had to be a natural progression that I was destined to meet the girl I was going to marry in a cinema. On my off-duty evenings I would go to a local cinema in Saltcoats, the adjoining resort to Ardrossan where I was serving at my first appointment, HMS *Fortitude* on the Clyde. There in the Regal, I began to notice a very pretty dark haired usherette with a sweet smile. Plucking up courage, I spoke to her one evening after the show to hear that she had 'noticed' that smart young officer, who was a regular patron. An invitation was accepted for us to go to Ayr the next Sunday afternoon, where I splashed out and took her to tea in 'The' Caledonian Hotel.

Our friendship developed; I was invited to tea at her home. We were to spend lovers' evenings in the front room, a very circumspect affair by modern standards, but no less romantic in our eyes. Jean was twenty-six and I was twenty-three. It was a Saturday morning in September 1940 that we were married, after I had been granted the Captain's permission to marry and a twenty-four hour pass. Perhaps it was as well that we married during wartime, when duty would call me away from home for long periods; in later life duty of a different sort would take me away from Jean again, but as our life together had always followed this punctuated tempo we could never really complain when we were parted and made the most of each other's company when we were together.

With Jean, 1940s.

HMS Macbeth.

It seemed as if my film life followed me around the world wherever I went during the war. One of the ships I served on, HMS *Macbeth*, was in the first convoy to sail to Russia. During our time in Archangel we were detailed off to take a Russian admiral out to meet the cruiser HMS *London*, which had brought Lord Beaverbrook and senator Avril Harriman on their mission to Moscow. As we went alongside the towering hull of the cruiser I heard a voice shout down from the bridge, in a strong Russian accent, 'Mitch, what you doing here?'

The voice belonged to Russian-born Sacha Fisher, on whose crew I had worked as a boom operator at Denham. Like me he was serving in the Royal Navy anti-submarine branch, but had somehow fiddled a temporary job as interpreter to the two visiting politicians.

Two years later I was serving as port anti-submarine officer in Mombassa on the Indian Ocean, when one day, to my amazement, I saw Sacha coming ashore there. He said he had been sent to relieve me, though the admiral in charge of the base took one look at my 'mad Russian' friend and quickly rescinded the posting; not that Sacha complained – he was sent to the Seychelles.

Another reminder of my film past came when I was waiting on the quayside in Mombassa for a launch to take me and Able-Seaman Martin to service the Asdic gear on a ship. The coxswain of another launch called out to Martin, asking him to give a hand with some large metal canisters containing cinema film. Martin glanced down at the label on one as he struggled with it onto the jetty and then shouted up at me in his broad cockney voice '*Four Fevvers* – more like four bleedin' tons.'

After two years I returned from Mombassa to an appointment at Dartmouth where over eighty gun boats were based to hunt down their German equivalents, the E-boats. Jean, who had joined the WAAF, and I were reunited after she was granted a compassionate posting to Torquay. It must have been pretty passionate because Jean became pregnant and our daughter Anne was born a month before D-Day.

There was a special flotilla of very fast gunboats at Dartmouth which took agents across the Channel to the coast of France. One of these boats had a very taciturn first lieutenant whose duty it was to launch and row a four-oared scow for the last mile to land the agents on the beach. The parent boat lay off shore with orders to return to Dartmouth before dawn come what may, and since locating the parent boat in the pitch dark proved to be impossible at times, Lieutenant Hamilton and his crew were often left on the beach, though they always showed up at Dartmouth a week or so later, courtesy of the French Resistance.

Hamilton had tried various methods of keeping in contact with the gunboat, silent and invisible. He enlisted my help and I made an underwater device that could pick up the gunboat's echo-sounder and guide him back to her. Everyone was delighted with this underwater homing gadget, especially me as because of it I was posted to an experimental establishment only twenty miles from Joan's family home.

Years later, in my early freelance days, I was given some daily rate work on a cinema commercial for Dubonnet. I noticed that the director kept staring at me until he finally came over and announced, 'You saved my life.' Lieutenant Guy Hamilton was now a successful film director, with whom I worked many times in the years to come, particularly on the series of films concerning another Royal Navy officer, Commander James Bond.

The Navy offered me a permanent commission at the end of the war, in contrast to their apparent reluctance to accept me at the outbreak of hostilities. At the same time Denham Studios invited me back to continue in my old post. Alexander Korda was no longer in charge, in fact Denham was part of the J Arthur Rank Organisation. I actually took up my film work again at Gainsborough Studios, which was also owned by the Rank Organisation. The film was called *Odd Man Out* and starred James Mason; Carol Reed was the director. To round off my war the production mixer was Sacha Fisher – madder than ever.

Goodbye Mr Chips *followed* The Four Feathers *in early 1939. It was to be my first meeting with Johnny Mills with whom I was to work on many films after the war.*

Chapter Six

POST-WAR DENHAM

I returned to civvy street at eight o'clock on a Monday morning. By the end of my first day the six years of war were already fading fast, apart from having to refrain from snapping up my right hand to make or return a salute. The microphone boom held no fears; but I encountered my first shop steward during the morning tea break, and that was another matter.

As official representative of our technicians' union he asked for my paid up membership card. He wasn't satisfied when I explained that after six years of serving King and country I couldn't readily produce a card, let alone a paid up one; I thought I did pretty well to remember my pre-war number, 168. He didn't and sent me packing to the union headquarters in Soho with the warning, 'With no paid up card, you cannot work on the set.'

In the Soho head office the full meaning of peace dawned on me when I was told that the union had no record of my pre-war membership, most certainly not a number as early as 168. With a new number, 2290, I returned to the studio to receive permission to start work as a fully paid up member. (Fifteen years later, as head of the sound department at Beaconsfield Studios, I came across the same shop steward on my staff, still checking the cards of all newcomers, but strangely enough not mine.)

The fact that I joined Sacha Fisher on my first morning probably helped to sweep aside the years in the Navy as we picked up our pre-war sound jobs and started work on a film that was destined to become one of the black and white classics.

As it turned out Carol wasn't totally satisfied with Sacha and I took his place, a step up the ladder to production sound mixer somewhat quicker than I might have hoped for.

On the completion of *Odd Man Out* I joined a by now famous director for the final weeks of a film he was making. His name was David Lean and the film was *Great Expectations*. I ended up recording all the sound effects which gave me my first experience of David's meticulous regard for detail.

Fame Is The Spur, a Boulting brothers production, came next, followed by

Sleeping Car to
Trieste, *Denham,*
1948. Myself, George
Brown (producer)
and Rona Anderson.

Sleeping Car To Trieste which took me to France for the first time since our return from *The Four Feathers* at Christmas almost ten years earlier. I spent all my time on a train too, working with a French sound crew recording thousands of feet of sound effects as we hurtled around France with microphones positioned in every part of the train.

In spite of this flurry of activity, having been less than a year out of the Navy I was the youngest and certainly least experienced sound mixer working for Rank. So the news from Cyril Crowhurst, Head of Sound, that I was to be assigned to the forthcoming film of *Hamlet*, left me in two minds. The thought of Shakespeare and the memory of reading Shylock in front of the class at school dismayed me more than a little. On the other hand with Laurence Olivier producing, directing and starring in the film it was obviously going to be a big budget, prestigious production to follow the enormous success he had had with *Henry V*. Stifling my dislike of Shakespeare I took up the challenge and went to meet Olivier, with whom I'd worked before the war when he was acting in Korda productions.

In the monitor room on one of the vast Denham stages he outlined his ideas. They were unexpected in several ways. He saw Hamlet in black and white, not colour. He also wanted to use a deep-focus technique that would allow him to have Hamlet close to the camera in focus with Ophelia eighty to a hundred feet away also sharply in focus. This required an enormous increase in light which called for four or five times the usual number of arc lights; it would be difficult for the actors, and a problem for 'sound'. They had to contend with the fearful glare, we had to cope with a five-fold increase in unwanted noise from the motors turning the twin carbons in each light, the bubbling from the white hot flames between the carbons and the creak of metal lamp housings continually expanding and contracting.

These technical problems aside, that first meeting with Olivier already began to reduce my reluctance – it would have been hard for anyone not to be enthused by his vision and the exciting ideas he had for the film. We parted with the first rehearsal date pencilled in the diary; Hamlet's soliloquies which he intended to portray in a 'spoken thought' form, that let the audience hear the lines overlaid on visual close-ups or scenes on the screen. I also left scarlet to the roots of my hair. 'Haven't you got a lot of dandruff,' Olivier had remarked peering at my forehead; despite six years in the Navy I was still prone to blushing.

We were still in the pre-production period when we rehearsed the soliloquies one Friday afternoon. I set up a microphone in a corner of the vast music stage at Denham, surrounded it with padded flats to cut down reverberation and settled down to record. Even though the proper recording was scheduled for a later date I wanted to go through the whole process from a technical point of view. In the days before the magnetic tape recording

Laurence Olivier directing Hamlet.

which allows instant playbacks, we made a sound copy simultaneous with the film recording using a sixteen-inch diameter aluminium record coated with a layer of acetate. A sapphire needle cut grooves into the acetate giving a fairly permanent recording which we could play back immediately. I decided to record Olivier on film that afternoon, although he had not asked for me to do so.

He went through the famous soliloquies one by one and then asked to hear what they sounded like. After listening to them he stunned me with the comment that there wouldn't be any need to go through them again; they would be the master recordings he would use in the film. I was amazed, but it was a salutary warning for my future work; no matter in what unlikely circumstances something was committed to soundtrack, there was always the chance it might end up being used in the final production.

With the afternoon nearly over he decided to use up the rest of the time in producing an effect for the disembodied voice of the ghost of Hamlet's father. We tried variations of microphones on his chest and his back, even standing Larry at one end of a twelve-foot length of drain pipe. None of them worked but as it was Friday he said we should think about it over the weekend.

On the Monday morning Larry came bounding in saying 'I've got it – I am going to stick the microphone up my arse!'

'Well, it'll be your discomfort,' I told him.

'But do you know why?' he asked.

I said I hadn't a clue.

He then told me he was really going to keep secret from his friends how he achieved what he knew was going to be a fantastic effect with the ghost's voice. Whatever we decided on, he would tell all his actor friends he had

On the set of Hamlet.

Drowning Ophelia in the stream behind Denham Studios. This was the only sequence filmed outside the studio – nowadays almost all outdoor shots are filmed on location.

simply stuck the microphone up his arse, knowing they would never believe him.

In fact we recorded the ghost's dialogue using a microphone strapped to his diaphragm with adhesive tape, then ran the recording slow, using much filtering and reverberation to achieved the desired effect.

Once filming started it was obvious that even my misgivings had underestimated the amount of arc noise caused by all the lights used for the deep focus technique, which I described at the time as like being in a boiler factory. The sound stages at Denham were some of the largest in the world, with reverberation problems to match. To reduce the din we had forty-foot by sixteen-foot felt baffles covered in hessian hung like huge curtains from the underside of the gantrys. During the whole production I had a team of stage hands who manhandled these heavy drapes to suit our requirements, carting them from stage to stage as we moved from one set to the next.

It wasn't long before we realised that Olivier's *Hamlet* was something

special. He knew the play and was word perfect. Chatting to him once, I commented how I envied anyone who could learn huge chunks of dialogue so effortlessly. His reply really shook me. He said it was absolute agony when he had to commit a new script to memory. He said he was impossible to live with and used to shut to shut himself away in a distant summerhouse at home at Notley Abbey with instructions not to disturb him for any reason.

It was extraordinary too to watch him juggling his roles as director and star, dressed in black tights and tunic, his hair cropped and dyed blond, peering through the camera discussing the set-up with Ray Sturgess, the camera operator,

Olivier, Norman Wooland and Stanley Holloway, the Grave Digger.

while Terence Morgan, also cast as Laertes, took his place on the set. When everything was ready, Olivier would step in front of the camera and play the scene. As soon as the take was completed, he would step out of his acting role again to discuss the finer points of the take from the director's point of view.

It was never a problem for him to persuade actors to appear in his productions and he was always very loyal to old friends who had proved themselves. One of these was Esmond Knight who had been blinded while serving on the *Prince of Wales* during the sinking of the *Bismarck*. Olivier had cast him in Henry V and it was no surprise to find him now playing Bernardo, one of Horatio's friends who keep guard on the battlements at Elsinore when the ghost appears.

Roger Furse, the designer, had built a twenty feet high rounded tower where the ghost is seen, with no parapet. High above the studio floor, surrounded by studio mist, it was often difficult for the sighted actors to know where the edge was. For Esmond Knight, whirling and twirling with a long halbert in his hand, the hazard was even greater. Not that he showed the slightest reticence up there. Once the other actors had paced out his moves for him, he strode about at the top of the tower fearlessly declaiming his lines.

The 'High Tor' revealed another side of Laurence Olivier's extraordinary range of ability. I shall never forget his fall on being confronted by his father's ghost. With arms outstretched, sword in hand he crashed back onto the stone floor flags, made not of studio plaster but solid slabs of York stone; we could all feel the sickening thud as he landed. I have always said that Olivier would have had a leg cut off if he had had to play a one-legged man.

It has always been my habit to walk on sets during their construction to check for squeaky floorboards, stair treads and the like. While I was checking the next set for the great throne scenes, marking the positions where sound dampers would be needed to cut down reverberation, I came face to face with Olivier who flung his arms back, looking skywards and muttering, 'Poor old Arthur Rank, I hope you can afford this'; he least of all never underestimated the drain Hamlet would be on the coffers.

Sound problems weren't restricted to noisy arc lights and squeaking sets. There were Russell Thorndike's ill-fitting dentures that clicked on every word he spoke as the priest taking Ophelia's funeral. That, at least, was only for one scene. I had to contend with another problem the noise from Hamlet's shoes through the whole film.

Not far into the filming I had become bothered by the distraction of the squeaks made whenever Larry moved his feet. Made from black suede, his shoes looked soft and supple; their appearance was deceptive. I was sure the wardrobe department would have a spare pair and I told Larry that I'd asked for them to be brought on set for us to try.

Looking me straight in the eye he said that nothing would persuade him to wear any other shoes. That pair had been made for his stage *Hamlet* which had caused a sensation at the Old Vic and on Broadway, and squeaks or no squeaks I would have to put up with them. I don't think he ever knew that I would get the wardrobe to soak the soles overnight whenever possible. Even

Hamlet with squeaking shoes.

so, I am still conscious of the odd squeak whenever I run the video of Hamlet with the sound turned up, though they had to compete with the dreadful noise from the arc lamps.

The design of the sets called for ingenuity too. One of the exits made by Osric, whose portrayal by Peter Cushing in one of the memorable comedy sequences in the film, was especially tricky. The script called for him to make his exit down a flight of stone steps, backwards and bowing to the prince, hat in hand, only to stumble and tumble down the last few. To follow Peter with a microphone on a boom cast a shadow from the arc lights. This little poser was solved by tensioning a length of piano wire following the run of the steps. Over this was draped a piece of raw ham rind to which we attached our smallest microphone. By allowing the contraption to slide down on the end of a length of black thread controlled from the spot rail, we covered all of Osric's dialogue and his ungainly departure.

Shooting the scene in which Hamlet gives advice to the players, whom he asks to re-enact his uncle's murder of his father, was almost as unorthodox from the cameraman's point of view. Larry had devised a camera movement using a semi-circular set of rails on which ran a specially constructed camera trolley. During Hamlet's speech to the player king he paraded across the little stage set with the camera travelling in a wide arc.

As often seems to happen, we were ready to shoot just as lunchtime approached. We made one take, the camera rolled and we all staggered through in a rather sketchy manner and got to the end of the speech without having to cut. Lunch was called.

After an hour we returned and found, rather surprisingly, that the camera track had been removed. When Larry came back on set he announced that the pre-lunch take had been fine; that was the one we would use. In my amazement I told him that if I had known it was to be the only take, I would have called cut for the various sound imperfections alone.

'If you had, I would have killed you,' was his answer. He knew he couldn't have played the scene any better, even if we technicians were not satisfied with our individual efforts.

Dudley Messenger with microphone boom on camera crane.

Larry receiving his Oscars for Best Film and Best Actor, Henry Vth.

One day on the set as we were getting prepared for a scene, Larry was sitting in his director's chair, removing the afternoon blue shadow from his chin with an electric razor, when a production assistant came on set with a package for him franked with American stamps. It looked as if it contained a couple of bottles of whisky. He gave it a cursory glance and stuck it into the pocket of his chair as the first assistant director called him onto the set. The scene completed, Larry returned to his chair. Remembering the package, he pulled it out, ripped off the paper to reveal two Oscar statuettes, which he'd won for best actor and best film with *Henry V*, and which he had been unable to receive at the Oscar Ceremony. They had been posted to Denham by a novelty manufacturer in Seattle.

In July we stopped shooting for two weeks; all the studios did, just like factories. Olivier had earmarked this fortnight to plan and block out Hamlet's famous duel with Laertes. He also wanted to be sure that Terence Morgan was adept at stage fights. He wasn't, as it turned out, but by the time we returned they both knew every move; cut, thrust and parry.

The scene was set in front of the thrones from which Claudius, Hamlet's uncle, and Gertrude, Hamlet's mother, would watch the duel at the end of the play. The master scene was set, cameras placed; and the two protagonists took their places with Peter Cushing as referee. Just before the camera rolled, Olivier told Terence that he wouldn't be sparing him. What ensued is probably one of the most convincing film fights ever with a demonic look on Hamlet's face as he fought Laertes back towards a stone pillar and Laertes in turn fighting back in sheer terror, eyes wide with fright. This was no acting. He was fighting for his life, parrying every thrust, beads of sweat on his brow as he used all his concentration to stay out of the way of Hamlet's swishing sword. A stuntman might have been easier on him, but Olivier was never one to pander to this convention.

The final day of shooting had been earmarked and reserved for Larry's most demanding stunt. Having killed Laertes and been mortally wounded by his opponent's poisoned sword, the plan was for Hamlet to rush up the steps to a balcony overlooking the King and Queen, to take a flying leap, sword in hand, onto his uncle, the King below. Basil Sydney, who was playing the King, would not agree to having himself jumped on from the parapet above, so stuntman George Crawford was dressed in his costume and crown and put in his place.

Two cameras were going to be used because for this scene there certainly wouldn't be a second take. That is why it had been left to the final afternoon of filming: just in case Olivier did break his neck, at least we had the film in the can. While Larry lined up the cameras, a second stuntman made leaps onto mattresses until the director was satisfied with the shot. The mattresses removed, Larry mounted the stairs, checked where the stuntman had started his run forward, called for the cameras to roll, took a mighty run and leapt. With arms outstretched and grasping his sword he flew horizontally through the air in an incredible dive onto Basil Sydney's double. They both collapsed to the floor motionless; the cameras were still rolling with no one to give the order to cut. Finally Olivier stirred, clearly winded and called out 'Cut the cameras'. Looking down at the still prostrate figure of George Crawford he muttered, 'Can't take it, eh?'

The two Oscars that Olivier won for Best Actor and Best Film aptly repaid the ten month's effort and expenditure that had gone into filming *Hamlet*.

From Shakespeare I moved to H G Wells and *The History of Mr Polly* in

The last 'shot' of the film.

which John Mills, like Olivier, had a dual role as producer and star. The same applied a year later when he made a film with Valerie Hobson called *The Rocking Horse Winner.*

Towards the end of *Rocking Horse Winner* John told me that he was next appearing in a submarine film, *Morning Departure.* As I had spent those six years in the Royal Navy serving as an anti-submarine officer, I was naturally keen to work on it too. Roy Baker, who'd been a contemporary of mine at school, was given the chance to direct his first big film.

The History of Mr
Polly, *Denham,
1949. A night time
shot filmed inside the
studio.*

The story was based on the sinking of the submarine *Thetis* just before the
war, when she went down during her sea trials in Birkenhead Bay with her full
crew and a large number of people from Cammel Laird who had been building
her. Only a few survived, even though the stern was sticking out of the water;
the rest were trapped and drowned and all as a result of a faulty torpedo tube
door. The submarine was salvaged, refitted and served throughout the war as
HMS *Thunderbolt*. The locations for the film were at HMS *Osprey*, the Navy's
anti-submarine base situated high above the dockyard on Portland Bill. For me
it was like stepping onto a time-warp and slipping back ten years to January
1940 when I had reported to *Osprey* as a probationary sub-lieutenant RNVR
special branch.

A great deal of our filming took place on HMS *Adamant*, an enormous
submarine depot ship, on which I had served in Mombassa in 1942. She
'mothered' ten or twelve T-class submarines, one of which, the *Tiptoe* was
allocated for our use.

When we first went aboard her the *Tiptoe* was lying alongside *Adamant*,
five boats out with only narrow gang-planks spanning the gaps between. Led
by Roy Baker we made our way across to be greeted on the upper casing of

Tiptoe where the assistant director, Bob Asher, had his arm grabbed by an officer who greeted him, 'Well done, sir. We had a Mr Dimbleby of the BBC aboard the other day. He came across on all fours.'

'You don't know how close I came to doing the same,' confided Bob.

Once aboard we clambered up the rungs of the conning tower to go below down through the hatch; our art director, Alex Vetchinsky, an enormous bulk of a man was discreetly led forward by the first lieutenant to be admitted by the much more capacious torpedo stowage hatch set at an angle in the deck.

Below decks I was surrounded by vivid memories. My first surprise was to discover that I knew the captain, Bob Smith, who had been a leading signalmen when we had met during the war.

Tiptoe was part of the Portland training flotilla which used her as a target for anti-submarine ratings and officers on surface ships to learn their search and attack skills. When we went to sea our filming had to be carried out without interrupting their training schedules.

The first time everyone was bundled below decks, hatches closed and secured, and the order 'Dive . . . Dive . . . Dive . . .' given, it unsettled most of the film crew; they were unnerved by the slight tilt of the submarine as she

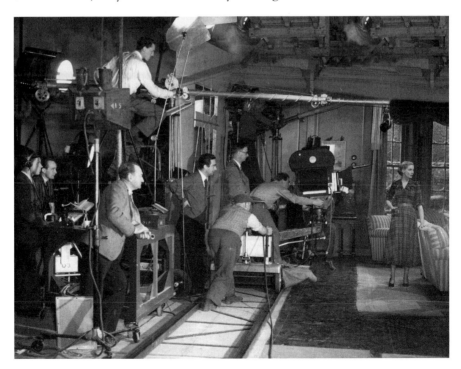

The Rocking Horse Winner, *Denham, 1949.*

Filming The Perfect Woman, *Denham, 1949, with Nigel Patrick and Patricia Roc.*

descended towards the bottom of Portland Bay with the sound of ballast tanks filling and klaxon blaring.

At first we were presenting a sitting target for craft searching above. The order 'Quiet ship' came over the intercom, followed by the sound of ship's screws overhead. The muffled explosion that came next jangled nerves even more until it was explained that this was only a small signalling depth charge telling us we could surface.

A great deal of my time was spent recording all the sounds needed for the final sound-track and here Bob Smith did me proud. He blew 'Q' tanks that made the submarine surface, rang every combination of ship's telegraphs, raised and lowered the periscope time after time, ran the engines at a range of different revs and operated the 'heads', which in a submarine has a lot more to it than just pulling a chain; as submariners will tell you, 'If you don't go through the right procedure, you're likely to get your own back.'

My final request to Bob Smith was to record the effect of a diver striking the outside of the hull with a spanner to simulate a message to the entombed crew. What could be better than the real thing? So a rating was detailed to go onto the upper casing and tap out a message in various places. The fact that it was pouring with rain only drew the comment from his skipper, 'He would

Filming Morning Departure, *1950.*

Johnny Mills bids farewell to Helen Cherry.

have been wet through anyway, if he was a diver.'

I met other wartime shipmates too. One day we were working on the floating dock in which a submarine was being repaired. I climbed down into the bottom of the dock and was looking at the anti-submarine search equipment, when a voice said, 'I think we shall have to change the dome, sir.' The voice belonged to Petty Officer Squance, who had been with me at Dartmouth just before D-Day.

To complete the filming schedule we returned to the studio to shoot the dialogue scenes in a mock-up of the interior of the submarine that had been set up with removable sides, to make our job easier, and intricately fitted out with all the correct equipment.

This must have been one of the last sets built at Denham because, unknown to us, the Rank Organisation had included them in their programme of post-war studio closures, which was to leave them with just the film laboratories at Denham and Pinewood Studios at Iver. For reasons that I never really understood I was the only sound mixer under contract with Rank, unlike several of my senior colleagues. So when Denham closed I was transferred to Pinewood where I was to work throughout the 1950s, whilst the others lost their jobs.

George Cole, Richard Attenborough and John Mills in Morning Departure.

Chapter Seven

PINEWOOD STUDIOS

Ship sound effects followed me to Pinewood; my first assignment there was the Paul Soskin production Waterfront. This was a typically run-of-the-mill post-war British film when cinemas still had a captive audience willing to queue in the rain for a second house, but still expecting a twice-weekly change of programme with a second feature. There was nothing particularly outstanding about *Waterfront*. The drunken ship's fireman was a clever piece of typecasting for Robert Newton who needed no persuasion to hit the bottle. Only two other names stand out: Michael Anderson who was later to direct *Around The World in Eighty Days,* and a young Welsh actor playing the ship's second officer. His name was Richard Burton.

Our last six weeks of location shooting comprised bitterly cold nights around Liverpool docks. The sound editor needed distant river backgrounds with ship's sirens if possible, so I decided to find a ship sailing that night on the tide and try to persuade its captain to sound the siren at pre-determined times as he approached and sailed past our position on shore.

The *Monas Queen* was due to depart well after midnight for the Isle of Man, by which time the dockside traffic would have ceased, making it quiet enough for our siren recordings. Having found where the ship was berthed, I saw the duty officer who took me to the captain's cabin and explained what I wanted to the captain, who was seated at his desk with his back to us. Swinging round, he looked at me and said, 'I know you, you bugger. You sailed on the old *Perveril* with me to Douglas before the war.'

I was eighteen in 1935 when we went to the Isle of Man with George Formby so it was amazing that he remembered me. An even bigger surprise was that he had been skipper of the *Monas Queen* throughout the war when, as a fleet auxiliary, I had been on board several times to check equipment during my time on the Clyde.

My first foreign location after the war came a couple of years after I started working at Pinewood. This was a Val Guest production called *Penny Princess;* it starred Dirk Bogarde and Val's wife, Yolande Donland.

Penny Princess was set in the mountains of Catalonia, in a village called Montseigne. This was the first time that a British film unit had gone to work in Spain, so we had no past experience to fall back on. The equipment was too bulky to be sent as freight and set off on a convoy of trucks to be driven down through France and into Spain, with the lighting generator following in the rear. We, the unit, were flown in a chartered Dakota to Barcelona, where we were driven by coach up winding roads and round hairpin bends until we arrived, weary, at the family-run pension that was going to be our headquarters. Accommodation here was so tight that apart from Yo Donlan, Val and some of the actors, everyone else had to share. Three of us were shoved into a room fitted out with camp beds, with a sloping roof over the kitchen. The consolation was that the warmth from the kitchen below kept us warm while others shivered in the mountain air.

The plumbing wasn't any better. Some thirty of us had to make do with only two toilets and no hot water. There was no bathroom and the shower next door to the kitchen consisted of a large round can suspended from the ceiling into which holes had been punched. Anyone wanting a shower called first at the kitchen where the services of a lady were procured. First she filled an enormous jug with hot water; then she stood upon a stool and poured it

Lunchtime on the set of Clouded Yellow *with Jean Simmons.*

into the shower can. It wasn't long before Yo had a tin bath brought up from Barcelona. At least we had plumbing. Dudley, my boom operator, and several of the camera crew were billeted in what was called the 'new house'. This was so new that apart from two toilets it had no plumbing. There was no glass in the windows either, only shutters.

Our arrival wasn't cheered when we heard from Val that the equipment hadn't arrived; it had been held up by Spanish customs at the French border for lack of proper documentation.

Our only link with the outside world was a primitive telephone with a handle that had to be cranked to call the operator. Calls to Barcelona and Madrid were difficult enough; trying to contact London was almost impossible. But for the fact that one of the Technicolor crew assistants, Johnny Cabrera, was a Spaniard whose father was a senior official in the government able to cut through the red tape, we might well have sat waiting longer than the ten days we did.

Every day we waited cut into the schedule and budget. Val changed some of the scenes to a nighttime setting, which meant we wouldn't be restricted to working only in daylight hours when we did get started. Meanwhile there was nothing for us to do apart from exploring the countryside or waiting for the next meal.

Val was regularly bombarded by telegrams from the studio demanding daily progress reports of the shooting to date. They could not believe that not a foot of film had passed through the cameras. In reply Val cabled back the message, 'No filming achieved to date, we have no equipment.'

When the convoy of trucks finally arrived in the village square there was a frenzy of activity to get something in the can that evening. Within three hours of their arrival we were ready to shoot the first scene, which in our case included a playback of music for timing purposes; our one problem being that a high wind kept blowing the pickup arm across the record.

Most of the filming was carried out in a very small area around the village. To save money the production department had given me a two-wheeled cart in lieu of a sound truck. The cart had rope-net sides and a planked floor and was just big enough to squeeze in our equipment. The motive power was a mule, the largest in Spain with the most malevolent pair of eyes. He hated us and took an even greater dislike to being backed between the shafts.

Like many remote Spanish villages, Montseigne was virtually run by the priest and the schoolmaster. Arrangements had been made with the former to

Dirk Bogarde and Yo Doulan in Penny Princess, *1952.*

ring the church bell when we needed extras for a crowd scene. People from the surrounding area would assemble in the square where the schoolmaster would stand on a box to hold a roll-call, register in hand. This system worked well until the first Sunday, when the priest realised we intended filming on the sabbath, and we realised that we wouldn't have any extras from his congregation unless a solution could be reached between him and Val. The compromise they struck saw Val and Yo attending mass, which the priest promised to keep short, and then his turning a blind eye to our working for the rest of the day.

As always, we settled into a routine for daily filming. We would walk down the hill to the square to be met by the 'new house' inmates coming up. They had solved their lack of hot water by commandeering an enormous black cauldron. Every morning this was filled with water and a fire was lit beneath using a large pile of rough poles lying by the front door. Every evening a suitable number of logs was sawn up for the morning kindling. This served them well for quite a time until the cauldron went missing one morning; they all arrived for work unshaven that day.

In the meantime the rest of us had heard a dreadful screaming coming from the butcher's yard where a pig was being slaughtered; by lunchtime we were unwittingly enjoying it as sausages. The cauldron had returned to its normal service and was bubbling with pig's blood, though the butcher was very accommodating. He told the 'new house' boys that they were welcome to use it for their hot water, except on Thursdays which was sausage day.

With Val Guest having rewritten much of the script for night shooting, as well as filming by day, we got little sleep. One evening we saw a squad of sinister shiny black-hatted Guarda Civile being deployed round our shooting area as the arc lights were lit. Apparently one of the men from our hotel family had broken out of jail in Barcelona, where he was serving time on a drugs' charge, and the police thought he might try to make a run for the village. I never found out if he did or not; in any case, our bright lights probably warned him off until the Guarda had left.

Towards the end of the film Val had a word with me about a scene that was scheduled for the next afternoon. He was stuck for actors to play customs men with Dirk and Yolande at a frontier post. As it was a montage sequence there was no sound to be recorded; only background to be laid over afterwards. So he suggested that the four of us in the sound crew might like to do it. People who work behind the camera are always loath to be talked into appearing in front of it. With no sound required, no actors available and Dirk tickled pink at the idea, we didn't have a leg to stand on. The next afternoon we paraded in front of the customs barrier decked out in khaki shirts, trousers, big army boots and peaked gendarmes' hats, except for Dudley Messenger who was such a big chap the only uniform he could fit into was an officer's, which set him off against we other three in our dingy garb.

The camera rolled. We did our stuff checking carts, questioning Dirk and Yolande, and waving them through with their load of smuggled cheeses. Val seemed satisfied with our performances though he was curious to know what my maintenance man, Austin Partridge, was doing in his cameo solo, scribbling away on his clip-board all through the scene.

'I was just making out my time sheet, old boy,' explained Austin.

We left the village with fond farewells to the friends we had made and went back to Barcelona for a few days filming and several steaming hot baths.

Killing time before catching the plane home on the last day I went shopping in and around the Ramblas; first for bananas, which Anne, who was eight by now, had still never seen one, then to a patisserie to buy cakes. Returning from locations with local goodies set such a regular pattern over the years that the crew got used to asking at the airport, 'Have you got your cakes?'

One of the jobs I have always enjoyed in my work is creating sound effects and a couple of years after going to Pinewood I recorded effects for a film produced and directed by Henry Cornelius which gave me full rein. I had known Henry before the war as an editor at Ealing. Now as a producer-director he had had terrible trouble raising the money for a script he believed would

The sound crew roped in as extras for Penny Princess.

The three-strip Technicolor camera used on Penny Princess.

turn into a comedy classic, but which Rank had dismissed as being of little consequence. Henry had mortgaged his house to scrape together the funds needed to make the film on the minuscule budget grudgingly provided by Rank. But his faith was well placed and *Genevieve* quickly established itself as an all-time favourite.

The shooting schedule was very short and most of the exterior filming had to be done at a time of year when the weather was prone to sudden changes. A cameraman friend of mine, Christopher Challis, was asked to take on the task of cinematographer on the understanding that the budget wouldn't allow for niceties like waiting for the weather to ensure continuity from one shot to the next. To Henry it didn't, or couldn't, matter that one scene might be filmed in sunshine, the next in rain, the next in sleet even. He couldn't afford any hold-ups. The crew only went down to Brighton for the closing shots. The rest was filmed around West Drayton and Moor Park with the two cars quite often mounted on trailers to be towed with the cameras.

By the time I came on the scene after main unit filming, to record all the sound effects and post-synchronising of location dialogue, Henry's coffers were all but empty. With limited funds and limited time we set to work creating effects for the cars and the town clock which drives Dinah Sheridan and John Gregson demented as it chimes right outside their hotel bedroom window. I wanted to make this pretty absurd. The basic noise of large cogs winding up the chiming mechanism we got from an old-fashioned mangle. Assorted springs were twanged. Chains were wound over large sprockets. And a football rattle was used to good effect.

As we worked on the sound effects Henry Cornelius was grappling with

Malta Story, *1952*.

With Alec Guinness.

the problem of what to do about music for the film, not having found a composer and knowing that he could only afford a much smaller orchestra than was usual.

At the end of the morning we had just finished recording the town clock, and I was getting ready to go off to lunch, when Larry Adler came into the effects theatre asking if we had a piano. Cornelius had shown him the film and he wanted to try a few bars of an idea he had had for a theme tune. He sat down and played the *Genevieve* theme. Henry Cornelius was impressed; even more so when Larry produced his harmonica from his breast pocket to play it again. Henry then asked me to record it, so that he would have an immediate copy with which to persuade the money men that it would do much for his film, as is so often the case with the right theme tune.

After its world-wide success, it is said that Rank approached Henry offering to buy him out of *Genevieve*, which he must have enjoyed turning down. Sadly he died within five years, having little chance to enjoy the fruits of his great success. But I believe that Larry Adler, who was offered a royalty in place of a composer's fee, has been benefiting from his inspiration since 1962. I am proud to know I made the first recording of the *Genevieve* theme.

Genevieve was followed a year later by another classic British comedy, the film version of Richard Gordon's highly successful book, *Doctor In The House*. I was delighted that the producer Betty Box had bought the film rights. I worked on eleven films with her and her director partner Ralph Box during my time at Pinewood and as a freelance.

Doctor In The House was enormous fun from start to finish. I have always felt that its great success came from the atmosphere of good-natured competition amongst the cast. Dirk Bogarde was already well-established as a star and Kenneth More, Donald Sinden, Donald Houston and the rest were not far behind him. Every day on the set, in sequence after sequence, we could sense them all striving to top the others. This camaraderie, with much laughter, spread to everyone on the unit. I don't think any of us will forget the day we filmed the scene in which James Robertson Justice (as Sir Lancelot Spratt) examined George Coulouris surrounded by the students. He marked out a large red line for the incision, right across the prostrate patient's chest, telling him to keep still – that this was no concern of his. Turning to Dirk, he snapped, 'You, Sparrow, what's the bleeding time?'

Dirk's memorable reply, 'A quarter to three, sir,' was followed by an hilarious uproar which almost drowned out Ralph Thomas's call 'Cut the camera'.

Doctor At Sea, which followed a year later, was almost as much fun. Who couldn't have enjoyed making a film aboard a luxury mini-liner sailing from Venice, through the Corinth Canal to Piraeus, on to Alexandria and then back to Venice?

As ship's doctor Dirk had hilarious scenes with a succession of patients, particularly Maurice Denham who was obviously trying to be excused duties as a steward. Dirk diagnosed 'pes planum', which completely confounded

Maurice, who enquired if it was serious, only to be told he had flat feet.

Noel Purcell, an Irish actor who had originally been stage carpenter at the Abbey Theatre in Dublin, was in his element as the ship's carpenter down to the fingers missing from his right hand, the legacy of an earlier accident.

Another patient was a young, little-known French actress. When Dirk was called to her cabin he found her naked in the shower. Forty years ago all the audience were allowed to see of her was a dim outline through the steamed up glass of the cubicle. Ralph Thomas and Betty Box were very taken with her and tried to persuade the head of the Rank Organisation to put her under contract. His reply was disdainful, assuring them he saw no great talent in her. Her name was Brigitte Bardot.

In 1954 Ralph Thomas and Betty Box planned to make a film based on a rather different story of the sea. *Above Us The Waves* brought to the screen the famous wartime attack by midget submarines on the German battleship *Tirpitz*, when she was moored in a Trondjen Norwegian fjord, protected by a barrier of anti-submarine nets and mines. This was another opportunity for me to renew my naval connections and to work with Donald Cameron RN, VC. He was our naval adviser on the film and one of the commanding officers of the three X-craft that made the attack; the other two were Lieutenant Place RNR, VC, later Rear-Admiral, and Lieutenant Henty Creer RNVR.

Henty was probably the saddest coincidence that cropped up in my career. He had been a camera assistant on *The Four Feathers* in the Sudan. Not long after joining the Navy I went back to Denham in uniform, only to have Henty say to me, 'They'll have to come and get me.' It was difficult to believe that he had been on that daring raid with Cameron; poignant too that Henty's had been the midget submarine to be blown up by a mine.

There was still an X-craft seaworthy and available for our film, which we used off the coast of Guernsey. The bulk of the work then took place at the submarine base HMS *Dolphin* at Gosport, where we went below decks once more in a T-class submarine. Several of the cast, including John Gregson and Donald Sinden, made a simulated escape from a submarine using the two hundred-foot high column of water inside the huge escape tower at Gosport.

For most of the time the three-man crews of actors were squeezed into a mock-up of an X-craft for filming. Donald Cameron was at hand to ensure authenticity, though this wasn't always predictable. At one point the director asked him, 'Now, Donald, in this scene we have the two midget subs, which have got under the nets. They are sitting on the bottom waiting for the third

Doctor in the House, 1953.

boat to rendezvous – Now what exactly would you be doing?'

Donald took his pipe from his mouth to say, 'Oh, I don't know . . . brewing up, I suppose.'

A year later I found myself back in Spain once more working on a film with Dirk Bogarde, whom the producer John Bryan had cast in the title role of *The Spanish Gardener*, a story set near San Feliu in a beautifully restored Catalonian farmhouse, owned by a millionaire lace-maker from Barcelona. Cyril Cusack was also in the cast, playing the chauffeur. He drove an open vintage Rolls-Royce, at least that is what the script said. No one had checked whether Cyril could drive; he soon demonstrated that he could not. So scenes of his arriving and departing had to be shot with a double at the wheel. For the closer shots, Cyril took his place in the driver's seat to be towed along at the end of a rope pulled by sweating prop men.

When I met up with Cyril two years later he had managed to acquire a

Above Us The Waves, *Guernsey, 1955.*

John Mills in Above Us The Waves.

The water tank at Gosport where trainee submarine crew learn the technique of 'free escape'.

driving licence. I was filming in Dublin and he kindly invited me and Chris Challis, our cameraman, to dinner with the airy comment that he'd pick us up in his car. This was evidently a recent acquisition. We pulled away with crashing gears. On the road his steering was erratic. His preferred method of stopping was to rub the wheels along the curb. And this was before we had spent the evening in a hostelry where he was obviously no stranger and where the local police joined us for a drink after gaining entry by a coded knock on the side door long after closing time. Perhaps it is just as well that I have no recollection of that return journey with Cyril.

After the great success of the 'Doctor' films, Ralph Thomas and Betty Box acquired the film rights of *The Wind Cannot Read*, which David Lean had once thought of filming. This told the story of the love affair between an English army officer (to be played by Dirk Bogarde) serving in India during the war and a young Japanese girl employed to teach Japanese.

For us it was exciting to be filming in India. For many in the crew it would be their first taste of the Orient. An Air India Super-Constellation had been chartered to fly us to Delhi via Beirut and Karachi. After a delayed departure from the collection of army huts and flapping marquees beside the Bath Road that in 1956 passed as Heathrow Airport, we took off eventually to fly into the night sky, lulled by the synchronised beat of the four Pratt and Whitney engines whose exhausts glowed red in the darkness. Beirut was reached after eight hours and we landed in the warm humidity of a Mediterranean night. From there we flew over Syria, down the Persian Gulf to land at Karachi in the midday heat. After refuelling, it was a relatively short trip to Delhi and the Cecil Hotel in the old part of the city.

The Cecil was laid out in spacious grounds in which stood the main building with lounges, dining-room, kitchen and reception, surrounded by a number of two-storey buildings linked by covered walkways; this was where the guests had their rooms. Every room was manned by a turbaned servant squatting outside the door, ready to run errands for his 'sahib'. India had been independent for nearly nine years by this time, but it soon became apparent that the servant class were missing the days of the White Raj, when paradoxically they seemed to have had better treatment than was the case now with middle-class Indians to boss them about.

Among the rules drummed into us before we had left were those concerning alcohol. We were told we could only drink in the dining-room and in our rooms and that Friday was 'dry day'. One of the party, a rigger by trade, claimed not to have been told about the drinking restrictions before he left England. He was used to enjoying his evening pints, he maintained, and if he couldn't have them in India as he had done when he was there during the war, he wanted to go home. He also saw fit to come into the dining-room without jacket and tie and in his braces, which did not go down well with the other diners.

This problem was solved very quietly by our production manager, Charles Orme, who presented him with a return ticket for London the next day. This horrified our rigger friend, who, after much haggling between Betty Box and the studio union shop stewards, had been the first member of his trade to go on foreign location. We heard he went sick on arrival back in London, never to return to the studio and the wrath of his trade union bosses.

For the rest of us the first few days in Delhi were spent retrieving our equipment from customs; a lengthy and laborious procedure which has not improved greatly in the intervening forty years.

The cost of air freighting the heavy car batteries that powered the sound equipment and cameras meant that we had to buy these locally. New ones were ruled out because of their expense so we spent ages combing the markets looking for reasonable second-hand ones. The short-sightedness of this penny pinching was soon revealed when, after several delays caused by flat batteries, we had to buy new ones and throw away the duds we had spent hours trying to find.

We started filming in the hotel gardens, moving from there to the crowded streets and markets of Old Delhi, and the Red Fort. Shooting in Delhi was completed after a near riot in a market scene when it was discovered that the art director had built his true-to-life set on a piece of waste ground (as he had been led to believe), which turned out to be an ancient burial site. The affronted spirits of the dead were calmed by the power of a bundle of rupees.

Our first location outside Delhi was Agra, where we were to shoot scenes at the Taj Mahal. Daytime shooting was carried out in spite of the crowds who did not take kindly to our clearing them out of the way for our long shots. The noise made by the crowds was so obtrusive that I had to make arrangements to return at night to record the strange wailing chant of the custodian. After dark, with shafts of moonlight shining through the tessellated screens into the large chamber under the dome, the atmosphere was a remarkable contrast to the daytime din – although as were packing up our equipment rain began pouring down, followed by flashes of lightning and the rumble of thunder.

This gave me a unique opportunity to make what I still regard as an historic recording.

From Agra we travelled to Jaipur, to film in many of the now-famous tourist spots of the Pink City, including an ancient fortress where Dirk and the little Japanese actress, Yoko Tani, made a pilgrimage by elephant, serenaded by three musicians playing a violin, a type of concertina and small finger cymbals. Their party piece was a haunting melody which I recorded later in

Producer Betty Box, and director Ralph Thomas, The Wind Cannot Read.

the day; it was used to great advantage in the final film.

Every evening our supper of steamed suet puddings, pies and jam and syrup sponges was accompanied by two little old men whose repertoire consisted of Ivor Novello and Noel Coward numbers. Their violins were hopelessly out of tune but the sound they made was sufficiently nostalgic to touch our heart and purse strings. We parted with a handful of rupees which turned into a bribe to make them go away when their limitations became more aggravating as the evenings passed.

Many of our facilities in Jaipur had been made possible through the good offices of a gypsum millionaire, whose daughter was due to marry as our filming came to an end. The preliminaries to the actual ceremony had been going on all day; while filming in the town we had seen the groom, mounted on a white horse, lead a parade through the streets to the temple. After finishing our shooting, we went back to the rest-house where we were staying to change into our best suits before getting Ram, our driver, to take us to the ceremony where most of the guests were already inside. A turbaned attendant there noticed us looking for somewhere to park, waved us across the street and motioned Ram into a space between two of the processional elephants.

With our invitations in our hands, we were met by the Hindu equivalent of an usher who asked us if we would like something to drink. After a day under the Jaipur sun he could have read our thoughts, though pint glasses of warm milk sprinkled with chopped candied peel wasn't precisely what we had in mind.

The ceremony was in full swing, presided over by a priest and two acolytes intoning from the scriptures. In front of them sat a handsome groom alongside his heavily veiled bride, surrounded by her ladies-in-waiting. To our surprise we were asked if we would like to see the bride, a privilege the groom had not yet been afforded; this was an arranged marriage and the happy couple would not come face to face until the ceremony was over. The veils were drawn back and we gazed on quite the ugliest girl we had seen in India; I only hoped it turned into a love-match.

Our return to Delhi was a nightmare for me. I was struck down by a bout of malaria and the journey seemed endless. Never was my room with its faithful squatting bearer more welcome. About the only good thing about malaria is that one seldom dies from it, provided the correct treatment is followed. But the blinding headache and vicious temperature has to be endured, followed by several days of weakness and dizziness.

By this stage in our stay Danny Daniel, my boom operator, and Ron Butcher, the recordist, had befriended Ram, who became the gentle butt of Danny's Welsh wit. Ram bore with good humour the persistent enquiries about his love-life and the 'dancing girls' with whom Danny fondly imagined him cavorting. In the end Ram called Danny's bluff by inviting the four of us to join him on a visit to the 'dancing girls'. This started with a drive to the bazaar in Old Delhi, where Ram parked the car and led us across an un-metalled street, into a building and up two flights of stairs. He knocked on a door, which opened to reveal a most extraordinary sight. Inside were three tiers of open,

The Wind Cannot Read. *Dirk Bogarde and Yoka Tani.*

cage-like, bunks on which sprawled girls of all ages from teens to twenties. All of them were heavily made-up, with large lipsticked lips, white-powdered faces and dark mascaraed eyes. A large blowsy woman who obviously ran the place made a bee-line for Danny and dragged him over to the girls to make his choice. He made his escape and tried to laugh it off as he joined us sitting cross-legged on the carpet, but still he was pursued and draped with flowered garlands. Highly coloured drinks in grubby glasses were proffered and cautiously sipped before we were able to make our exit with much bowing and hand clasping, leaving Ram to pay for our entertainment which I suspect was only partially fulfilled.

Most of our work was completed, the only further shooting to do was in the hotel grounds and also to record sound effects of marching and drilling at the barracks of the Rajasthan Rifles. A visit to the colonel with my list of requirements led to the suggestion that we might like to be present at a passing-out parade in a couple of days' time, a ceremony that should give us all the material we might need.

Two mornings later we reported for duty at eight o'clock to find the entire contingent on parade and a raised dais from which we were to be honoured reviewers. It took some diplomacy to explain that we would be busy recording the ceremony and moving around with our equipment. A suitable compromise was reached and my maintenance engineer, Van de Goor, took the place of honour on a high-backed chair under the canopy.

The marching and counter-marching was first rate, though visually quite extraordinary, for marching alone between the head and tail of two columns was the tallest man I have ever seen; his stride equalled two paces of the other soldiers. I found out later that he was only twenty years old and had been enlisted as a visual mascot.

As the parade progressed I became aware that all the shouted orders seemed to be in English, which was ideal for my purposes. In actual fact all the commands had been given in Urdu. Someone had ingeniously translated the commands so that the length and command of each one still sounded as if it was being bellowed by a sergeant major in the British army.

While we were dismantling our equipment for the pre-departure customs check, a note came round from the production office telling us all to attend a unit meeting in the evening. Rumours began to spread that there was a problem and when we assembled later we were told that Ronald Lewis, one of the actors, had suspected typhoid fever. Ronnie was safely tucked away in isolation in his bedroom, with nurses in constant attendance. If word got out there was a risk that all fifty of us might be slapped in quarantine, the thought of which must have sent the production manager's temperature soaring.

The solution offered by the unit doctor was that we should all be inoculated immediately and sworn to secrecy. There was only one dissenter, one of my crew. But I stood up and took responsibility that he would keep quiet; none of us fancied an enforced stay in India after being away from home so long. So, we all bared our arms, took the jab and agreed to keep silent.

To speed our passage through customs someone had the idea of inviting the customs men to the end-of-film party. They turned up in force and much scotch was consumed, which looked promising. It was just a pity that a completely different customs crew was on duty when we arrived next morning at the airport. Every item on the packing lists had to be inspected and every entry had to be rubber-stamped five times.

Showing my daughter
Anne a film studio for
the first time, 1950s.

Chapter Eight

THERE IS NOTHIN' LIKE A DAME

Back in Pinewood I was walking through the studios some months later when I met Laurence Olivier and his associate, Anthony Bushell. Larry told me that he was planning a film of Terence Rattigan's play *The Sleeping Prince*, in which he had appeared on stage alongside Vivien Leigh, though her part was to be taken in the film by Marilyn Monroe and the title was to be changed to *The Prince And The Showgirl*.

By all accounts the American backers were only interested that Marilyn play the part, while Olivier only wanted to get the film off the ground and shot as a means to find backing for the next projected Shakespeare epic, *Macbeth*. He asked if I would like to join him and I was delighted to accept. It sounded a very exciting project with a wonderful cast and a credit list made up of the cream of British film technicians.

The sets were a triumph, designed by Carmen Dillon who had worked with Roger Furse on *Henry V* and *Hamlet*. The Ruritanian embassy she created captured the atmosphere of the play perfectly. Good to look at, her sets were also masterpieces of practicality. Walls could be moved in or out at will to accommodate the camera; and a sweeping horseshoe staircase could also be trundled out of the main entrance hall to make space for reverse shots.

With the sets built, we awaited the arrival of Miss Monroe. She had recently married the playwright Arthur Miller, and this was to be a combined honeymoon-cum-business trip to Europe. The press followed every movement from the moment she arrived at Southampton and we were getting ready to work a 'closed set' with no visitors, certainly no press, during filming. Extra security had been brought in and everyone was stopped at the studio gates and asked to identify themselves and show their credentials.

Olivier had been warned by most of his director friends, particularly those in America, such as William Wyler, Billy Wilder and John Huston, that working with her wouldn't be easy. So he had decided to have two-to-three weeks of theatre-type rehearsals before the actual filming. A studio had been prepared for this purpose, where we had gathered to await her arrival.

Escorted by a smiling Laurence Olivier, Marilyn Monroe walked down the long corridor flanked by Arthur Miller and her drama coach Paula Strasberg, the wife of Lee Strasberg, the founder of the New York Actors Studio, home of 'method acting'. As if to emphasise this, both she and Marilyn were dressed in black.

Despite the efforts to keep the press away a photographer did manage to get into the corridor and pounced from a doorway with his camera and flash. He might as well have spared the effort; his film was confiscated and he was escorted away to the main studio gate.

Larry introduced us in turn before setting to work on rehearsing the famous couch seduction scene, where the crown prince has sent for the little blonde he had seen in the theatre chorus the previous evening. Marilyn teetered on stiletto heels into the empty rehearsal room marked out on the floor with lines showing walls and doors. The prince greeted her in the mid-European voice Larry had copied from Alexander Korda's Hungarian accent and there was a long pause. Marilyn looked around bemused and then explained that she always had to have her dialogue for each scene typed in double-spaced capitals

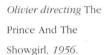

Olivier directing The Prince And The Showgirl, *1956.*

on white cards. She didn't know a single word of the script; in fact we began to wonder if she had even read it. Olivier, who as always was word-perfect, looked shaken. His friends had had trouble directing her, now he was planning to direct and play opposite her at the same time. The rehearsal was cancelled. We never went back to that room again during the whole production.

More was to be revealed as time went by. Paula Strasberg held an almost Svengali-like sway over Marilyn. Arthur Miller, while having an affinity with Olivier, was very much her guardian, spending every day beside her portable studio dressing-room; never obtrusive but always there to walk her off stage as soon as a scene had been shot.

Marilyn brought her American make-up man Whitey Snyder, who had worked on every one of her films. It was claimed he would even fly to New York from Hollywood to make her up for a particular evening function, and then fly back to Hollywood on the night flight ready for work on his current film set the next morning.

Milton Green was another of her tight circle of trusted confidantes. He was the stills photographer famous for the pictures of Marilyn nude on the beach, and on *The Prince And The Showgirl* he was also co-producer. He had bought the film rights to *The Sleeping Prince* on Marilyn's behalf, and also had a free hand to take stills throughout the production.

This tightly knit quartet formed a barrier round Marilyn that Olivier found hard to penetrate. This wasn't helped by Marilyn's concern that he did not like her. He certainly found it hard to accept her apparent lack of professionalism which was made worse by similar lack of understanding that in film making time really does mean money.

Nevertheless, she did have that indefinable 'something' – an instinctive understanding of when to give a line, when to give a look. This often amounted to an inspired flash in what had otherwise been an impossible take. It was from an enormous collection of 'out-takes' that our veteran film editor, Jack Harris, painstakingly pieced together scenes, using a line or a look, maybe just a single word or part sentence from many takes, to give the finished film the appearance of sheer genius from her.

As we progressed, Larry and I agreed that we had to make every effort to avoid post-synchronising with Marilyn. It was bad enough that she couldn't remember lines and neither of us could face the prospect of her re-speaking those lines in the post-synch theatre, exactly matching her lip movements on the screen. In 1956 we didn't have sophisticated miniature microphones attached

to pocket-size radio transmitters. At times it wasn't possible to use the boom microphone because of the shadows it would have cast from the cameraman's lights. So I had to use a miniature Lavalier microphone, about the size of my thumb. I suppose I can claim to be one of the few people to have positioned a microphone between Marilyn Monroe's bosom. A cable led from this down the back of her dress, which was paid out by one of my assistants as she moved through the scene, often up and down the vast horseshoe staircase.

Long delays were common from the day we started filming. We had to wait for Marilyn's belated arrival from the mansion that had been rented for her at nearby Englefield Green. There were even longer delays while she was in make-up and hairdressing before she was ready to be sewn into her figure-forming dress. Many, many times Dame Sybil Thorndyke would be kept waiting on the set, word-perfect too for her role as the Grand Duchess. Never once did she show impatience, only an even greater desire to help.

The same couldn't be said of Paula Strasberg; very early on it was clear that she and Olivier didn't hit it off. His disapproval of method acting was well known. He also resented the barrier that she was creating between himself and Miss Monroe. Paula Strasberg's behaviour on set was certainly most unprofessional. She used to watch each rehearsal and then move in just before a take to say something to Marilyn. Through my headphones I obviously heard more than anyone, except Marilyn, of these prompts from Paula, comments like, 'Now Marilyn, remember a tree is a tree. There are oak trees, beech trees, apple trees, and peach trees. Remember Frank Sinatra and the three little bears.' Poor Marilyn invariably looked totally blank, answering with a vague, 'What – Oh, yeah.'

Then Olivier would take his place in front of the camera, having walked away while Paula was whispering to her. The camera would turn; many times Larry had to feed her dialogue, particularly if we were shooting over his shoulder onto a close-up of her. So much of her best performance was wheedled out of her by this method, almost line by line, by a patient Larry; not that she was ever sufficiently at ease with him to call him that. Quite often it would be a querulous 'Sir Laurence'.

At one point Paula Strasberg had to go back to America for a week to see her daughter Susan opening in a play in New York. For Olivier this was the opportunity he wanted to try to get closer to Marilyn. And it worked. We made good progress and she seemed far more relaxed, if for no other reason than only having to pay attention to one set of directions. When the time came for Paula Strasberg to reappear we heard that Olivier had refused to allow her back on the set for the rest of the film. Marilyn countered by refusing to start any of the new scenes without Paula. The New York Actors Studio won and the strange whisperings continued while Olivier waited patiently off-set until Paula Strasberg had finished – although he was not deaf to comments from other quarters.

After listening to several rehearsals of my friend Richard Wattis, playing the part of the equerry, I was convinced that one of the lines didn't ring true.

I mentioned this to Larry, 'I don't suppose you'll agree with me, but don't you think Richard's line is completely out of character?' To this I received a curt, 'No'. I put my headphones back on but noticed Olivier looking across at me before he walked over to say something to Dickie Wattis. Then, crossing to where I was standing, without any comment, he put his hand in his pocket, took out a penny and pressed it into my hand. The line was changed.

When shooting was over an end-of-picture party was held and a totally different Marilyn Monroe appeared. Breaking free of Paula Strasberg, Arthur Miller and the rest, she chatted to people she possibly had not said a word to during the past fifteen weeks. It came as a surprise when she addressed me by name as she gave me a pig-skin wallet as a memento. She looked genuinely disappointed when the 'bodyguard' broke up the party to take her away just as she was starting to get into the swing of things, dancing with whoever happened to be passing. I have often wondered if she would still be alive if only she had been allowed to act naturally, without always being sheltered by her oppressive entourage.

Inevitably we did have post-synchronising to do with her. Larry thought we might need the theatre for three days. When she had not shown up by lunchtime on the first day even that looked on the short side. At two-thirty she arrived, again dressed from head to toe in black, as was Paula Strasberg, who followed close behind.

I asked Marilyn if she would like to stand in front of the microphone or sit. She opted for a high stool and wiggled herself on to it while we ran the first picture and the sound loop. Pressing a single earpiece to her ear, she spoke the line. It perfectly matched her lips on the screen. What a fluke!

The next time round we recorded it, with just one more take for safety, I called 'Print' and we moved on to the next loop. In that extended afternoon we completed all the outstanding post-synch. As Marilyn unwound off the stool I congratulated her. With her innocent, wide-eyed look she replied, 'It's the only thing I can do properly.'

The Prince And The Showgirl, as the American distributors insisted on calling it, was not a great commercial success. *Macbeth*, with all its locations sited and planned in western Scotland, was never made. It would have been a fitting fourth Shakespeare film for Laurence Olivier, no doubt every bit as good, if not better than the three we do have for posterity.

The next time I saw him was at Shepperton, where he was filming his stage production of *Othello*. I was talking to the cameraman, Geoff Unsworth, when a voice in my ear said, 'We don't want no white trash in here.' I spun run and looked blankly at a black man staring back at me. It took a second or two before I realised it was Olivier. For once I had the right answer and strode off, calling over my shoulder, 'I don't talk to niggers.' Olivier fell apart with laughter; for the only time ever I'd caught him off guard.

From *The Prince And The Showgirl* I was allocated to the next Betty Box and Ralph Thomas production, an updated version of the *Ninotchka* theme, *The Iron Petticoat*. This gave me the chance to work with two more of Hollywood's greatest stars, Katharine Hepburn and Bob Hope. The script depicted Katharine Hepburn's character as a Soviet fighter pilot sent on a mission to London, where she met Bob Hope playing an American Air Force officer. The plot followed that of the Garbo *Ninotchka* in which the stern Communist and strict observer of Marxist principles gradually falls prey to the temptations of capitalism.

Before the stars arrived the crew were briefed that it would be wise to tread warily with Miss Hepburn and only to speak when spoken to. Soon after news came through from the main gate that she had arrived, the lady in question strode onto the sound stage wearing a khaki bush jacket and slacks, topped by a matching baseball cap. She walked over to a chair, her freckled face glistening with Vaseline, sat down, and peering round said in that unique voice, 'If I don't appear to recognise anybody that I ought, forgive me, but I'm so bloody blind. Forgive me too for the Vaseline, but it's to cover up my skin cankers.'

Ralph Thomas started to introduce individual members of the crew. My turn came. She listened to my name, then peered closely at me before saying, 'You're not the John Mitchell I know – he was a drunk. Nice to meet you.'

She was right on both accounts. The other John Mitchell had worked as the soundman on *The African Queen* when Kate, like everyone else who worked with the poor fellow, soon got to know of his fondness for scotch. (When I went freelance several years later his reputation went before, often causing doors to be slammed in my face; it took some living down.)

Day one of *The Iron Petticoat* saw Miss Hepburn at Pinewood Studios early on a freezing winter's morning. By that time she had already driven the twenty-six miles out from the Connaught Hotel in her open-topped Hillman Minx. Phyllis Wilbourn, the English spinster who was her assistant-cum-secretary, had barely survived the journey and had to be helped from the car blue with cold.

That morning, as on every other, Kate indulged in her morning ritual of a

The Iron Petticoat,

1958.

bath in freezing cold water, followed by standing on her head in a yoga position. She used to say how much she enjoyed the Pinewood water, which came from an enormous, uninspiring steel tank perched on a high girder by the time-keeper's lodge; it remains there to this day, still uninsulated, the water icy cold in winter.

Miss Hepburn was never late; that we quickly realised. She was on set a good half-hour before the call, when not even the director had arrived, dealing with her own face at the portable make-up table and mirror just off set, which she preferred to the portable dressing-rooms favoured by other stars.

Our first set-up of the day was worked out without any sign of Bob Hope. When he eventually ambled through the sound-proof doors he led in an entourage of manager, dresser, bodyguard and gag writers, soon nicknamed 'the seven dwarfs'.

'You're late,' Kate called across to her co-star, formidable in her Soviet colonel's uniform.

'For Christ's sake, I'll get one of those clock things from the gate-house to clock in every day,' he snapped back.

'You'd better had,' she answered, adding, 'Did you get the flowers?'

'Sure. My dressing-room was full of flowers. Who sent them?'

Kate replied, 'I did. I knew you'd be too bloody mean to have sent me any.'

Any idea of rapport between them was rapidly dismissed. They were complete opposites; she an individual, he a unique industry: the product front-man to a high-powered team of people who fed him material to be put over in his own special way.

Many times during filming he was called to the studio phone to take a call from one of the 'seven dwarfs' suggesting a new gag for the scene we were going to shoot. Hope would listen, give it some thought, reject it, or accept it with a 'That's great – I'll use it.' Minutes later it would have been skilfully slipped into the script, replacing the original lines with no sign of effort on his part.

I was intrigued by this. His explanation was that his early training in radio had taught him how to cope with script changes right up to broadcast time. His major contribution to the film in fact was his timing, his ability to pick precisely the right place to pause and for how long. There were occasions too when Katie would suggest an alternative to the gag writers' offering. Often hers was better, so much so that Bob accused her of having more writers in the cellar of the Connaught than he had at the Savoy.

'I don't need gag writers,' she told him. 'I write my own!'

Bob Hope had other interests that made their presence felt on *The Iron Petticoat*. One day, just before lunch, we set up for a scene in which Bob was to be driven away in an American car. He came back on the set, took one look at the car, and walked off. It turned out that, unbeknown to producer Betty Box, Bob had a contract with a particular car manufacturer. All his film appearances had to be in that make of car and, more specifically, it had to be blue. Ours fitted neither criteria. It was black. Filming the scene was postponed until the next day when a blue car could be found.

Katie's life seemed altogether less complicated. She spent her weekends driving out of London to visit stately homes and I was happy to suggest places that she might enjoy seeing. Just before the Easter break she said that she did not want to spend the holiday in the Connaught, so I suggested she try Wales, taking pot luck on accommodation.

Katharine Hepburn,
1956.

The morning we got back to Pinewood she came bouncing onto the set full of her Easter experiences. She had, as predicted, had trouble finding a hotel with a free room. Late in the evening she knocked on the door of a pub somewhere in the valleys of South Wales. It was after closing time and the landlady told her that they didn't have rooms to let. Still, she took pity on the lone lady motorist and offered their spare bedroom and some breakfast before she set off to find more suitable accommodation in the morning.

Neither the landlady nor her husband appeared to have a clue who their unexpected guest might be. It was not surprising to hear that Katie did not move on after breakfast, but stayed at the pub for the whole Easter weekend, serving pints, washing dirty glasses and generally enjoying herself chatting up the locals. She told us it was the best Easter she had ever had and she managed to drive away on Easter Monday without anyone realising who she was.

Meanwhile I had spent Easter with my wife and daughter in a caravan; not in some pleasant seaside spot, but on a building site in Chalfont St Peter. I had bought a plot of land there, on an estate with private roads and gated access. The cost of the land was seven hundred and fifty pounds, but by the time we had plans drawn up I was committed to an outlay of nearly four and a half thousand pounds – a huge sum to find on my salary of thirty-five pounds a week. In those days, building societies were not falling over each other to lend money.

In addition to this, my daughter Anne was nearing the age of eleven when she would be ready for a change of school. We were anxious that she receive a good education and therefore applied to St Mary's, a highly thought of Day Public School in nearby Gerrards Cross. One of the conditions of her being given a place was that she commenced at the start of term. So it was that we decided to live on site, in the caravan, where we could also be on hand to monitor the building. Needless to say it was my long suffering wife who bore the brunt of dealing with the builder each day, passing on my comments on progress or lack of it following my previous evening's inspection.

Katie and I had become good friends by now and she used to ask for progress reports, always wanting to know what kind of kitchen we were having, or the colour of the bathroom we were planning; grey as it happened. When she found out that I used to ask the actors if I could sneak a bath in their dressing-rooms she would call out across the sound stage, 'John Mitchell, time for your bath – you haven't had one for a week!'

She took a close interest in the other members of the cast as well. Richard

Wattis had been cast as an assistant in a smart ladies boutique that was displaying a saucy little hat and even saucier negligée in the window. Comrade Kovelenco, as Katie was called in the film, had been intrigued by these until she could resist the temptation no longer. Striding into the shop she demanded to try on the hat.

Dickie played the scene beautifully; Katie certainly thought so. After Ralph Thomas had called 'cut', she went over to him and asked for Dickie to be given more 'cover', more separate close-ups to match hers. The scene would get a better balance and Dickie would enjoy far more attention on screen. Such selflessness was not common amongst film stars; they were much more likely to count their number of lines in a script, as well as the number of close-ups.

Katie was to show the same consideration to Anthony Hopkins after being impressed by his performance in *The Lion In Winter*. She recommended him years later to David Lean, suggesting that Tony would be perfect for the part of Captain Bligh in the film he was considering about the *Bounty*. David's film was never made, though Tony did play Bligh in the one that was.

Richard Wattis and Katie Hepburn.

The film progressed; our house progressed, in spite of awful winter weather. It was probably too much to expect that we could live in a caravan through those bitter months without going down with something. Sure enough Jean and Anne went down together with flu. I used to leave them in the morning as cosy as possible with soup to be heated in case I couldn't drive the nine miles back at lunchtime to look after them.

When Katie heard about them she volunteered her assistant to go over to help. Poor Phyllis looked the type who would have succumbed to the flu bug as soon as she opened the door of the caravan. I persuaded Katie not to send her, to which she agreed, on condition that Jean and Anne moved into the Connaught as her guests to convalesce for a few days.

With only some night work to be shot at an RAF airfield, we reached the time when on most films goodbyes have to be made. Katie had spent the last few weekends shopping personally for gifts for everyone, carefully selecting things that she hoped they would remember her by. On the last day she went from person to person handing out packages. Our production manager, of whom she was not over-fond, received a vicuna scarf from Jermyn Street, very expensive, but in a terrible muddy green colour. The continuity girl got a beautiful cashmere twin set from Fortnum & Mason, again in a frightful colour. Bob Thompson, the camera operator, whose film career had started when silent films were still being made, which intrigued Katie, had asked her once to help his wife out with a pastry recipe in an American cookbook. Inside the large box she gave him was a Kenwood food mixer.

By the end of the day it looked as if I was to be the only non-recipient.

'It looks like you've blown it, mate,' Danny, my boom operator, cheerfully commented as we were putting away the equipment.

Just as I was about to leave for home Katie hurried onto the set, followed by Robert Helpmann who had a part in the film, saying she thought she had missed me. From behind her back she produced a small parcel wrapped in white tissue paper. I took it, thanking her and saying I'd open it at home. She countered with the command, 'Open it!'

'You'd better open it, John,' Bobby said.

Inside was a picture, a framed water colour sketch by Katie, showing her with her hair in pigtail, lying full length in a grey bath, with her red varnished toe nails showing where her feet rested on the taps. She seemed really excited. It was then that my fingers touched some padding on the back. I turned it over and found an envelope, held in place with sellotape. It was full of five pound

*Katie's present to my
wife and I – a
bathroom.*

notes. Looking back at the picture, the wording at the bottom of the picture struck home, 'To John – Mrs John – Anne – Happy baths! Comrade Katharine'. She had paid for our bathroom.

I felt terribly embarrassed and tried to give back the bundle of white flimsy fivers.

Bobby Helpmann insisted I took the envelope, with Katie saying, 'I've never given anyone a bathroom as a present before.' In any case, she said, the safe at the Connaught was full of five-pound notes in unopened envelopes that our film accountant had handed over to her as expenses every Friday.

That night Jean and I pondered how we could reciprocate. What do you give a very wealthy lady who does not use make-up or perfume, and dresses most of the time in an old bush jacket and slacks? It was not easy. Then, at the weekend, I found a beautifully illustrated book of stately homes. At an RAF airfield on the following Monday I gave it to her while she was taking shelter in the sound-truck; she preferred it to her caravan. She tore off the paper, looked at the cover and with the famous Hepburn tears trickling down her cheeks said, 'Nobody ever gives me presents – just wait until I show my father.'

Quite recently I heard through the film grapevine that Phyllis Wilbourn had died at Katharine's house in New York. She was aged ninety-two; she had no relatives. Katharine had her cremated and took the ashes to the Hepburn home in Connecticut, where there was a family plot. She buried them there and planted flowers on the spot.

I wrote to Katherine to express my sadness, and received the following note: 'Dear John – Thank you for your sweet letter – Yes, Phyllis was an angel – I'll certainly miss her. K. Hep.'

Chapter Nine

BREAKING FREE

After six years at Pinewood I was beginning to chafe at the bureaucracy of the Rank Organisation and the idea of going freelance looked increasingly attractive. However, a hefty mortgage and school fees made me more cautious. Even after Jean and I had agreed the time would come to quit Pinewood, several more years passed before a suitable film presented the opportunity to make the break; when I did many fellow technicians thought I was committing professional suicide.

The production that tempted me away from the shelter and security of the studio was Carol Reed's film version of Graham Greene's novel *Our Man In Havana*, which was going to be made at Shepperton Studios and on location in Cuba. My recommendation came via Cecil Ford, the London boss of Columbia. I had known him on Carol's production of *Odd Man Out* immediately after the war; two years later he had also been second assistant director on *Hamlet*.

At the time the sound boss at Shepperton had no staff mixers to work on the film and agreed to break his rule of not admitting freelancers. He did, however, insist that I accept his nomination of the rest of the crew. So I started on the rocky road of freelance work with a female recordist who was his girlfriend and who had never been on a location film; a boom operator who was a nut case; and a maintenance man to whom I will always be grateful. He proved to be my mainstay in spite of never forgetting his loyalty to the studio.

Eighty of us climbed on board a well-laden Argonaut, its hold stuffed with camera, wardrobe and sound equipment, for the first leg of our flight to New York. At Idlewild Airport most of us had our first experience of American immigration. Although we were 'in transit' we had to go through a passport check; this entailed being goaded into line by airport police wearing revolvers, which took some getting used to in real life. One by one we passed through the counter where an unsmiling official took my passport, and opened an enormous ledger thicker than a London telephone directory to run a forefinger down the row of Ms for Mitchell.

The next question was totally unexpected, 'Have you been in Manchester recently?'

I had not, which was just as well. There had been an outbreak of polio and no one who had been to Manchester was going to be allowed past that barrier.

When the aircraft had been refuelled we took off – next stop Havana. That was the intention at least. Half an hour into the flight the intercom clicked on and the captain told us that one of the engines was overheating and we were turning round.

Back at Idlewild we were taken by airport bus and dropped at immigration once again. Marshalled into line we went through the procedure we had been through only an hour or so earlier with the immigration: looking through the ledger for miscreant Mitchells, making enquiries about our travelling habits and never a smile to welcome us to the New World.

We spent an hour waiting in the transit lounge until the plane was ready. The second flight was uneventful and after a brief stop-over in Miami we made the short hop to Cuba and landed at Havana, only to be greeted by more officials with even bigger guns. This time they were soldiers, teenagers as far as I could judge, in camouflage jackets and caps, toting Sten guns. The regime of Fidel Castro was still in its early days. The jails may have been filled with

Alec Guinness and Burle Ives, Our Man in Havana.

supporters of the ousted dictator, Batista, but for ordinary Cubans it was one long joyous carnival.

We settled into filming, closely watched by our Castro-appointed censor, film script in hand, but unable to read much English. He and his wife soon got on Carol's nerves, often preventing him from filming things he had spent some time staging. A shoe-shine boy on a street corner was picked by Reed for his cheeky face and torn shirt, grubby from weeks of wear without laundering. The censor told him he must give the boy a clean shirt; Cubans did not dress in rags. Another time a tiny donkey drawing a grossly overloaded cart was sent through a crowded traffic intersection. Neither the animal's pitiful condition nor its load caused comment, but the driver's clothes did.

The regime had closed all the brothels and casinos, one of which had been owned by George Raft, American star of numerous gangster films. Our script had scenes set in this and one of the former establishments, both of which were temporarily re-opened for a few days, after a great deal of negotiation. This pleased the 'ladies', who were now obliged to ply their trade on the street, and George Raft's employees, who were out of a job.

Noël Coward, who was playing Alec Guinness's under-cover contact, arrived after the rest of us. We had all been told not to approach 'the Master' under any circumstances and when he joined us in one of Havana's many squares his chair was promptly produced by a prop man with his name newly painted on the back 'Sir Noël Coward'. He accepted the chair, with what we were all going to learn were his natural good manners, but with the whispered request to the prop man, 'Could you have the "Sir" painted out, dear boy?'

We had four knights on our film – Sir Carol Reed, Sir Alec Guinness, Sir Ralph Richardson and Sir Noël Coward – and they caused considerable amusement to the American actor playing the Batista-inspired police chief, Ernie Kovaks, when it came to addressing them. One day I heard him telling Alec Guinness, 'I don't believe in this "Sir" shit; to me you're Al, he's Carol, he's Ralph and he's just Noël.'

Ernie was expansive in every way; big in stature and rarely seen without an enormous Havana cigar stuck in the corner of his mouth. He did say that he had only accepted the invitation to appear in *Our Man In Havana* so that he could buy up a large stock of the very best hand-rolled cigars to take back home to the States, where they had been black-listed since the coup. In any case, he claimed, he was proving his dislike of the Castro regime by helping to set fire to some of its crops!

I introduced myself to Noël Coward after a day or so, just saying that I was in charge of sound and would try not to cause him any trouble. His reply was typical of the man, saying that he had worked on very few films and would welcome any help. That was a considerable understatement for someone who had appeared in some of the earliest talking pictures and had been responsible for the production of such films as *In Which We Serve* and *Brief Encounter*. On the last day I was delighted to receive a copy of one of his books, inscribed on the flyleaf 'To John with grateful thanks, Noël! – Sound without Fury.'

It is strange how often situations arise on location that are just right for a particular scene in a film. While shooting in the streets we had noticed a little band of musicians who sang to the accompaniment of guitar and maracas. Carol Reed, who had a great eye for opportunity, used them in one of Noël's earliest shots in which he appeared striding round a corner, a typical Englishman with his rolled umbrella, to be followed by the band. They added so much to the scene that Carol used them many times in the rest of the film as Noël moved through the city for his assignations with Alec Guinness. Their presence heightened the intrigue surrounding this shady character – could they possibly be Cuban intelligence men?

Noël Coward in Our Man in Havana.

I thought their singing was so effective, so delightfully unprofessional, that I persuaded Carol to let me have them for a session in the studio in Havana one evening when I recorded much of their repertoire, which, I was pleased to discover, was used to advantage in the finished film.

One of our film sets, the interior and exterior of a bar, was built in the middle of a five-road junction in the busiest part of Havana. The noise was indescribable, for Carol wanted to see traffic passing in the background accompanied by the shrill whistle of a traffic policeman who had been seconded to us. He proved to be quite a character – very tall, with arms that flailed like a windmill as he controlled the seemingly impossible rows of cars and buses which bore down on him from five different directions. As if with eyes in the back of his head, he would point an imperious white-gloved finger, screech on his whistle to command a stop and wheel on his feet like a ballet dancer to fling a beckoning arm in the direction of the next line of traffic to move.

While this racket was going on we were struggling to record dialogue between Alec Guinness and Burl Ives, just enough to be heard, as a guide track for post-synchronising. Carol, however, decided not to wait for post-synchronising. He wanted to make wild tracks, a process in which an actor listens to the original recording and records it immediately afterwards trying to maintain the same tempo and cadence. Unlike post-synchronising the actor doesn't have the advantage of seeing his lips moving on screen in the recording studio. Some actors prefer wild tracks, though not I imagine on humid tropical nights in a corrugated iron studio.

We spent evening after evening with poor Alec and his fellow actors, sitting in a booth lined and roofed with felt and blankets to cut down reverberation and noises outside. Carol Reed painstakingly made take after take, with always a 'just once more' until Alec would ask in exasperation how different did Carol want it. 'Just one more, exactly the same,' Carol would answer.

Towards the end of location shooting I spent an enjoyable time recording wonderful sound backgrounds: going into bars with a hidden microphone; catching women talking outside their tenements, or dropping a basket from a fifth floor balcony to a street trader below shouting what they wanted in strident Spanish.

Perhaps because he could not understand all that was being said, our censor became increasingly wary of Carol as the shooting came to an end. On the day we were due to leave, when all the equipment had been loaded onto a British Airways Britannia we noticed that neither Carol nor Alec was in the departure lounge. They had been detained at emigration. The authorities refused to hand back their passports unless the film negative, which was still in Cuba, was handed over. It seemed like hours before they were allowed out of the country with the cans of film. However, the exposed negative rolls had been transferred into unexposed film cans with only Kodak labels, whilst the original cans with their *Our Man in Havana* labels and roll numbers were handed over containing unused film!

Back at Shepperton I was appalled to find that all the sets designed by the Oscar-winning art director John Box had been laid with hard-glaze Spanish tiles; very attractive to the camera, but a sound man's despair. Maureen O'Hara was wearing the highest of metal-sheathed heels to walk across these floors. Carol saw me attempting to have small rounds of felt stuck to the bottom of the heels by wardrobe, but in spite of Maureen's insistence that she did not mind, he had them removed. My purpose for the felt heel pads was to eliminate the clatter as she talked and walked across the room.

At the end of that week all of the senior technicians were expected to meet, as we did every Saturday morning during filming, at Alexander Korda's HQ at 146 Piccadilly, near Hyde Park Corner. Here we sat in the private theatre to review the week's work while Carol watched, grim-faced, to pick up on anything that displeased him.

That first day's work on the Shepperton set came up on the screen. Click, clack went Maureen's shoes as she walked and talked the entire length of the room over to a window. I slunk deeper into my seat, cringing at every footstep, not wondering, but knowing what Carol was going to say.

The house lights went up at the end of the reel. Carol made straight for me to say, 'You didn't tell me, dear boy, that it was so bad. We'll have to post-synchronise the whole scene, which means bringing her back from the States.'

What was the point of arguing? Of course I had; my notebooks there to prove it, but what could I say?

The heel clicks could have been removed in editing, but they are still there in the final version. The effect grew on Carol and he used it dramatically. Perhaps if I had persisted in sticking on my felt pads, it would have been the wrong thing to do after all.

The final day came and with it my letter of termination of contract. I had never been sacked before, but this was to be the pattern of my future work. On average it happened three or four times a year.

At the end-of-film party I was aware for the first time ever that most of the conversation was about what people were going to be working on next; some were spoken for, some not. For someone new to the process it was unsettling.

During the drinks I was called to the phone to take a call from Julian Wintle, for whom I had worked on several films. He wanted to know what I was doing and when he heard that I had just finished making *Our Man In Havana* that Friday, asked me to join him the following Monday to start work on a film at Beaconsfield Studios. Julian's film, *Battle Of The Sexes* starring Peter Sellers, may have been a more modest affair lasting seven weeks, but it gave me the confidence that the end of one film could often be the start of the next.

I have to admit that there was a five-month gap before the next film materialised. I spent the time at home redecorating, waiting for the telephone to ring, while the bank balance shrank. When the vital call came through I was on top of a ladder and Jean had to call me to the phone. Chris Challis, my cameraman friend, who was photographing *Surprise Package* for Stanley Donen, told me that Stanley was planning a production of the stage success *The Grass Is Greener* as his next film, in co-production with Cary Grant. Chris had been talking to Stanley about my recording of the Havana street musicians and Donen had said he would like to meet me.

Knowing Stanley as I do now, it comes as no surprise that I had to present myself at Shepperton Studios at eleven that morning, which gave me a bare three-quarters of an hour to get out of my decorating garb and drive over there.

When I was shown into his office he directed me to a seat while he spoke on the telephone to the States. This lasted quite a time. When he put the receiver down he excused himself, went to the toilet, and shaved his dark overnight stubble to reveal a sallow face with sensuous lips and a sharp nose, surmounted by piercing eyes. I always maintained he would have made a good lawyer with his searching questions and razor-sharp mind. Fortunately for me he was a good director and offered me the sound job on the film which was to start in a few months' time.

Before then Ralph Thomas and Betty Box asked me to work with them on *Conspiracy Of Hearts*, the true wartime story of some Italian nuns who hid a large number of Jewish children in their convent on the outskirts of Florence. We used a Carthusian monastery set on a hill top outside Florence as our convent. The building remained open to the public during filming and one day a party of Americans were being shown round where the novice monks did their studies. Opening a door the guide said, 'And this is where our younger brethren work,' only to be confronted by Sylvia Syms in bra and panties about to be dressed in her habit and wimple by the wardrobe lady. No doubt the brethren found amusing the sight of Sylvia and our other actress nuns sat out in the sun between takes, skirts tucked up to tan their legs while they puffed away at cigarettes.

Conspiracy of Hearts was being made on a modest budget and it occurred to me that I might find a choir locally that would suit the film without being too expensive. Our go-between on the film was a young Italian called Carlo, a member of the Ruffino Chianti family – he knew everybody. It was he who suggested a choir in his home town, Certosa, about ten miles from Florence. They were an ancient order of nuns renowned for their singing, and Carlo suggested that I should drive over with him one evening after filming to meet the Mother Superior. He promised he'd have a word with the archbishop beforehand.

I had not realised that these nuns belonged to a closed order. When we rang the bell in the little porchway the voice that answered came from behind a rotating wooden cylinder in the wall. This was how they passed small objects into the convent without the nuns on the other side being seen.

At Carlo's request the Mother Superior came to the grille, listening while he outlined my requirements. She was prepared to let me record her choir, but she made it quite clear that I could only have one hour in which do it. Their working day started at dawn, she told me, and they were tired by evening. That was agreed and a date was fixed for me to come with crew and equipment for our session.

When we returned, we carried our recorders and microphones into the centuries-old church, waiting in the gloom, not quite knowing what to expect. Suddenly lights came on halfway down the left wall of the nave, revealing a completely modern transept running off at right-angles. Rows of nuns stood silently down either side. The opening between us was completely glazed except for a small hinged glass flap. Through this we were allowed to push our telescopic pole and microphone but it was very obvious that we were not to be allowed in among the choir.

The first rehearsal showed that it was not possible to strike a good balance between the voices and the portable electric organ, which I wanted to be unobtrusive. Through Carlo I asked the Mother Superior if we could move the organ. Immediately six or eight novices left their places and tucked up their skirts to manoeuvre the heavy instrument to a position further away. There was time for one more rehearsal before I had to start recording. I let the choir run through a considerable number of pieces to get as much on tape as I could before time ran out. Finally the singing stopped and through the flap the Mother Superior said that that was as long as she would allow.

I knew it wasn't going to be good enough, so I got Carlo to ask if she would like to listen to the recording, played back through a large speaker I had set up when we arrived. I was delighted when she agreed, and the choir sat down to listen as well. After the familiar embarrassed giggles when they heard the voice of the sister conductor preparing them for the first down beat they listened in silence. I was expecting the Mother Superior to call a halt. Instead she let the tape run through to the end and then had an intense discussion with Carlo.

She was not entirely happy with what she had heard. Did I need to make any adjustments from a technical standpoint, if they were to go through the repertoire again? She was certain they could do better and the sister conductor also wanted to try to improve the performance. All question of our restricted time was forgotten.

Two hours and many more recordings later, the result was transformed and we left a smiling choir with my grateful thanks and I hope a suitable, but discreet, donation to the convent. I was pleased for them, as much as for myself, when I ran the choir tracks months later for the Italian composer Angelo Lavagnio, who was going to write the music for the film. He pronounced them perfect. They would provide the ideal background effect, leaving him to come up with the orchestral composition for specific timed sequences.

After the familiar routine of working with Ralph Thomas and Betty Box, starting with Stanley Donen was a step into the unknown. He was the Spielberg of his day, long before the term 'whizz kid' gathered its current meaning. He had started in showbusiness as a dancer in New York, graduating to the chorus in Gene Kelly musicals. By all accounts his keenness to progress to choreographer/director wore Kelly down so much that he gave him his first break in *Singin' In The Rain*. Stanley Donen made his name with this film of course, and it was soon to be followed by *Seven Brides For Seven Brothers*. After turning his back on musicals he formed Stanley Donen Enterprises, later to become Grandon Productions with Cary Grant, for which *The Grass Is Greener* was the most recent in a line that had started with *Indiscreet* in which Cary

Cary and Jean in
The Grass is Greener,
1960.

Grant had starred with Ingrid Bergman.

When I made my usual pre-production visit to the sets to sort out any sound problems beforehand I found that at a very late date the film's backers had forced Stanley into filming in Cinemascope, the letter-box shaped screen that had become all the rage.

By the time they dropped this on him, the sets had been built to the conventional format, much the same as the proportions of a modern television screen. This meant they were far higher than Cinemascope required. There wasn't time to make the set walls lower and this meant added problems for all of us. Chris's lights on the spot rails were much higher than necessary. As a result our microphones would cast shadows unless they were raised higher than was a good position for recording.

On this film my problems weren't confined to technicalities. Stanley introduced me to Cary Grant on the first day. He was very polite; charming some might say, but he left me with a feeling that I should be on my guard. He was very helpful and even warned me that he was the bane of sound men by using very little voice.

Our first set-up had the camera panning across the full width of the studio mock-up of the Wedgewood Hall at Osterley House; Cary Grant was playing an English lord. We completed the scene after several takes, during which Cary had checked whether he was giving enough voice. Faced with a familiar problem of a balance between footsteps and voice level I replied that since he'd asked, a little more voice would be of help. After lunch I was walking back to the set with Chris when Stanley Donen called me over for a word. I could not believe it when he asked why I had asked Cary Grant to give more voice on the scene before lunch. I gave him my version of what had happened. Donen fixed me with his piercing dark eyes saying, 'Are you sure you didn't approach him with a request for more?'

This was make or break time. My first day working for Stanley Donen could well have been my last, but I felt he believed me, even though he was Cary Grant's partner. According to Cary Grant I had completely thrown him during the scene by demanding that he gave more voice.

Once that episode was behind me the shooting settled down to a very pleasant routine. Deborah Kerr and Robert Mitchum really enjoyed their scenes together, with Robert pulling Cary Grant's leg during the scenes they shared. No one could ever fault Cary Grant for his style of film acting – his sense of timing was perfect. Like so many famous film stars his performance from success

Murray Watson,
Robert Mitchum and
Cary Grant.

to success depended on playing the stereotyped character of Cary Grant. There was never any call for a great actor to tackle a range of different parts. He was also an intensely selfish actor, making the others wait. Moments before the camera rolled for a scene he was checking that every hair of that immaculate hair style was in place, when through the headphones I heard him muttering, 'I like me.'

On another occasion Deborah and Jean Simmons came on set wearing beautiful model gowns complimented by some exquisite jewellery. Again, over the headphones I heard him call Stanley over to say, 'Get those jewels off them.' In reply to the query, 'Why?', Stanley was told that the audience would be looking at the jewels, not at Cary Grant!

Cary had a scene where he was about to leave the room and in answer to Deborah's enquiry where he was going, replied that he was going for his 'bathrobe'. Somehow to my ear this didn't sound right. No English lord would say 'bathrobe', particularly in a transatlantic accent. I suggested to Stanley that dressing-gown would be more appropriate – after all, Grant was born Archie Leach in Bristol. This was met by an outstretched arm appeal from Cary to the crew, 'Say, fellas, would I say "dressing-gown"?'

Behind the camera Chris Challis took his pipe from his mouth and called out, 'Yes you would, and what's more every one of the Pilgrim fathers on the *Mayflower* had one.'

To please both factions one take was made using 'bathrobe', another 'dressing-gown'. In the final version 'pyjamas' was dubbed in!

Chris had his own problems with our co-producer who would not wear make-up, but insisted on maintaining a strange tan. On Monday mornings Chris would always find it several shades darker after a weekend under the sun-lamp or splashing on the contents of a man-tan bottle.

'He looks just like an old mahogany sideboard,' was the verdict of my cameraman pal.

Chapter Ten

BEACONSFIELD STUDIOS

Beaconsfield Studios had been built in the early 1930s to provide Edgar Wallace with a studio where he could produce his own sound films from his books. In 1960 it was being run by the Independent Artists Production Company, which had been formed two years earlier by Julian Wintle and Leslie Parkyn. I had first worked for Leslie on *Morning Departure* and it was Julian who had called during the party at the end of *Our Man In Havana*, to ask me to work on *The Battle Of The Sexes*. That was a pleasant fill-in for a few weeks.

Julian and Leslie had mentioned that they were thinking of increasing the capacity of the studio by building another sound stage. If they went ahead with the project, they wondered if I would be interested in joining them to run the enlarged sound department. I replied that I would certainly think about it and we left it that they would get in touch if and when the new stage was ready.

Once more luck and good timing were on my side. They did build the new sound stage and as I was completing *The Grass Is Greener* they telephoned asking me to start helping with the installation of sound recording facilities, popping over on evenings and at weekends. The only problem as far as I was concerned was that one of them had to tell their present sound mixer that I was joining them as head of department. This they promised to do. There was no risk to the man's job; it was just a matter of courtesy, but they were the ones to tell him, not me.

I had been asked to begin working on a Norman Wisdom film, on location, not in the studio. The start date ran alarmingly close to the scheduled end of *The Grass Is Greener* and I ended up driving to Weymouth right after the end-of-shoot party, to be ready the next morning for the first day on *The Bulldog Breed*.

I again felt completely at home back in the Portland naval base, filming around the dockyard and on board various frigates. The film was the usual Norman Wisdom riot in which our star taxed Bob Asher, the director, with his insistence that he could do all the stunts himself without calling in the stunt man.

Norman asked me one evening if I would like to go with him to see the summer show in Weymouth in which a couple of his pals were appearing. He did not mention who they were; anyway, the presence of Morecambe and Wise in the programme meant nothing to me at the time. Only a few minutes into their spot I and the rest of the audience could see that that would change; here was an act that was going to go a very long way.

Our location work went fairly smoothly, apart from my having to manage with a boom operator I did not know. He was a great socialiser, the sort of fellow who was missing when most needed. One morning when we were due to spend the day at sea on board a frigate, he failed to show up at departure time. We cast off and spent a busy day filming without. He was waiting on the dock as we came alongside late in the afternoon, blustering and complaining that we had left without him. The Royal Navy does not wait for late arrivals, nor do I. His name was erased from my crew list.

Back at Beaconsfield, a more serious problem was in store. I was appalled to find out that Len Page, the resident mixer, had not been told about my appointment. Naturally he was very upset when he found out and handed in his notice on the spot. He had intended to retire at the end of his current film, after a long career in sound, but when we heard that he had died of heart failure two days later there was much bad feeling around the studio, most of it directed at the management. That was not the best of starts for me at the studio.

Independent Artists had quite a programme of modest budget films. *Very Important Person*, a light-hearted story of British POWs, starring James Robertson Justice and Leslie Phillips, turned out to be a very successful launch for a less well known Scottish comedian, Stanley Baxter. The producers were so taken with him that they had the script for another comedy, *The Fast Lady*, re-written to suit him. While this was taking place, we got on with another film with Peter Sellers. *Waltz Of The Toreadors* was a very successful play by Jean Anouilh. Wolf Mankowitz had adapted it for the screen and Peter was playing the part of on elderly general with a roving eye. I thought the film was one of Peter's best, although it was released without much comment. Cyril Cusack added his own sparkle to the cast and Prunella Scales played the part of a young assistant in a hat shop and even in that small role gave a tantalising glimpse of what her career held in store.

The script of *The Fast Lady* was ready when work finished on *Waltz Of The Toreadors*, the 'lady' in question being a four-and-a-half-litre vintage Bentley.

At that time the streets around Beaconsfield were in almost as much use for filming as the studio itself. We would often pop out to snatch a scene because the light was good, or maybe by arrangement with the Fire Brigade to use their fire-engines or tower as a back-drop. A number of scenes for *The Fast Lady* were shot on one carriageway of the unfinished M4 motorway, between junctions eight and nine.

The episode when we filmed a little cameo with Frankie Howard at one of the intersections in the Beaconsfield shopping area was a memorable example of this sort of improvisation. In the script Stanley drove the Bentley round a corner to straddle a manhole cover. After the car had passed, Frankie was supposed to push up the cover to see the receding Bentley. The studio carpenters had made a suitably coloured wooden replica of the manhole cover, to make it easier for Frankie to lift. This was put over the manhole in place of the cast iron cover after Frankie had disappeared down the rungs inside. 'Fast Lady' rounded the curve. Stanley got his bearings slightly out and instead of straddling the cover, drove one wheel over it, before carrying on. We all waited for Frankie to pop up, but the wooden cover was firmly jammed like a cork in a

Waltz Of The Toreadors, *1962.*
Peter Sellers and Cyril Cusack.

bottle. Down below Frankie's muffled voice exclaimed, 'Ooh – ah! Get me out'. That took some time and then we had to do it all over again for take two.

Another member of the cast was a shy young actress called Julie Christie, appearing in her second film. She seemed terribly unsure of herself, suffering agonies under the director's, Ken Annakin's, not-too-understanding approach. On the set she kept to herself, frequently chewing well-bitten finger nails. I remember the second assistant director, whose job it was to give her the 'call' for the next day's work, saying that she didn't seem to have a permanent address. She used to say to him, 'Just tell the driver to pick me up at Kensington underground station', or at a variety of different places, rarely the same one twice. It needed a more sympathetic director, John Schlesinger, with whom she made her Oscar-winning film *Darling*, to draw out her real potential and make her a world-famous star.

The last feature film of my time at Beaconsfield was the most memorable: *This Sporting Life*, which earned its stars, Richard Harris and Rachel Roberts, Oscar nominations for their performances. Karel Reisz was the producer, Lindsay Anderson the director. Both were men of the theatre, colleagues from the famous days of the Royal Court in the fifties and early sixties.

The film was set in Yorkshire and most of the exteriors were filmed in my birthplace, Wakefield. Richard Harris was playing an ex-miner-turned-Rugby League player and many of the scenes were to be filmed at the Wakefeld Trinity Rugby League club. They were high in the league at that time and though it was poorly paid, the game attracted many young men with necks like bulls from the coal pits and other heavy industry in the area.

The first scenes we filmed were simple background snatches of play on the pitch. I knew I was going to have a problem recording good close-up sound from out of camera vision. In those days there were no directional microphones, let alone radio microphones, to make the job easy and I was left to come up with something of my own.

I had been impressed with the performance of the parabole as a 'collector'. You see them today on the walls of most houses that have satellite television, but if I wanted one thirty-five years ago, I had to make it myself. My maintenance man, Frank Slogett, helped to make a mould in the plasterer's shop, from which a fibre-glass dish was cast. I positioned a conventional dynamic microphone to face into the parabole and was delighted by its performance. The dish itself measured about thirty inches in diameter and was quite heavy. Frank and I had set two cast-iron cupboard handles into the back of the bowl which made it manageable. In fact I used it to great advantage on lots of films all over the world until the advent of modern condenser directional microphones, the sort that are hidden away in 'shaggy-dog' windshields. It always surprised me that other soundmen did not cotton on to the benefits of the parabole.

Richard Harris joined us soon after finishing the second of the American *Mutiny On The Bounty* films, with Trevor Howard as Captain Bligh and Marlon Brando as Fletcher Christian. Without any doubt Richard had acquired Brando's mannerisms and gait, as well as the American habit of chewing gum.

His first day was spent on the pitch being tackled by the players. All went well until the continuity girl queried a script detail with him. He scowled in the Brando manner and then swore at her. His fellow players, all Methodists, did not take kindly to language like that being used to a woman. For the rest of the afternoon they drove home their tackles with all their strength. We could almost feel the ground shaking as time after time he was felled by sixteen- and seventeen-stone hunks. To give Richard his due, he took it in good heart; during our time in Yorkshire they all became good friends.

At the ground we were filming crowd reactions too. We advertised for extras in the local paper and although we were swamped with hundreds who wanted to appear in front of the camera, we kept the numbers down. We only used real people in the front rows of the stands. The spectators in the middle and back rows were painted cardboard cut-outs, like the ones that 'watched' the Olympic Games twenty years later in *Chariots Of Fire*, which was also made on a tight budget.

Rachel Roberts came up north to play a scene with Richard at a wedding. In the film she was a widow with two young children, who had lost her husband in a pit accident; Richard was her lodger. In the script they had an argument at the church during which he had to slap her face. Whether by accident, or intent, I do not know, but Richard hit Rachel so hard he almost knocked her off her feet. That ruled out any question of another take.

Later we had to film a picnic sequence at Bolton Abbey with Richard, Rachel and her children in the film. Richard was in a foul mood after differences of opinion with Lindsay over the interpretation of the script had reached stalemate with Karel Reisz. The property men had set out the picnic on a travelling rug by the river. Richard was locked in his caravan, refusing to budge while we waited and tried to make embarrassed conversation with the priest in charge of the abbey, who, with his wife, had been invited to watch the filming.

Scenes from This
Sporting Life, *1963.*

Then the caravan door was flung open and Richard dashed towards the river tearing off his clothes and chucking them into the water as he ran along the bank. Jimmy the wardrobe man and half the film crew chased after him. Down to his Y-fronts by now, Richard stomped back to his caravan, slammed the door behind him, yelling 'Fuck you, Lindsay! Fuck you, Karel!' That seemed to settle him and the idyllic little scene was filmed as if nothing untoward had happened.

The rest of the day was spent with Richard, Rachel and the children playing an earlier scene in the script in an open car which was tied down to a flat-bed trailer, towed by the camera car as we drove up and down the down road. Everything was sweetness.

Back in the studio, our location work well over schedule, work progressed just as slowly. By now Richard was completely immersed in his portrayal of Frank Machin. He lived and slept the character, as Lindsay tried desperately to placate him and keep the film limping along.

Lindsay, of course, was a very strange person whose brand of left-wing politics made me wonder if he had been one of the Cambridge University 'reds'. More than once he walked on the set at the start of a day, draped in a red flag, complete with hammer and sickle.

The only time when Richard relaxed was when the two little Yorkshire children playing Rachel's kids used to run over to him on the film set after one of their breaks at home in Leeds. They rushed up to him yelling, 'Richard! Richard!', hugging him round the legs until he hoisted them up in his arms. They really loved him, with that simple honesty that children have.

I only crossed swords with him once. Between takes in a scene I went over to make the legitimate 'sound comment' that his Irish accent was creeping in. He yelled at me to 'Fuck off'; which I did – right off the film set into the recording room, telling Ron, my recordist, to switch off the recorder. An assistant director was despatched to ask me to return. I said I would if Richard apologised.

Lindsay and Karel had to spend months in the cutting rooms after filming finished. Even post-production did not go smoothly. The film was dubbed by Anvil Films and dubbed a second time at Pinewood. Then when *This Sporting Life* was eventually released the public didn't take kindly to it. I suppose it came too near the end of the kitchen sink era. Leslie Parkyn confided that the returns from general release were very poor; *The Fast Lady* had taken much more money. These days, of course, *This Sporting Life* is considered to be one of the classic black and white films from the 1960s.

During the time I had been working with Lindsay and Karel, Julien Wintle had turned his attention to television, concentrating on a series called *The Human Jungle*, which proved to be a good starring vehicle for Herbert Lom. Each episode took two weeks to film with a different director assigned to each one. I recorded the first three of these, then went out on loan to EON productions to work on two films with producers Cubby Broccoli and Harry Saltzman. By the time that secondment was completed, Beaconsfield Studios had closed. *The Human Jungle* was transferred to Elstree where it grew into a successful series.

When Beaconsfield re-opened it was as the headquarters of the National Film School. Only recently have they moved to the more spacious surroundings of my original 'film home' – Ealing Studios.

Chapter Eleven

SPIES, MOSES AND AIRMEN

While at Beaconsfield, I had been lent out to take over and complete a film at Pinewood, *Call Me Bwana* starring Bob Hope and Anita Ekberg. This was a Cubby Broccoli and Harry Saltzman production; they had just finished the film version of the first of Ian Fleming's James Bond books, *Dr No,* its leading actor a then unknown Sean Connery.

The two producers had shown a rough cut of *Dr No* to Gordon Douglas, who was directing *Call Me Bwana*. His verdict was not encouraging. He thought it lacked pace, which prompted them to give to it their editor, Peter Hunt, telling him to be ruthless in re-editing. History has proved them right. *Dr No* opened to glowing reviews. James Bond caught the public imagination on both sides of the Atlantic. Sean and Ursula Andress became international stars on the strength of it and United Artists gave Cubby and Harry *carte blanche* to hurry another Bond film on to the screen.

My chance meeting with them led to the offer to work on *From Russia With Love*. This time the budget was greatly increased. Location shooting started in Istanbul before the unit went back for the studio work at Pinewood.

The superior status of a Bond film had already been acquired when we took our chartered plane to Turkey – there were specially printed menus on the flight and plenty to drink. Shooting began in many of the famous sites of Istanbul: the covered bazaar, the Blue Mosque, even the gated streets of the brothel area. As always, I made friends, in particular in the bazaar, where every day I set up my recording equipment in an open-fronted shop belonging to a carpet dealer. Some of his carpets were very valuable, though they were not necessarily the ones that most appealed to me. He plied me with small cups of Turkish coffee throughout the day and did not seem to mind that I never bought anything. Perhaps he knew that Harry Saltzman would make up for my lack of interest. I found out over the years I worked for him that he was a voracious shopper. No one with any sense ever got behind Harry at Heathrow customs; his checking always took ages.

Sean's female companion was a little-known Italian actress, Daniela Bianchi,

Sean Connery with the late Cubby Broccoli.

a very pretty blonde, but hardly in the same league as Ursula Andress or any of the subsequent Bond girls. The story goes that Sean had received a very modest sum for *Dr No*. Now, with *From Russia With Love* and possibly many more films from the pen of Ian Fleming, he was playing hard to get.

Part of what was to become the typical Bond chase was filmed in a Roman sewer beneath the streets of Istanbul. This was an extraordinary place, approached down long flights of steps from an inconspicuous manhole in a side street. Terence Young, the director, had devised a long tracking shot with the camera alongside the water's edge. We had several rehearsals until the decision was made to shoot. The camera turned and Sean ran until I noticed that the camera speed was fluctuating on a frequency meter and called out 'Cut'. Harry came charging over yelling, 'Now what's the matter with sound?'

I let him rant on and then told him, calmly, that it was not sound but the picture camera. His attitude changed instantly. What could be done to fix it? As was usually the case, 'sound' in the person of my maintenance man, Charles Van De Goor, traced the cause of the problem. Harry Saltzman was added to the list of difficult people with whom I managed to get along.

We shot a lot of the early scenes of Sean joining the *Orient Express* at

Istanbul station. On the platform I got into conversation with an elegantly dressed Englishman who turned out to be Ian Fleming. His own background in the foreign office during the war was fascinating, but his mother sounded a more exotic character. In later life she had a wealthy boyfriend somewhere in Europe and used to travel out regularly on the *Orient Express* to see him, in the days when it did carry spies and beautiful women agents.

I made my usual arrangements to record train sound effects, concentrating on the steam locomotive that was still hauling the *Orient Express*. We booked a compartment for the journey from Istanbul to near to the Bulgarian border. This gave us time to collect all sorts of different effects, one of the best being in the toilet with the lid up. That gave a wonderfully hollow rumble which added the right atmospheric touch to our wagon-lit compartment back in the studio.

When it was time for something to eat we found the dining-car was

This poster was featured, amusingly, in From Russia with Love. Call Mr Bwana *was one of Cubby and Saltzman's earlier films.*

equipped with a coal-fired range but no menu. That was because you had to accept dish of the day or nothing at all. Dish of the day seemed to consist of black peas in a kind of gravy.

Back in our compartment we had a visit from the guard accompanied by two plain clothes policemen. They looked at our recording equipment and our passports. Before leaving they pulled down the window blinds and indicated that we should stay put with our recorder switched off. Some while later the guard came back, pulled up the blind, smiled and said 'OK'. It seemed that we had been passing through a secret military area and they were suspicious that we might have been monitoring radio transmissions.

The last sequences were due to shoot in Turkey: the famous power boat chase in which Sean and Daniela in one speed boat were being chased by five boatloads of villains. A motley collection of craft had been assembled for this action-packed high point to the film. Two boats closely resembled the sedate 'slipper' launches that glide up and down the Thames. They quickly shipped water and sank, rather setting a tone for the whole project which had to be cancelled in Turkey, to be filmed at a later date in the UK.

As the studio work progressed at Pinewood Harry Saltzman and Terence Young spent their weekends flying in a helicopter round the south-west coast looking for a suitable location for the boat chase.

When it was obvious that they were not having any success, I suggested that they should try looking at the Western Isles, north of Jura. They thought this was a crazy idea. Filming was scheduled for September. Whatever would the weather be like at that time of year? Thanks to the Gulf Stream, I told them it could be superb. So the following weekend they travelled north to see for themselves and fell in love with the islands of Rhum, Eigg and Seil. That took care of the location. Now they needed half-a-dozen high-speed sea-going launches.

During my time in the Navy I had got to know the commander of a torpedo boat. His name was Charles Currey and I knew from having stayed in touch with him that he was now manager of Fairey Marine, builders of the Hunter and Huntress class of power-boats. As the mere sound man, getting hold of speed-boats was really none of my business, but the production manager, Frank Ernst, seemed grateful when I offered to investigate the Fairey connection and I gave Charles a call. He sounded interested and told me to bring Frank down to meet him on a rest day, while we were night shooting on the Pinewood lot.

Ian Fleming and the
Orient Express.

Charles already had a chart of the Western Isles on his desk when we saw him. He suggested it would be a good idea to base the boats at Crinan, on the western end of the Crinan canal, where there is a sea lock into which the boats could be taken in the evenings for any repairs or maintenance.

'I suppose this Bond chappy, with his dolly bird is being pursued by the bad guys,' Charles said. 'That means you'll need boats of comparable performance.' A call went out for his power boat manager and a short time later Peter Twiss appeared.

Peter had been the first man to fly at one thousand miles an hour, in a Fairey Delta aircraft, and he used all his panache to put one of the Fairey Hunters through its paces on the Hamble. Jean, who had driven down with us for the day, and I were his passengers; Charles was at the helm of another Hunter, carrying Frank.

My wife did not particularly like boats, not even my Albacore dinghy. She stood with white knuckles wrapped round a grab rail, legs rigid, while Peter flung the boat round like a mad thing. I loved it as we creamed past Calshot, where two enormous Princess flying-boats lay mothballed. I don't think poor Jean opened her eyes until we were back alongside the jetty. As we helped her ashore, she hissed at me through clenched teeth, 'Don't you ever do anything like that to me again.'

Frank Ernst was more favourably disposed. The outcome of our visit was that Faireys sent six boats up to Scotland by road. Peter went along to look after them, assisted by a shipwright and an engineer.

We were housed up and down the shores of Lochgilphead. In my case I shared digs with the art director, production manager and continuity girl in a mansion typical of those built at the turn of the century by wealthy industrialists. Stone-built, with a panelled hall and impressive double staircase, it took on a slightly sinister air when we were greeted by our landlady, a woman with staring eyes and a distinctly odd manner. Our discomfort was not eased when we caught sight of a strange figure on the landing, obviously mentally retarded. However, we were fed magnificently, slept well and set off for our first sight of Crinan after a splendid Highland breakfast.

Peter Twiss had all six boats alongside the jetty, waiting for instructions. Everyone in the unit wanted to jump on board and there was a mad scramble until the director called them all off and allocated the two camera crews to two of the boats and put Keith Pamplin, who had replaced my original boom operator, and me in a third. Terence, his first assistant director, and the continuity girl were in another boat, while the rest of the crew, make-up, hair, props, carpenter, painter and the rest were put on to a motor fishing vessel, with orders to anchor in one of the foul weather anchorages reconnoitred by Peter during his working up period. There they were to await a call over the radio if they were needed. Those of us on the action boats were issued with black roll-neck sweaters, to disguise us as baddies if we were ever caught on camera. Terence had already worked out his sequence on a story board and started shooting long shots with one camera perched on the summit of an escarpment overlooking the water.

Keith and I had been allocated to the boat in which Walter Gotell, playing a chief villain, was riding. A large man with a balding head, I didn't like him at the time, though I changed my attitude when we worked together twenty years later; we became good friends.

Walter stumped down the quayside in jack boots and onto the deck of the Fairey Huntress to dive out of sight below. I was less than impressed by his

From Russia With
Love.

unseamanlike behaviour. He could have been wearing deck shoes like the rest
of us because his jack boots were never in camera.

That first day's shooting revealed that the ex-Navy Petty Officer driving
our boat was deaf and could not hear orders over the radio. Fortunately, our
function was to record sound effects mainly; the script had little dialogue other
than shouts. Terence knew that I was used to handling boats and asked me to
take over the helm of Walter's boat for the rest of our time on that location.

Our days were long. By the time we got ashore and then drove to Ardrishaig
to see the rushes, I was rarely back in my digs until after eight. Our landlady
was very understanding, serving us wonderful meals of venison, game and of
course fish. It was just a pity she was so unsettling. After dinner one evening I

had been telephoning Jean when she came into the lounge, and asked, 'Was that your wife?'

Then she really did surprise me. She could see Jean, she said, and described her so accurately that she might as well have been in the room with us. I suppose I should not have been surprised when she explained she was psychic and held seances. But the knowledge did nothing to dispel the general air of disquiet. This was not helped by the bursts of organ music that periodically erupted from the 'chapel' where the mentally retarded occupant of the house (her son as we discovered) used to exercise his unusual talents. The first to leave was the production manager who moved out with his wife to stay in Lochgilphead.

At breakfast one morning our landlady greeted the young assistant art director with the chilling news, 'I see trouble today – do take care.' Down at Crinan, Terence Young decided to take a quick look at a proposed location. Our Bell helicopter was parked nearby, so he climbed in with the assistant art

From Russia With Love, 1963. I was driving the boat behind, but never featured in the film.

director and the pilot. Whether it was caught by a gust of wind or never worked up full power I do not know, but the helicopter toppled over and plunged into the harbour. The art director managed to jettison his door and all three of them struggled out. They had life jackets and none of them was badly hurt, though Terence had to continue the filming with one arm in a sling.

There was another exodus from our digs that evening. The assistant art director departed, so did the continuity girl. That left me as the sole remaining guest.

After moving into the hill country to shoot scenes of Sean and Daniela on the ground being pursued by helicopter gunmen, we returned to Crinan to film the climax of the power-boat chase. As usual, I was reading the script for the next scheduled scenes when I realised that the boat I was on would be in camera for the final part of the chase. The script called for Sean to dump a twenty-gallon drum of petrol into the water from off the stern of his boat and then set fire to it, with tracers sending up a wall of flame in which our boats would be engulfed. To achieve this, the special effects team had strung a row of petrol-filled plastic bags across a narrow passage between the mainland and a small island. The bags were fitted with detonators to be fired electrically from the shore.

We had several dummy runs, checking timing and positions. Terence was happy and we got the message to shoot. Sean in his boat was positioned ahead of the fire bags, the rest of us were lined behind them. Each of our boats had a stern line out to a kedge anchor. On the order 'action' Sean was to start moving forward. A second order to 'slip' was our cue to move off at full throttle. A further order was to be given to 'fire' as we were clearing the flame wall. When we got the order to slip a stunt man in the stern let go of the line, but he did not fling it clear and the line caught in one of our propellers. This only left me with one engine, so that we could not run towards the fire bags at full speed. They were detonated a fraction early as we cleared them. This was when Walter Gotell remembered he had some urgent business below in the cabin and dived for cover. I was too busy trying to pull away from the flames to notice this. Apart from the odd singed eyebrow we were unscathed. Thank goodness it looked good on camera and did not require another take.

'Where the hell is Walter?' called the director. I shouted back that he was down below.

'Why?'

Diamonds are Forever. *Blofeld was played by Charles Gray.*

'Because he's yellow – but I don't blame him.' That brought a great laugh from the onlookers.

Every member of the unit had crammed in to see the rushes the next evening and everyone booed as poor Walter disappeared out of sight. The sides of our boat had been too hot to touch; we had diesel engines fortunately. Walter had been screaming obscenities at Sean through one of my loudhailers which he had thrown down as he scuttled below. The plastic mouthpiece had melted in the heat, but the loudhailer still worked. I presented it to the makers, Pye, for them to put on show at that year's Boat Show as the loudhailer that defied the flames in *From Russia With Love*. We had a good presence at that Boat Show; Fairey had Sean's powerboat prominently displayed on their stand.

Keith and I were not forgotten either for our exploits in the wall of flame. We were each given five pounds by a grateful film company! Although when I got back home I was grateful for a fiver from any quarter. The news that

Beaconsfield Studios was closing looked as if it was going to shatter my comfortable little world.

I was on location in Padua again with Betty Box and Ralph Thomas on their film *Hot Enough For June* starring Dirk Bogarde. A cable arrived one morning which could be the confirmation I had been dreading. How wrong could I be?

The message inside was from 20th Century Fox offering me a new Robert Mitchum film, *Mr Moses*, which was to be filmed entirely in Kenya. The cable was signed Richard McWhorter, who wanted me to telephone him in Wardour Street. When I got through to him McWhorter proved to be an American who told me in whining tones that the director, Ronald Neame, with whom I had worked when he was a cameraman before the war, wanted a British crew but that Fox favoured Italians. He added caustically that he didn't know me. In fact he didn't even know if I was 'blonde or brunette'. I told him I was brunette, going grey at the edges. By the way, what was his hair colour? He did not answer.

I was not to meet Mr McWhorter until the film was under way, but when I got home from Italy the job was mine with ninety pounds a week and my own crew.

Mr Moses was the tale of a quack doctor, played by Robert Mitchum, who was the only person who could persuade an African Masai tribe to move before their land was flooded for a water catchment scheme. The female lead was played by Carol Baker who had achieved something of a reputation early in her career in *Baby Doll*.

Most of the location work was shot in a magnificent village that the film company had built on the side of Lake Naivasha. When it was ready a whole Masai tribe had been invited in to set up home, so that by the time we arrived three months later the place looked lived in.

The Masai were the lucky ones as far as the working day went. We had a fifty-mile drive daily from our accommodation in what had once been a famous colonial hotel, The Brackenhurst. The hotel had fallen into disrepair after the war but had been refurbished for the film unit. If it had not been for the distance from the location it would have been an ideal choice. There was a large main building with a lounge and restaurant, surrounded by smaller buildings ideally suited for offices and technical departments.

We had had an eventful departure from Heathrow. Keith and I were in the lounge when a message over the public address system called us onto the

Harnessing and motivating Suzy.

tarmac. There we found the microphone-boom crate sitting dejectedly under the door to the cargo hold; it was too long, by one foot, to fit inside. Some judicious measuring and a borrowed saw helped to squeeze it in.

I have a paranoia about missing planes, in fact about being late for anything. When Ron, the fourth member of my team, still had not shown up I made a desperate call to his home, hoping he was on his way. My nerves were not calmed to hear Ron's voice at the other end laconically telling me that the hire car had yet not arrived to collect him and that he had opened a bottle of Chianti whilst waiting.

Luckily our charter was not tied to a scheduled departure time. I told Ron to call a local cab and make it hot-foot to the airport. A good hour passed. We were sitting in the plane when Ron ambled up the steps and the door shut behind him. 'Waiting for me?' he asked. His hire car had finally turned up having gone to Haselmere in Surrey, not Haselmere in Buckinghamshire.

Our first evening at the Brackenhurst was given over to a cocktail party so that we could 'get acquainted' as the Americans say. A man with piercing blue eyes and not a hair on his head came over and introduced himself as Dick McWhorter. I recognised his American accent and started to laugh, telling him, 'Now I know why you wouldn't tell me if you were blonde or brunette.'

My previous impression of Dick was wrong. Once I had met him I discovered that he has a great sense of humour. We became firm friends and worked on many films together in later years.

At that period film crews on location worked a three-week, non-stop schedule, with one rest day every twenty-first day. To be on set by eight in the morning we had to leave Brackenhurst well before seven. There was only a half-an-hour break for lunch, which had to sustain us until work finished at dusk. The day ended with a dusty, bumpy drive back and a return to the hotel after eight in the evening.

Mr Moses was hard work, but not without its compensations. Coming off the escarpment from Limuru we followed a curving road past a beautiful miniature church, built by Italian prisoners of war. After one more bend in the road, all the vastness of the Rift Valley lay before us. From there on, the road was fairly smooth and we could speed along in our VW combis. Around us giraffes lolloped across the scrubland, stopping to munch away at thorn bushes. Several times we saw a leopard. It was always at the same spot. One morning we passed its body on the road, a victim of car or truck.

The chief of the Masai tribe living in the film village had negotiated terms for their services as actors and crowd extras. He collected the regular payment, giving small amounts to be spent on goodies in nearby Naivasha. The bulk of the money was banked, to pay for a cattle dip and a tractor when they returned home.

In the script the character played by Robert Mitchum travelled about the country with an enormous gypsy-type caravan pulled by an elephant called Susy. In the original story she was a large-eared African elephant, but as they cannot be domesticated successfully, ours was an Indian elephant which had come from a circus in Durban. She had travelled to Mombassa by sea, accompanied by her trainer and a second elephant, a companion without whom she would not budge. The three of them travelled in a cattle truck by train from the coast to Nairobi and had then walked the last fifty odd miles to Lake Naivasha.

Frank Ross, our American producer, was anxious to see Susy pulling the caravan on which so much depended. The harness was attached to the shafts into which a very unwilling Susy was coaxed. I was reminded of my Spanish mule that took exception to pulling my sound cart on *Penny Princess*. At least it had not bolted. That first trial with Susy ended in catastrophe. On her flight with Robert Mitchum's caravan she careered through a Masai rondaval hut, smashing it to pieces. It was empty, luckily; and not occupied by a Masai family.

Frank Ross was livid. He had been assured that there would be no problem in Susy being harnessed between the shafts of the giant caravan. A breathless, dusty trainer was hauled before him and explained in a strong German accent, 'Susy, always she push – never she pull.' Her early working life had been spent in the teak forests of India where she had rolled tree trunks around with her tusks like a four-legged fork-lift truck. They found that the only way to keep Susy reasonably calm was to have her elephant friend close by at all times and through the whole of the filming she was barely more than a trunk's length away, just out of camera. Wags on the unit suggested that they were a couple of lesbians.

Before we had left London Dick McWhorter had telephoned to say that Frank Ross had wanted recordings of tempo tracks, to be used as playbacks for Masai dances. John Barry, famous for having written the title music for the James Bond films, had been brought in to compose and conduct our 'Masai' music. He and I spent three hours in a recording studio, with fifteen musicians playing an assortment of percussion instruments, making several takes of various tempo themes.

Just as Frank Ross had been impatient to see Susy put through her paces, he was eager to hear his tempos at work with the Masai. We rigged up the speakers at the end of filming one day. Ross gave the word for the playback to start. The effect was extraordinary. Everyone in the film crew started jogging about to the rhythm but not a single Masai moved or paid the slightest interest to our 'jungle drums'.

The producer was amazed. I switched off the recording and asked the interpreter if the Masai would show us how they danced. This they did to the perfect rhythm of a chant led by one of their number. We never did use those expensive London recordings. The Masai's own rhythm was so precise we found we could edit from one take to another with no change in tempo whatsoever.

As shooting progressed, a routine evolved in which the majority of the men in the village were busy as film extras from early morning until dusk. This ran pretty smoothly until one morning our caravan of minibuses rolled up and we saw all the women squatting with their children in a large circle beside the road, across from the village, while several of the younger women harangued them from the centre. We had no idea what was going on. The Masai men were grouped inside the village, standing sheepishly in little groups by their huts. Interpreters were sent for, but striding towards our production team came the chief, looking more noble and commanding than ever. In one hand he carried a horse-hair fly swish, in the other his hard-wood club with its mushroom-shaped knob.

Keith Pamplin and me with our famous parabolic microphone, Lake Naivasha, Kenya, 1965.

A great discussion with many interruptions from the women took place. Slowly we understood that they had a complaint. By tradition their men folk normally spent the day on the grazing grounds tending their cattle. At dusk they returned to their respective huts where they were expected to take their wives to bed for a little intimate satisfaction before the evening meal. Now that the film unit was working their husbands from dawn to dusk, they were too tired to attend to their pre-supper duties. A compromise was struck with the chief and a rota was drawn up to a give a certain number of men a day off film work. This was put to the ladies with all the solemnity of a trades union dispute and they voted to give it a try.

Near the end of the film was a scene that called for several huts to be burned down. Careful preparations were made to avoid setting light to any of the occupied ones: there were well spaced fire breaks and a fire engine for good measure. The scene did not run as intended. One hut caught alight, the fire got hold of others and soon the whole group was ablaze. The director used every available camera and got all the footage he needed. There was a break for lunch during which the firemen doused the embers.

We had nearly finished eating when there was an enormous explosion from the direction of the village. Women were running from their huts, clutching children and sobbing hysterically. When the dust and smoke settled, the body of a Masai man could be seen, his stomach torn open, very obviously dead.

The atmosphere changed instantly and our friendly Masai became quite menacing. We were told to evacuate the village as troops based nearby were called in. When things had settled down the cause of the explosion was discovered. An empty air cylinder had been left in one of the huts and had exploded in the heat of the fire, showering shrapnel in every direction. Shooting stopped for the day. Common sense prevailed, for death was accepted as an inevitability by these pragmatic people. Compensation was agreed with the chief and two cows were duly handed over.

An unexpected and not wholly welcome visitor to the location was a journalist from *Newsweek*. He had written a scurrilous article about Carroll Baker, after *Baby Doll*, who was amazed to hear from our publicist that the man was over from the States to interview Robert Mitchum and had been brazen enough to have asked for an interview with her. She refused, but could not avoid seeing him when he arrived.

During our lunch break Carroll moved up to the desserts, and loaded a large plate with trifle, fruit and dollops of whipped cream. On her way back to her seat, she tripped beside the journalist's table and tipped the whole lot over him, with protestations of how sorry she was.

Carroll did not know that the journalist was a friend of Mr Block, the very wealthy owner of the land on which we were filming and even after independence one of the most influential men in Kenya. An apology was called for. Carroll refused. Block gave the film unit notice to quit and a very ugly scene erupted. In the end Carroll was persuaded to express a form of regret over the 'unfortunate' accident, which was accepted with ill grace.

While we were still in Kenya, I had a cable enquiring whether I was available for a film that 20th Century Fox were planning to make in England during the summer. When I heard that it was all about vintage aeroplanes I could not wait to get home and by the time I was back and ready to start work, preparations were well advanced on *Those Magnificent Men In Their Flying Machines.*

The idea of making a film about the London to Paris air race of the early 1900s was brilliant, but also expensive. Very few aircraft of the period had survived and those that were still around were mainly museum pieces, so replicas would have to be made. It was possible to get some idea of the size of the aircraft from original photographs, using the height of the pilot to gauge the overall dimensions. In the case of Santos Dumont, the actual winner of the race, it was calculated that his Demoiselle aeroplane was tiny, for he was a very small man himself.

A replica of this little plane was built by Doug Bianchi at Booker aerodrome in Buckinghamshire. He used aircraft alloy tubing painted to look like the original bamboo frame and powered his little machine with a modified VW Beetle engine. On the test flight at White Waltham he found that it handled very well. However, when he took the plane up to Booker airfield near High Wycombe, where much of the filming was going to take place, he could not get it off the ground. Booker must be six hundred feet higher than White Waltham and that made all the difference; there was not enough power for Doug to get airborne.

Back at White Waltham was a very famous flying instructor named Joan Hughes. During the war she had ferried all types of aircraft from Spitfires to four-engined bombers. A charming lady and a brilliant pilot, she had the major advantage for our film that she was tiny. On her first take-off the little aircraft rose off the runway, performed some gentle turns and climbs and returned safely to the ground to the delight of the team that had built it. Joan doubled as

Terry-Thomas in Those Magnificent Men In Their Flying Machines.

the pilot, played by Jean Paul Cassell, for the whole of the film.

The plane that James Fox 'flew' was an Allouette; a large monoplane which was built at the Airspeed factory at Portsmouth. This had plenty of power in its Gypsy Moth engine but suffered from being almost impossible to control in the air. Modern planes have ailerons on the wings. The Allouette did not. Its pilot had to twist the wings to make it go the way he wanted, which called for some delicate handling. The wing warping system was far too hit and miss for our purpose and discreet ailerons were fitted to our mock-up to make it usable in the film.

The Box Kite was the only machine built from original plans; the Bristol Aircraft Company still had copies. This was a biplane with a pusher propeller facing towards the tail and the engine mounted behind the pilot. Ours was fitted with a modern Rolls-Royce continental engine and was without doubt the most successful of the planes we had, the pride and joy of its well known champion glider pilot, Derek Piggot. Derek's other plane was a mock-up of a German biplane, flown for Gert Frobe. As time went by, the pilots became more familiar with their machines and the Civil Aviation Authority lifted some of the restrictions imposed on the heights and distances they were allowed to fly. By the end of the film they were flying from location to location, obviating the costly and time-consuming need to strip them down and transport them by road.

On one occasion Derek had to fly from Booker to East Anglia where he was to double for Gert Frobe in a fly-past of several of our aircraft. He took off wearing Gert's uniform, topped by his Prussian Pickelhaube helmet. This caused more than a stir along his flight path, particularly in Dunstable where he made a dive towards the Gliding Club. On the ground in Kings Lynn he presented the mayor with an illuminated scroll. It was all excellent publicity and for some of the scenes enormous crowds gathered to watch the filming. The early summer of 1965 had perfect weather and this continued for the whole period of filming. We were still at work outside in the first frosts of early autumn.

Those Magnificent Men In Their Flying Machines had an international cast who were soon competing to make their performances stand out. Who could forget Gert Frobe's party piece of mimicking a German military band through his lips. We had not heard this until a scene in which the German contingent were pulling their aircraft out of the hangar and quite unscripted Gert started up with his wonderful one-man band. Once heard, that was in the film for good.

It was one of those films in which well known faces kept cropping up in all sorts of strange parts. A team that I thought worked particularly well was Terry-Thomas and Eric Sykes; Terry playing himself, hilariously as usual and Eric taking the part of his down-trodden sidekick. They worked so well together in *Those Magnificent Men* I wonder more was not made of that pairing in other films.

Tony Hancock was in the cast too as the inventor of an incredible-looking but completely unflyable machine. Tony was inclined to bend his elbow and had taken a tumble and broken his leg a day or two before the start of filming. There was one scene in the script in which he was supposed to run after his brainchild as the pilot wrestled to get it off the ground. He insisted he could still do what was required in spite of plaster cast – and he did, hopping and skipping across Booker airfield shouting, 'Up! Up! Up!'

The nearest we came to a serious accident was the day Tim Clutterbuck,

The artist's chairs, the Blériot, Benny Hill's windmill and me, Booker Airfield, 1965.

piloting the Allouette, took off in the direction of the windmill from which Benny Hill, as the fire chief, kept watch. Tim just cleared the sails and the trees behind and disappeared in ominous silence. Everyone expected to hear that he had crashed, but he managed to skim the treetops until he spotted a clearing just big enough to put down in. The mechanics' team soon stripped off the wings and the Allouette was returned to Booker none the worse for its close shave.

Our farthest flung film location was Dover, where we shot the bathing scenes over several freezing cold days. Then we moved up to the field where Blériot had landed after making his first flight across the Channel. From here we filmed groups of our aeroplanes passing over Dover Castle, out over the Channel, some behaving very like the original contestants, wave hopping at heights dictated by their seriously under-powered machines.

From the point of view of the sound department it became very apparent that the modern engines did not produce the right sort of period noise. We also needed to give each of the featured aircraft its own distinctive sound. It took over a month to achieve the results we wanted, working after the main filming had finished late in the autumn of 1965. Air Commodore Alan Wheeler, who was in charge of all matters aeronautical on the film, was both a very accomplished pilot and a founder member of the Shuttleworth Trust, owners of the largest collection of vintage aircraft in the country. He put all their aircraft at our disposal, a gesture which transformed the sound on the film. He flew a First World War Sopwith Pup for us and an Avro 504, powered by radial engines that gave a very distinctive note and an even more distinctive smell of burnt castor oil, which they used as a lubricant. We even persuaded him to start up an original Blériot aircraft in the collection, allowing it to be flown in short airborne hops as we made our recordings. Back at Booker a famous expert on exhaust systems, Vic Durrington, was making up some extraordinary snake-like pipes. These gave us out of phase exhaust notes.

One of the most successful noises was created from fastening a model aircraft engine, with propeller, to the end of a wooden batten and having one of the sound crew run up and past the microphone, weaving and diving with it to create the changing Doppler effect. The sound was far too high in pitch like this, but re-recorded and played back at slow speed it produced a wonderful slow revving 'tock-tock' noise which sounded just right.

Our stint was completed with the handing over of the many rolls of tape for the dubbing sound editor's attention. Then we moved on to work on our next film during the post-production period and saw nothing more of *Those Magnificent Men In Their Flying Machines* until the night of the royal premiere at the Dominion Theatre. That was also the first time we heard Ron Goodwin's wonderful theme tune which has helped to make *Those Magnificent Men In Their Flying Machines* one of the best loved films.

My, by now, good friend Dick McWhorter had called during *Those Magnificent Men* offering me the sound job on a film he was setting up for the director Martin Ritt. *The Spy Who Came In From The Cold* was based on John Le Carré's novel and starred Richard Burton and Claire Bloom. The bulk of the filming was scheduled to take place in the Republic of Ireland to avoid Burton having to pay UK income tax. Our production base was to be the Bray Studio outside Dublin. This suited us well. It had been well-built and was ideal for a one-off production like ours, although the studio had been mothballed for two years and the Western Electric sound recording installation had suffered from

Eric Sykes in Those Magnificent Men In Their Flying Machines.

this lack of use.

Dick is a belt and braces man and sent a sound maintenance engineer over to Bray a good month before filming was due to begin. He also insisted that I take a complete portable recording channel as back-up.

I met Martin Ritt at the Paramount Offices in London. Dick had obviously put in a good word for me and I left with *Spy* in my pocket, very pleased to be working with the director of *Hud*, which had achieved best actor Oscars for Patricia Neal and Melvyn Douglas.

Over in Ireland we settled into the studio and familiarised ourselves with the sound department. At the same time the art director and construction crew were building the first sets. Richard Burton and Elizabeth Taylor arrived and were mobbed by the large crowds gathered outside The Sherborne in Dublin, where they were staying. Elizabeth was always being mobbed during her stay; it was difficult to wander incognito through the streets of Dublin dressed in a white mink duffel coat.

The first scenes shot were of Cyril Cusack in a small office set. Marty was not the most explicit of directors, Cyril not the most receptive of actors. Combined with the vagaries of the script, which John Le Carré had written himself, it was heavy going. Worse was to happen at the rushes the next day. The sound quality was awful. The scenes ground on and I sank deeper into my seat. I had no idea what had gone wrong. We were recording on magnetic tape. As I always monitor through the headphones from the tape 'playoff' and not direct from the microphone, I knew that the original track was OK. But that was not going to satisfy Marty who could only judge the sound quality by what he heard coming out of the speakers. And he did not like what he heard.

We spent hours that evening checking the whole reproduction system from sound heads to speakers. The fault was in the amplifier. Convincing Marty that all would be well was not as straightforward. Directors do not quickly forget mishaps like that.

Elizabeth used to come out to the studios on most days, driven in her Cadillac by Gaston, her faithful French chauffeur. We could all see she liked to be in evidence when Claire Bloom was on call; Claire had been a friend of Richard's long before Liz Taylor had come into his life.

The crew got on well with Richard. Marty was a teetotaller and frowned on his fondness for scotch, but Richard never showed any sign of having had a drink when he came on set. That was not the case with Bernard Lee. Bernard, best known as 007's boss 'M' in the Bond films, also had a reputation for liking his drink. Marty knew this and it took a lot of persuading from Richard before he agreed to cast Bernard as an under-cover agent running a grocer's shop.

On the Bond films Bernard had always been scheduled for morning filming; the lure of Pinewood's famous bar had derailed many promising careers. Flying out to join us, Bernard was in trouble by the time he got to the airport. Boarding an Air Lingus plane to Belfast he tucked into the in-flight hospitality and had no idea he had arrived in the wrong part of Ireland until he asked a taxi-driver to take him to the Bray studios. It was a long ride down to Dublin and Bernard arrived unshaven and hungover the next morning.

Martin Ritt refused to accept his apologies and ordered him back to his hotel. Richard got him to postpone Bernard's filming until after lunch, promising he would have slept it off. After lunch Bernard reappeared and gave his usual brilliantly underplayed performance behind a shop counter. Twenty-four hours later he failed to make it to the studio for a second time, after a day drinking with a couple of stalwarts from the Abbey Theatre, Jackie MacGowran and Noel Purcell. Marty put him under strict surveillance until his filming was finished and he could be poured on to a plane heading back to Heathrow.

Filming progressed with regular hold-ups over what was actually meant in the script. Marty used to call for Angela Martelli, the veteran continuity girl, to bring the 'book'. Le Carré was on set for one of these consultations and even he did not seem sure about the meaning of what he had written.

Check Point Charlie, the famous crossing-point between East and West Berlin, had been recreated in a disused market in Dublin. We filmed there at

With my wife, daughter and Sophia Loren at Ascot during the filming of Arabesque, *1965.*

night in freezing weather, under the high curved lamp posts which were familiar landmarks in Cold War newsreels.

Dick McWhorter was there each night in a lounge suit; his only concession to the bitter cold was a trilby covering his bald pate. I could not understand this until he lifted a trouser leg to reveal thermal long johns. I had never seen them before and I suspect that Dick was creating ammunition to fend off demands from the crew for 'cold money'.

On another bitter night we were filming a scene with Richard in a particularly rough part of Dublin. He was filmed walking along a deserted street, shoulders hunched, the collar of his raincoat turned up against the dampness of the night. The usual crowd of on-lookers were watching, when the shiny black Cadillac nudged its way through. Out stepped Elizabeth in her white mink. Richard turned, saw her, and ran towards her shouting, 'Get back in that car, you stupid bitch', then to Gaston, 'Get her out of here.' Even before she arrived the crowd were not that happy at our being there.

The final scenes of *The Spy Who Came In From The Cold* were filmed in a beach-side house on the Dutch coast at Noordwyck, where the weather was even colder than it had been in Dublin.

When I got back from Holland, Jean and I received an invitation to a party Richard and Elizabeth were holding in the Oliver Messel suite at the Dorchester, in which they always stayed. This happened to be on the same evening that we had arranged to take Anne and a group of friends to dinner in Knightsbridge to celebrate Anne's twenty-first birthday. I called Richard to make our apologies.

'Bring her too, after your party,' he answered. 'Ours will go on into the small hours!'

Anne was thrilled. She had met Richard in Ireland and had fallen in love with his voice.

We arrived at the party some time after eleven. Anne got a big birthday kiss from Richard and probably did not wash for a week afterwards. Shirley Bassey appeared a little later, coming straight from her own West End show. She was soon standing by her musical director at the piano singing for over an hour, to the delighted shouts of 'More! More!' whenever a song finished.

More singing and several drinks later we made our excuses to leave; I was on call in the studio at eight. Richard, by now well refreshed, called for everyone to sing 'Happy Birthday' to Anne, and he and Bernard Lee led with a splendidly drunken duet.

It was a twenty-first birthday any girl would envy.

Chapter Twelve

007 DOUBLE

Film technicians become identified with certain films in the same way that actors do. So after my work on James Bond films with Cubby Broccoli and Harry Saltzman it came as no surprise to be offered a production of *Casino Royale.* Somehow this had been left out of Cubby and Harry's film rights' deal with Ian Fleming and they were livid.

The owner of the film rights was Charles Feldman, a New York impresario who had had a script written as a send-up of Fleming's story. Peter Sellers played Bond, heading a cast that included Ursula Andress, David Niven, Orson Welles, Deborah Kerr, Woody Allen and Charles Boyer. By the time the film was released it had had almost as many directors as actors. Joe McGrath was the first. He lasted two weeks and was replaced by Bob Parrish. Over the months that followed portions of the omnibus project were directed by John Huston, Ken Hughes and Val Guest. Veteran stuntman turned director, Richard Talmadge, occupied the director's chair for just one sequence, a casino decked out as a circus big top.

Feldman was obsessed with security. He had decreed that the script was only to be issued a page at a time, sufficient for each day's shooting; the master script was always kept locked away in the producer's office. Presumably this was to guard against any chance of the Broccoli-Saltzman team getting sight of it. If they had they would not have found anything to jeopardise their plans for more Bond films. Nevertheless, our individually numbered daily sheets were collected at the end of shooting and shredded.

Security aside, my lasting impression of *Casino Royale* was one of bewilderment, shared by cast and crew alike. No one had a clue what it was all about. Complications mounted when Sellers and Welles, who had taken a dislike to each other from the outset, refused to play a game of baccarat together. To film the scene, all the close-ups of Sellers had to be shot over the shoulder of a look-alike double for Orson Welles and vice versa. The two actors never came face to face on any occasion.

From week to week we floundered through our daily allocations of script, often arriving at work on Monday morning to find we had a new director. In the end the film was in such a mess Charlie Feldman called a halt to the production while efforts were made to rough-edit the material shot to date. We were all given two weeks' notice with no certainty that the same shooting crew would be used when the production resumed filming.

Hardly had my enforced rest started at home than a call from EON Productions' headquarters in Tilney Street offered me the next real Bond film, *You Only Live Twice*. There was location shooting in Japan, a very long schedule of five or six months and good money for me and all my crew. The plan was to prepare equipment at Pinewood Studios for two weeks before flying to Tokyo.

Almost as soon as I had accepted, the *Casino Royale* office was on the telephone to say that they were resuming shooting within a week and wanted me to return. I had no doubt that the 'proper' Bond was the one to stay with, but I agreed to return to *Casino Royale* for a month.

Never have I worked on such an incredibly ludicrous piece of film-making. For Richard Talmadge's casino-cum-circus sequence, we had all the paraphernalia of a casino spread out under green shaded lights inside a Big Top. There were cowboys and Indians riding through while people abseiled down ropes and a high-wire and a trapeze act performed up above.

Other extraordinary scenes were shot. Peter Sellers came out of the casino at night, calling for his car. Sterling Moss, in chauffeur's uniform, drove up in a Grand Prix Formula One car, which Peter straddled saying, 'Home, Moss, and go easy on the bends.'

Another sequence that took a good week was filmed on the largest sound stage at Shepperton Studios. The best part of one hundred kilted pipers marched through thick smoke produced by the fog machines. Machine gunners appeared, shooting at James Bond as the bandsmen counter-marched through the swirling mist.

After four weeks of mayhem we left to settle back into the calm professionalism of EON Productions for the fortnight's equipment preparation, looking forward to our trip to Japan.

On arrival in Tokyo, after a twenty-four hour flight, Harry Saltzman had wanted us to travel directly to Japan's southernmost island, Kyushu. Our understanding production manager, David Middlemas, persuaded him to let us stop over in Tokyo to re-adjust our body clocks. Then the weather came to our assistance and blew such a storm over Kyushu that all the exterior shooting was ruled out and the whole schedule was switched around. Filming would start in Tokyo instead.

The evening after our arrival a buffet was laid on for the British and Japanese to meet each other. On the way in we passed two immaculately clad Japanese nurses, dressed from head to toe in white. Each of them had a hypodermic syringe, which they filled from a box of phials. They had instructions to give each of us a shot of haemoglobin in our bottoms. No jab – no party!

In Tokyo we shot scenes in the traditional gardens of the then new Otani Hotel; our production headquarters. The next stop was Kyushu and our first location at a small fishing village called Akimi. The unit was staying a fair way inland from the coast, in the town of Kagoshima. On the first morning we moved off just after dawn. Even that early in the day it was very humid. Two hours driving over bumpy roads brought us to Akimi, exhausted and saturated with sweat.

Cubby Broccoli, who had gone on ahead in an air-conditioned car, stood in amazement as the buses disgorged his crew, dishevelled and covered in dust. By that evening he had chartered a twin-rotor twenty-six seat Boeing helicopter from Nippon Airways and a helipad was hewn from the hillside above the village. In four twenty-minute air-lifts he was then able to deliver his film crew, fresh and ready to cope with Akimi's punishing climate.

Except possibly for Cuba, the humidity in the south of Japan was the worst I ever experienced. Stepping out of an air-conditioned hotel, the laundry-like atmosphere was suffocating. In minutes shirts, slacks, socks were soaking and we had to spend the rest of the day looking as if we had just stepped out of a shower fully clothed. My headphones would stick to my ears. Drops of sweat would run down my nose to plonk on the meters of the mixing panel. Even re-threading a new roll of magnetic tape was a chore as I tried to avoid salty sweat getting on to the sensitive recording heads.

A lot of our time in Akimi was spent on a raft moored out in the bay. This acted as a platform for crew and equipment to film Sean swimming around with the little Japanese actress, Akiko Wakabayashi. They did not know how lucky they were, even if the sea was the temperature of a tepid bath. Our consumption of cool drinks was enormous, so the sight of the sun dropping in late afternoon was always welcome. When the call came for a 'wrap' there was a wholesale scramble onto the launches to get back to the shore. The actors and director were always away first in the helicopter. Struggling with the equipment we were lucky to make the last flight.

The schedule in Akimi was so tight, the only time I had to record the sound effects I required was our rest day before moving up into the volcanic region. Keith and I were dropped off from a small Bell helicopter and trudged off down the village with equipment slung over our shoulders. I had to take a boat out into the bay to record tracks of rowing and the sound of water slopping against the hull. Back on shore we needed general village background sounds: distant chatter, children playing, chickens scratching around, in fact anything that would be useful for our sound editors back in the studio.

What we had not taken into consideration was how we were going to communicate without interpreters. No one in the village spoke English and neither Keith nor I spoke a word of Japanese. Signs, gesticulations and the old dodge of playing back recordings to let people hear themselves and their friends, won the day. We got our boat, roamed the village for the right effects and were offered, and accepted, hospitality all over Akimi.

Our next location was up in the mountains. The big Boeing airlifted us to Kirishima, a nice little town full of hotels which does an enormous trade in honeymoons. Japanese newly-weds prefer the company of others to getting away together somewhere quiet. One hotel we stayed in later by the coast was more like a holiday camp. There were a thousand rooms and a gigantic, factory-like glazed building housed numerous pools, where nude bathing could be enjoyed under full-grown palm trees and exotic shrubs in a variety of baths offering water at various temperatures and with a variety of scents: sulphur, banana, herbal, even strawberry.

The whole place was stiff with people. When we stepped into the foyer it was crammed with gambling machines being played by hundreds of young couples. All of the restaurants were full; without a table reservation there was no hope of getting a meal.

We were in the mountains for the next sequence. This was set on the rim of an extinct volcano into which a tiny single-seat helicopter flew. In the final film the floor of the crater opened like a gigantic sliding roof, through which the aircraft dropped into Blofeld's secret space stronghold. The fantastic set that amazed audiences everywhere was the brainchild of Ken Adam, the production designer on the Bond films. This had been built on the back lot at Pinewood using miles of tubular scaffolding that supported plaster rocks inside the volcano. A monorail train ran round the floor. There was even a rocket topped by a space capsule which could rise towards the sliding aperture, apparently taking off with all the smoke and flames of a Cape Canaveral launch.

Donald Pleasence as Blofeld, You Only Live Twice.

Our job in Japan was to film Bond's point of view from the crater's rim with Akiko and a famous Japanese actor, Tetsura Tamba. The landing site on the rim was too narrow for the big Boeing, so a minimum shooting crew plus equipment was taken up in an Alouette helicopter that could carry five at a time. This restriction did not apply to guests, of course. Despite trying to work on a twenty-foot wide strip high above two precipitous drops, we were joined by Roald Dahl (the script writer), Patricia Neal (his actress wife, partly paralysed from a massive stroke) and the director's wife and family, all of whom had to be provided with production chairs. When everyone was settled, filming commenced.

The little helicopter, operating close to its maximum ceiling, flew down into the crater without difficulty but found it a very different story to climb out. With the engine at full-throttle it spiralled up in a series of wide circuits, making an agonising climb while we all looked on apprehensively. A loud cheer went up when it eased over the rim at last, scattering the guests who fell flat on their faces as it staggered across a few feet above them.

After a snatched boxed lunch (raw fish, sour pickles, cold coagulated rice – the works) we started filming the actors reacting to the helicopter. As this was going on I noticed that the weather was starting to close in. The first assistant director scoffed, especially when I said the guests should be taken down to the safety of our car park base below.

My sound crew was in the habit of carrying shoulder bags with foul weather gear, so we were all right. The rest of the crew were only wearing t-shirts, shorts and sandals. The predictable panic calls were soon being made to fetch the guests down in the Alouette. By the second landing on our crater heavy mist was swirling around. The base camp had disappeared in the cloud and

The film set of Blofeld's secret stronghold, an extinct volcano.

the pilot doubted if he could risk another landing.

A radio call from base confirmed this, leaving us to scramble down with the equipment as best we could. On the way down I saw the clearest proof yet of the difference between western and oriental cultures. In the scene Tamba had ridden a little pony and I naturally assumed that he would give up his mount now to let Akiko ride it on the way down. Not a bit of it, Tamba stayed resolutely in the saddle, the only member of the group not carrying something; even the little actress shouldered one of the continuity girl's scripts.

The docks of Osaka, back on the mainland, was our next destination, to film scenes of Bond being chased by villains. Sean Connery, wary of exerting himself unnecessarily, made sure that all the long-shots were carried out by his personal stuntman, Bob Simmonds. Bob had mastered Sean's walk, his stance and the way he ran, so that the real Bond had only to dodge out from behind a pile of crates, or other hiding place, into which Bob had fought, dived and dashed.

From Osaka we had an electric train laid on specially to take us to the ancient capital, Kyoto. There we filmed many scenes in the fantastic castle that towers over the city, scenes that showed the training of the Ninja teams that helped Bond in the assault on Blofeld's base at the climax of the film.

Black-garbed warriors wearing cane masks fought with staves. Others practised kendo and judo. Most fascinating of all was a display of swordplay between half-a-dozen warriors. They attacked one lone figure armed with a gleaming broad-bladed sword that he wielded in both hands with flashing sweeps. When the filming was finished, the main unit moved on, leaving me to record additional sound effects of clashing swords, swishes and grunts.

The lone warrior had remained behind and treated us to an extraordinary sight. He was the least approachable of all the Ninjas, the one who always kept himself aloof. We knew that the discipline they practised was taken very seriously, with great observance to tradition and much emphasis given to status, grades of proficiency and dedication. This warrior personified all of it.

He measured up to the straw dummy of a man with woven arms, legs and body, topped by a cane head stuffed with straw. Drawing his lips back over his teeth in a frightening snarl and with a demonic look in his eyes, he set about the dummy. In five masterful, sickening, swipes, he first struck off the head, then sliced off both arms and both legs, one after the other, leaving the hollow cage of the torso to tumble to the ground. The sword was replaced in its sheath with a flourish. Then he just walked away.

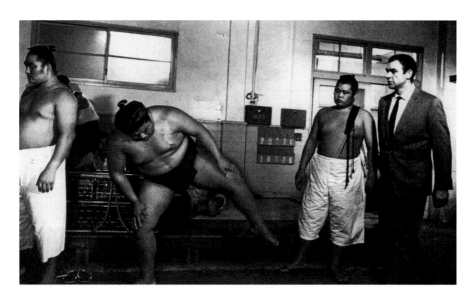

The Ninja team came back with us to London for more filming. It was their first time away from Japan and all but the lone swordsman loved it. For most of their free time he remained in his room at the Holiday Inn in St John's Wood. He did not like English food. He never smiled. In fact he was completely disdainful of England and everything English.

Sumo wrestling was another aspect of traditional Japanese life reflected in the film. We spent five nights at a stadium filming the bouts and behind the scenes. Backstage away from the arena was fascinating. Here the wrestlers lay in stalls, rather like stables, where they were tended by their managers and hairdressers before the contests. They were all young men, heavy and enormously fat, force fed on high-calorie diet and weighing up to thirty stone.

When the main unit flew home, a second unit directed by Peter Hunt stayed on in Japan to film the chase by Blofeld's helicopters of Bond in his tiny autogyro. Peter had already been responsible for much of the success of the earlier Bond films, using his editing skill to turn an average sequence into an outstanding one with great pace and excitement.

Our role in this part of the film was solely to provide radio communications. We had already recorded soundtracks of the Bell helicopters, later having the chance to record a library of effects of the remarkable tiny autogyro built and flown by Ken Wallis, a retired wing commander who doubled for Sean. We had met him on the set of *Those Magnificent Men In Their Flying Machines*, when he flew for us for sound effects recordings. One of our tasks was to set up an emergency procedure in case of an accident, using the facility of a hospital up in the hills where difficult surgical and orthopaedic cases were treated.

The cameraman who filmed the aerial battle was Johnny Jordan, one of a small band of highly skilled operators who sit on the left-hand side of a helicopter with the door removed, feet braced against the skid and operating the camera on very complicated mounting that cancels out the helicopter's vibrations.

Johnny and Ken were as intrepid as each other. We had already witnessed Ken's steely nerve when he had radioed Johnny to say that he was low in fuel and would have to land on a nearby road and then brought his little craft down, skimming over the roof of a car and giving the Japanese driver a hell of a fright. Johnny was soon hovering overhead in his helicopter, lowering a can of aviation fuel to Ken's autogyro parked by the roadside. Ken filled his tank,
007 flies the Wallis   waited for the traffic to clear and then took off to carry on filming.
Autogyro.

Our return from Japan was hilarious. In 1967 the pound bought a lot of

Trip to a Geisha House during filming of You Only Live Twice – *all work and no play makes John a dull boy!*

yen. There was an Aladdin's cave of goodies in the shops that we had never seen at home: tape recorders, hi-fi equipment, cameras, toys, wonderful porcelain and household goods, all incredibly cheap. I had bought vases, tea sets, ikibani dishes with special spiked supports, pebbles, tools and books on Japanese flower arranging; all of which had been shipped home in advance. My real regret is that I did not spot the enormous potential there would be at home for small Hitachi barbecues. Little cast-iron hibachi barbecues were there for the asking. I know the man who did see the opening and made a fortune importing them, though he now has them made in Taiwan – Japan is too expensive!

We touched down at Heathrow, after our long flight via Bangkok, at four-thirty in the morning. Immigration officials checked our passports without comment. We collected our luggage and then presented ourselves to customs. For our arrival the 'Queen's' men had been briefed that this was a 'revenue party'. I took my place in a queue behind our standby carpenter with his assortment of suitcases and newly purchased tools.

'Have you purchased anything of value while you've been abroad, sir?' asked the customs officer. His apparently innocent tone was all that was needed to disarm Jim, who answered that he had bought a few clocks. Asked to show them, he opened a large suitcase to reveal twenty-eight! They ranged in size and complexity from small digital ones to a couple of handsome traditional mantelpiece clocks. The customs man had never had such a haul openly declared to him.

We had been back at Pinewood Studios for about a month when word reached us one Monday morning that there had been an accident involving the crew still working in Japan – just that, no details. Cubby Broccoli came on the set later, called for quiet and announced that one of the Bell helicopters from Blofeld's attacking force had collided with the camera helicopter carrying Johnny Jordan, who was reported injured.

Another day went by before we got the full story. The Bell had misjudged a near-miss approach on the camera helicopter and had sliced through the left-hand skid on which Johnny's feet were resting. He had kept his camera turning during all this, even after the Bell had plunged away below to make a forced landing on the slopes of a volcano. Johnny was aware that he had felt an impact on his leg; he panned the camera down further to photograph a foot dangling on the end of his leg. He always had a Nikon stills camera with him and took a few more pictures, for the insurance people he maintained, before radioing Ron at the base to say they had had a 'prang' and needed an ambulance.

The pilot brought the skidless helicopter down to a hover, so that Johnny could be lifted from his seat and taken by ambulance to the emergency hospital nearby. He was still conscious in spite of his terrible injury and was even able to yell at the driver when he was about to take a wrong turn.

The late aerial cameraman Johnny Jordan filming action sequences for the Bond films. PHOTOGRAPHED BY LARRY ELLIS.

Johnny was in luck that day. Two eminent surgeons had arrived that morning from Tokyo to operate on a patient who needed a complicated bone graft. Their patient was returned to his bed as Johnny was taken straight into the operating theatre where they set about trying to save his foot.

Masumi Maeda, one of the two Japanese nurses who had joined our film unit, took great care of Johnny. She was the only nurse in the hospital who could speak English. She was with him constantly as he recovered from the operation and only agreed to take some rest when Johnny had been given a whistle and trumpet to call for assistance – the whistle was for little requests, the trumpet for more urgent ones, like the bedpan.

Cubby was magnificent. He flew Johnny's wife out to Japan to be with him and when he was fit to come home, Cubby had a special stretcher area created on the plane. He also paid for Masumi to come back to the UK to carry on her looking after him. Cubby also booked Johnny into the London clinic and made sure he had top medical attention. On arrival at Heathrow, however, Johnny insisted on stopping off at the studio to see us all before he disappeared for his treatment. He breezed into Blofeld's volcano hideout in a wheelchair to everyone's delight and amazement.

Johnny was in what he affectionately called 'the bloody London clinic' for a long time. In spite of Masumi's efforts to keep his leg free of infection, his surgeons decided his foot would be so deformed it was better to amputate it

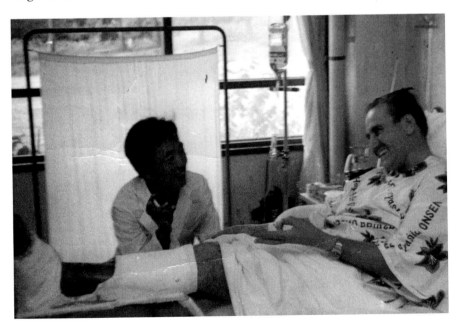

Johnny with his Japanese Orthopeadic surgeon.

and fit a modern artificial limb. For a fiercely active man this could have been a serious setback. True to character, Johnny saw it as a new skill to master. Roehampton, where he had the new limb made, was a revelation. Even before arriving there he had ordered an artificial flipper that he could attach to his stump so that he could carry on scuba diving. He quickly mastered the difficult transition to his tin foot, despite intense pain from sores that developed on his stump. His inventor's mind was hard at work as well coming up with ways of improving the mechanics of the ankle joint. Johnny was soon a star patient the staff co-opted him into helping and encouraging other patients who found the experience almost more than they could cope with. Johnny's cheerful, determined, stubborn persuasion helped many to succeed. By the time of the premiere at the Odeon Leicester Square Johnny was confident enough to stump up the stairs unaided; for all of us who had worked on the film there was only one star that night.

Chapter Thirteen

BANG BANG AND BOND

Ian Fleming's writing was not confined to the James Bond books. Although it came as news to me, he was also the author of a delightful children's story, the strangely titled *Chitty Chitty Bang Bang*. Cubby Broccoli had the film rights and a year after the completion of *You Only Live Twice* rumours started that this was going to be his next production.

The rumours turned into fact when Cubby asked me to go and see him to talk through the idea. Roald Dahl, no stranger to popular children's stories, had written the script for what Cubby saw as a big budget musical film starring Dick Van Dyke, a follow-on to his great success in Walt Disney's *Mary Poppins*. Cubby had drafted in the Sherman brothers, who had written the music for the Disney film, and their musical director, Irwin Kostal. The husband and wife team of Marc and Dee Dee Braux had also been engaged to repeat their success as choreographers in Mary Poppins.

Irwin was in England at the time, finishing his work on *Half A Sixpence*. He was keen to meet me to discuss the sound on the new film, because he had been very unhappy about the quality of the playback system used on *Half A Sixpence*. His real concern was the limitations of the speakers that had been used for the big production numbers for which there had never been enough power output from the amplifiers. If Cubby would stand the cost, Irwin wanted us to construct a custom-built system for *Chitty*.

Hollywood had always been in the forefront with musicals: *My Fair Lady, The Sound of Music* and *Mary Poppins* had set a standard that few could match. Cubby realised that and I was not surprised to hear he was seeking help and advice from the Hollywood studios. What did come as a complete surprise was his asking me to go to Hollywood for him to find out how the studios dealt with playback. Cubby's office made all the necessary arrangements, helped by United Artists in Hollywood, and in a matter of days I was on my way to Los Angeles flying first-class with Pan-Am.

On arrival a blue-suited chauffeur, who introduced himself as Al, 'floated' me away to Beverly Hills in the longest car I had ever seen. At the check-in desk at the Beverley Wilshire Hotel I was greeted with the news that Mr Broccoli had asked them to look after me; I had only to let them know if there was anything they could do to make my stay a pleasant one. Up in my suite I found a note from Hernandez Cartwright, the justifiably famed owner and a book of matches with my name in gold letters. A bottle of champagne completed my welcome. I found out later that this was routine practice.

United Artists had their offices at the Goldwyn Studios, where Al drove me after breakfast the following morning. There a Mr Lee Katz briefed me on my itinerary. Most of the main studios were on the list for me to visit: MGM, Columbia, Paramount, Fox, Warners, Universal, Disney and RKO. Al, who seemed to have worked for every studio transportation department in Hollywood, proved to be invaluable. He knew every security man at each of the entrance barriers, where access is only gained with great difficulty and after careful scrutiny. Al just called out cheerfully, 'Mr Mitchell, from London, England' and we were waved through.

Cubby's introduction ensured an easy ride wherever I went. At every studio the technical staff went out of their way to show the way they did things. Several times I was lucky enough to see playback sessions in progress; in particular Julie Andrews shooting a Gertrude Lawrence number in *Star* on the Paramount lot. I was surprised to see them using sixteen-inch acetate discs. Another shock was the turntable on which the record revolved. That was a disc cutter as big as a workshop lathe which dated from the 1930s. The whole thing had been taken to Austria for the filming of *The Sound of Music* and manhandled on to the slopes above Salzburg where Julie Andrews had sung her opening number, 'The hills are alive.' No wonder the Paramount people were aghast when I told them I was planning to use a quarter-inch tape recorder as my playback machine. They were convinced the tape would stretch; but from hundreds of test runs with a single roll of tape, punctuated with sharps, stops and starts, I knew it would not.

As I moved around the studios I realised that we either followed the traditional Hollywood methods or backed our own judgement for portability, speed of operation and flexibility. I knew which I preferred, but I still made the most of the opportunity to see Hollywood working at first hand. I found a situation that was very similar to the studios I was used to working in at home. There was the same reluctance among die-hard heads of department to install modern equipment. This gave freelance specialists like me the chance to introduce innovations and prove their value, profiting from them at the same time.

I had built up a considerable equipment facility company by now, starting with a loudhailer. This was needed for a film being made in Spain, but the studio head refused to allow one of his to be taken out of the country. So I bought a loudhailer; hired it to the production for nine weeks and covered its cost of £50 in that time. For several years Jean made do with less house-keeping than my crew took home to their wives, so that I could invest in the latest recorders, microphones and ancillary equipment, always staying ahead of the competition. I never borrowed from banks or finance houses, always paying out of earnings from equipment hire.

But Hollywood was suffering a recession by the end of the 1960s. On my first Sunday I walked from the hotel to Century City, a newly built hotel, office and shopping complex, standing on part of the studio lot that 20th Century Fox had been forced to sell off.

One innovation really impressed me in Hollywood, the Todd-AO camera system with its huge projected picture and six-track stereo sound. This had been dreamed up by Mike Todd, Elizabeth Taylor's husband who was killed in an air-crash in 1957. Mike was essentially a financial wheeler-dealer, but he conceived the idea for a system that was so practical it is still in use thirty-five years later. He shot his own film *Around The World in Eighty Days* in Todd-AO and proved its worth by winning himself an Oscar; the AO stood for American Optical, the company that developed the lenses for his cameras.

We had shot tests on the volcano set for *You Only Live Twice* using a lightweight Todd-AO camera which had been brought from the States for Cubby and Saltzman to see. I got to know Don Rogers, the Todd-AO assistant who had come with it and we had exchanged business cards. I certainly did not think at the time that within the year I would be calling on him in Los Angeles to see round the Todd-AO plant.

Don introduced me to Fred Hynes, a real veteran of sound men, sixty years old and the originator of the six-track stereo system. They ran their demo film in their main theatre, which had quite the biggest screen I had ever seen. The effect was amazing and I left determined to convince Cubby that that was what we needed for *Chitty Chitty Bang Bang*. The trouble was that when I went in to see him the day after I got back, bound report under my arm, brimming with technical analysis, Cubby just said. 'Hi, John, did you have a good time?'

In my absence the production departments had been busy. Ken Adams, the production designer, had drawn up plans for the fabulous 'Chitty' cars and three were being built. Two were complete road cars with modern Ford Zodiac engines under the bonnets (with automatic gearboxes for Dick Van Dyke who had never driven a car with a gear shift). Another had been built with air-flotation to serve as the 'floating on the water car'. The fourth car was the engine-less lightweight version, the 'flying car'. The fifth was a car without wheels which sat on a flat bed trailer towed by the camera car. There were also miniature models perfect down to the last detail.

My crew had been busy ordering massive speakers from Tannoy, together with high wattage amplifiers. To satisfy Irwin Kostel we were building our own playback units with plenty of power. We were also preparing in built-speakers for the road cars and flying car, as well as a complete rehearsal unit for Marc Braux in his dance rehearsal studio.

A day or two after I had got back I had another summons from Cubby. He told me that he had decided to release *Chitty* in 70 millimetre big screen with six-track sound and had asked his people at United Artists to get him information

The original six-track-wide screen Todd-AO Dubbing Theatre, 1955, with Fred Hynes and crew.

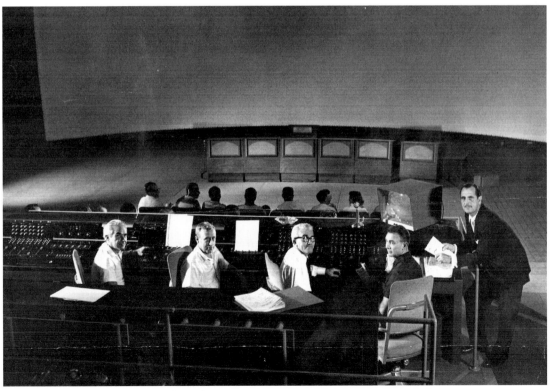

on such processes. It took a moment for this to sink in. Had this not been one of the reasons for sending me out to Hollywood?

I produced my dossier, gave him the information I had carefully collated every evening in my hotel. It seemed to have genuinely slipped his mind that I had been to California and back for this very purpose. Anyhow, he thanked me, asked his secretary to put a call through to Todd-AO and asked Fred Hynes to come to Pinewood to discuss the proposal. Two days later Fred arrived and the deal was struck. Then we got to work.

We began the recording sessions with Irwin Kostal and musicians at the Denham Music Stage of Anvil Films. First were the dance numbers for Marc and Dee Dee to choreograph. They were followed by the vocals: Sally Anne Howe's solos followed by Dick's with his two film children. Neither of the children had ever sung in public, let alone made a recording. They did their best, but the only way we could get them to maintain the tempo was for each

Opposite.
Chitty Chitty Bang Bang.

Grandpa Potts sings 'Up Grows the Ashes' with his fellow prisoners in the Baron's dungeon.

of us to hold a child under the armpits, and literally to pump them in time to the music heard in our headphones.

Few sounds are stranger than a vocal track played back without its orchestral background. Even professional singers dislike hearing themselves like this and the piping tones of a couple of eight-year-olds are no more pleasant on the ears. Once all the tracks, from the orchestra, Dick and the children, were brought together, balanced and mixed the finished number was terrific and repaid all the effort and patience it had taken.

The Sherman brothers had written a very fast tempo number for Dick Van Dyke's 'Bamboo' dance, for which Irwin booked eight xylophones for the test recording. After several rehearsals, each one being played faster than the previous one, he decided to make a take, which was played faster still. Irwin decided he could not do any better, though he was sure that Marc Braux would kill him for presenting the dancers with such a challenge. Marc was in total agreement; his verdict on the recording was 'impossible'. Still, it must have kindled something inside him because that ended up as the recording we did use in the film, producing one of the fastest and most exciting dance routines ever filmed.

Ken Cameron, who was head of Anvil Films, had all the best attributes of a Scot. He looked magnificent in the kilt, which he always wore, and he was generous with his whisky. After one evening session on the sound stage he invited several of us to have a 'wee dram' in his office. Dick was fascinated by his kilt and Ken offered to let him try one on – he kept four in a cupboard in his office.

After a lot of coercion from the rest of us, Dick slipped off his trousers and donned a kilt, complete with sporran. Some time after that his trousers mysteriously disappeared and he was forced to go home in the kilt. This was not too bad as his rented house was only a few miles away and his Morris Ten was parked outside. As he told us the next day, he had pulled into a lay-by to adjust his unfamiliar dress and was joined by a passing policeman on his bicycle who wanted to know what he was up to. It was quite late by now and when he was asked to identify himself, and replied that he was Dick Van Dyke, it did not go down well with the policeman, who cautioned him to drive carefully and go straight home.

Still wondering about his reception from the family, Dick had not got beyond the hall when his wife and daughter caught sight of him. After the first gales of laughter they ran for cameras to make sure there was a permanent record for the Van Dyke family album.

Rowland Emmett, famous for his crazy inventions, was hard at work in the pre-production period too. He had the job of producing incredible working models of bizarre inventions for Caractacus Potts, the inventor who Dick Van Dyke was playing. We got to know Rowland well and always looked forward to the next invention to emerge from his workshop-cum-forge in Sussex. What we enjoyed most was his incredible eye for the absurd. Everyday items like egg whisks, spoons and bicycle chains were used to fashion his absurd contraptions which, to our delight and amazement, always worked. As far as we were concerned, the breakfast machine was his ultimate triumph. Chugging along its rails suspended across the kitchen, with its little steam engine puffing away, the breakfast machine collected fried eggs, sausages and bacon to deliver them on a plate at the breakfast table.

In the story Dick's home and workshop was a windmill and for the film

Sally Ann Howes examines Caractacus Potts' inventions.

the production had refurbished a famous windmill at Fingest in the Chilterns, even giving it a new set of sails with an electric motor to turn them. We spent many weeks up on the ridge above the village. That was also where the first 'Chitty Chitty Bang Bang' song started when Dick and the two children piled into the car and drove off. It was also the first test of our in-built playback system which we hoped would work in later scenes as the car trundled through the lanes of Buckinghamshire. Observant viewers might spot that one part of the song seems to have jumped to the Mediterranean. The weather had turned so awful at this point that shooting was postponed until we were on location on the Riviera where the song could be completed on the outskirts of St Tropez as vineyards whizzed by in the background. Not many bars later Dick is seen stopping the car outside a country pub near Henley. I wonder how many people have spotted that over the years?

France was not our only foreign location. We went to Rottenburg, the medieval German town whose timber-framed buildings had been copied in Disney Land. We also went to Hohen Schvangau, one of mad King Ludwig's fairy-tale castles in Bavaria. Disney copied this too for his centre-piece at Disney Land. There we filmed Robert Helpmann's evil child-catcher scenes.

Chitty pursued by Gert Frobe.

Robert Helpmann,
the 'Child Catcher',
with choreographer
Marc Braux, director
Ken Hughes and
veteran continuity
girl Angela Martelli.

My own daughter was occupying a fair bit of my time away from work. Anne had become engaged eight months before our French and German location work and the wedding had been fixed for the following September. I had no idea where I would be or what I would be doing, so gave her the go-ahead. *Chitty* cropped up in the meantime and with it the scheduled departure for Rottenburg on the very Saturday when I was due to lead her up the aisle. An understanding Cubby arranged for Jean and me to travel out a day later.

At a music session a few weeks before the wedding I had invited Marc and Dee Dee Braux, and Irwin Kostal and his wife to join us at the wedding. None of them had been to an English wedding before and as I was explaining to Irwin that he could hire a 'split-tail coat, tall hat' and the rest of the outfit he wanted from Moss Bros, Dick Van Dyke appeared and asked why I had not invited him too. An invitation to Mr and Mrs Van Dyke followed swiftly. Sally Anne Howes could not join us, but she generously offered to lend her limousine and chauffeur to ferry Anne to and from the church.

The wedding was held at Old Windsor church, the reception was at Gerrards Cross and little maps were given to each of the guests to help them find their way about. The day came, the bride was given away by her father and the service was almost over when I spotted Dick slipping into the back of the church. None of us had the slightest idea why he was late and I only caught up with the story at the reception.

Dick had found his way to Windsor and had assumed that where the castle was must be Old Windsor, not appreciating that it is actually half-way to Runnymede. He asked for directions at the police station and the sergeant on duty, recognising who he was, arranged for a car to escort them to the church. The police car turned off the main road towards Windsor Lock and, seeing a marquee, pointed Dick towards the wedding reception. Inside he was handed a glass of champagne and wandered round among the guests looking for familiar faces. There were none. He was at the wrong wedding.

One of the guests explained that they were at the wedding that had taken place immediately before Anne's and sent him off in the direction of the church where he was just in time to see the bride and groom leave together as man and wife. We have a marvellous picture of Dick telling Anne the story; he had never been to two weddings on the same day.

By the time all the main unit shooting was completed it had been decided that the director, Ken Hughes, would not be sitting in on the dub in Hollywood. Instead Cubby told me I would be going to Todd-AO for what are called the pre-dubs, all the piecing together of individual effects, footsteps, post-synchronised dialogues and music. This was a five-month stint for me, and Cubby, ever generous, insisted Jean go too. He also suggested that we might like to stop in New York for a couple of days and asked his United Artists man there to make all the arrangements for us.

Myer P Beck, better known as Mike, was totally blind, though meeting him for the first time you had no idea. He moved about as if he was sighted, even shuffling papers on his desk convincingly. Mike was hospitality personified. Detecting a slight hesitation when he asked how we liked our hotel room, which was pretty poky, he immediately called to his secretary, 'Ada – call the Warwick. Tell them to move John and Jean to a suite.'

Had we got dollars?

I said I had travellers cheques of my own.

'You don't want to spend your own money,' protested Mike. 'Ada, make out a cheque for five hundred dollars for John. Bring it in and I'll sign it.'

Next he said that we must not leave New York without seeing at least a couple of shows. Once more Ada was called in to be asked what shows we should see. Tickets for *Cabaret* and *Fiddler On The Roof* were handed to me the next day. Before we left New York Mike took us out with his wife for lunch

Anne and Peter's wedding.

in his favourite Italian restaurant, leading the way as if sighted, only just lightly holding my arm.

In Los Angeles another stretched limo was waiting to take us to an even more opulent suite at the Beverley Wilshire Hotel. This one had his and her bathrooms with phones by the loo and sun lamps overhead which switched on when you sat down. Now I knew why Californians had such marvellous tans. We only stayed in the hotel a few days, preferring to take an apartment in a service block near Westwood Village, where Jean was in walking distance of shops and could do other things while I was at work.

I had been working at Todd-AO two weeks when Fred Hynes told me he was putting us on 'nights'. The current Barbra Streisand production, *Funny Girl*, needed to be re-dubbed and they were given 'days'. I knew that Hollywood studios kept their plants working round the clock and now I was to experience it for myself. I told Barbra years after, when she was interviewing for her production of *Yentl*, that I had worked the night-shift at Todd-AO, in order that *Funny Girl* could have the daytime slot. She was not impressed and I did not get the job!

Cubby telephoned occasionally to check on how things were going. I used to ask if he wanted to come and see for himself but the answer was invariably the same. He was in Las Vegas and did not want to leave because he was winning, or he was in Vegas and could not leave because he was losing. Either way he did not want us to miss the fun and when he heard that Jean had never been to his gambling mecca, he asked us to name a date and he would take care of everything else.

After finishing at Todd-AO and organising a special showing of *Chitty* in Hollywood for Dick Van Dyke, Jean and I drove the couple of hundred miles across the desert to Las Vegas, where Cubby had booked us in to the Tropicana hotel. The experience was a sensation in several ways.

Stepping from the air-conditioned car, we hurried through the roasting desert heat of the parking lot and hustled into what felt like the arctic temperatures of the foyer. On our way to our suite two of the peculiarities of Las Vegas struck us: there were no public clocks and no matter where we wanted to go in the hotel, we had to pass casino tables and one-armed bandits.

The accommodation was excellent – cool and quiet, with double-lined curtains covering the windows, even though it was afternoon; in Las Vegas, we learned, daytime is for sleeping.

A knock at the door revealed the vice-president of the hotel company, who introduced himself as an old friend of Cubby's. If we needed anything, we had only to call room service. We were to let the desk clerk know which shows we wanted to see while we were in town. And when we left we just had to sign the bill. Cubby would take care of the rest, with one proviso – he would not be responsible for our gambling debts!

Las Vegas was a fitting end to our American trip, though not quite enough to tempt me to take up an offer from Fred Hynes to join him at Todd-AO as his deputy. Todd-AO was thinking of setting up a British counterpart, perhaps in association with one of the existing studio organisations. He thought that my background could be useful. He also promised to groom me to take his place once he retired. I was pleased to have been asked, but for various reasons I never made the move. The Hollywood slump of the 1970s, before television finally made its full impact was one reason. So was Fred's robust constitution. He was still a consulting vice-president up to his eighty-second birthday. As heir apparent, I would have been waiting in the wings for a couple of decades or longer.

By now Johnny Jordon had completely mastered his artificial leg and was back at work darting around the sky in his Alouette helicopter. He worked on

Chitty, announcing his arrival for his first aerial camera job since the accident by waving his stump to us from his familiar exposed position behind the camera as he flew past Dick Van Dyke's windmill. Over our ground radio came the message, 'That's one the buggers won't get.'

When he had finished his assignment on Cubby's musical, Johnny moved on to Harry Saltzman's aerial epic *The Battle of Britain*.

In 1969 we joined forces to work on the next James Bond film, *On Her Majesty's Secret Service*, the first without Sean Connery in the title role. George Lazenby, whose screen credits to that point were topped by his appearance in a television commercial for Fry's Turkish Delight, had taken over as 007, partly because Sean was driving ever harder bargains with the producers and partly because he did not want his whole career to be overshadowed by Ian Fleming's character.

As so often with the Bond films we were soon off on location, this time to Switzerland, where we were based in Mürren, just down the valley from Interlaken, and living at five thousand feet. Our main shooting area was on top of the Schilthorn, the mountain rising a further five thousand feet above Mürren, which can only be approached by cable car.

Right on the top the famous Piz Gloria revolving restaurant was nearing completion. This looked an ideal setting for Blofeld's headquarters and Cubby and Harry had the clever idea of offering to finish off the fitting-out in return for the use of the site during the making of the film. The contractors had no objection, it was going to save them a lot of headaches. The deal was struck, Blofeld got his headquarters and we inherited a whole lot of unexpected problems.

The first was electricity. There was only a small supply at the top of the ten thousand foot mountain and Hubert Froelich, our German production manager, who seemed to be able to manage anything, had two generators taken up in bits and pieces and reassembled in a sound-proof room. He had a helipad built for use in the film and to give Cubby somewhere to land when he came up to see how we were getting on. His ingenuity knew few limitations; the helipad could also be flooded and frozen and used as a curling rink.

The second problem was snow. Looking across the valley, the Eiger and the Jungfrau were covered in snow, but we had not got any. Twenty-five years ago snow machines were nothing like as efficient as the ones in use today, so making enough snow, even at the altitude we were working at, was a problem.

Jean had come out to Mürren with me and we had a little apartment right opposite the cable car terminal. Every morning I would say goodbye and walk

over to catch the cable car to work, five thousand feet above Mürren.

Shooting went surprisingly smoothly. Our Swiss-born assistant director, Frank Ernst, seemed to have some difficulty assembling all Blofeld's girls for their scenes, once commanding them in his amusingly formal English, 'Ladies, ladies, please put down your reticules and come on the set.'

George Lazenby turned out to be a very pleasant chap, though I always felt he had been ill-advised by someone when he landed his starring role. Whoever it was had told him to insist on the same star treatment that was being handed out to his co-star, Diana Rigg. That was not so bad. More serious from his point of view was his refusal to sign the contract. Harry Saltzman asked him repeatedly to sign, but for reasons I will never understand he always put it off. In the end I was told that he never did sign the contract and was paid off, after the film was finished, with only a small proportion of what he should have received.

On Her Majesty's Secret Service. Blofeld's girls included Joanna Lumley, Anushka Semple and Jenny Hanley.

There was little rapport between George and Diana Rigg. At lunch, immediately before they were due to shoot a love scene in a Swiss barn, he ate an enormous quantity of garlic, which did not endear him to Diana. These minor hiccups aside, the production moved through the script on schedule.

Before we finished in the Alps above Mürren Johnny appeared to film the spectacular flying sequences. He had been frustrated for some time because his camera could not pan upwards without photographing the helicopter rotors, which restricted potentially good shots of aircraft flying above him. The solution he came up with gave all the professional pilots the shivers. To get around the problem Johnny proposed attaching parachute shrouds to a large diameter hoop fastened to the helicopter skids. He was going to dangle from this in his harness, at the full length of the shrouds, operating the camera which was suspended on an elasticated rope from the centre point of the hoop. He reckoned that hanging down below the helicopter like this would give him a much greater upward field of vision away from the whirling. He was right, but only Johnny would have been prepared to put his idea to the test.

The first few flights with the new rig were anxious but Johnny, his pilot Captain Crewsden, and the ground team worked out a routine that got Johnny and the camera safely airborne without the shrouds becoming tangled. Johnny's artificial leg was an added complication. The alloy foot conducted sub-zero temperatures to his stump. To get over the discomfort, he disconnected his leg

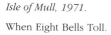

Isle of Mull, 1971.
When Eight Bells Toll.

once he was in the harness and pulled on a thick mountaineering sock to keep the stump warm.

Some incredible pictures were taken of Johnny soaring past the alpine background, though perhaps his most-hair-raising exploit displayed his wicked sense of humour. Johnny had formed the opinion that the Swiss were a stuffy lot and needed taking down a peg or two. What better way was there than to make an assault on the summit of their beloved Eiger? Late one afternoon, he put his plan into action with the help of Captain Crewsden. Johnny's idea was to plant a James Bond 007 flag right on top of the Eiger, for all to see across the valley at Mürren.

The helicopter took off and rose in ascending circles until it was hovering over the summit. Johnny slung in his rig, quickly chopped a hole with an ice axe, rammed home the flagpole and poured in the by now warm water from the bucket of boiling water he had loaded into the helicopter, securing the 007 emblem fluttering over Swiss territory. The affronted reaction of the good citizens of Mürren the next morning gladdened Johnny's heart. They demanded the immediate removal of the flag, but Johnny Jordan had made his point. He left us when filming finished in Switzerland and joined Mike Nicols who was having problems with the aerial filming of *Catch 22*, which he was making in the USA and Mexico.

Our final locations for *On Her Majesty's Secret Service* were in Portugal. One Sunday afternoon we were filming on the suspension bridge over the Tagus in Lisbon when we got a message that Johnny had been killed. There were no details, just the awful, numbing realisation that our friend would no longer enthral us with his exploits behind the camera or make us laugh as he waved two fingers at fate.

From what we found out later, he had been filming the flying sequences for *Catch 22* from the converted rear gun-turret of a Mitchell bomber. In one scene Johnny was shooting a formation of aircraft flying behind. In order to reload the camera, he had undone his harness and was lacing up the film when his aircraft hit a particularly vicious air pocket. The pilot had to dive to avoid colliding with the planes following right on his tail. This flung the camera assistant and grip against the aircraft's ceiling. Momentarily stunned, they took a few seconds to realise that where Johnny had been crouching all that remained was the camera in its mount with no sign of their friend.

Later that day, Johnny's body was picked up by Mexican fishermen, having fallen four and a half thousand feet to a terrible death.

Chapter Fourteen

LE MANS

As we were completing the work for *On Her Majesty's Secret Service* Hubert Froelich, our resourceful production manager, got in touch with me. He had been asked by Steve McQueen to get together a scratch unit to shoot a series of tests during the Le Mans 24-hour race of that year. This was to be the prelude to a full-scale production planned for the following year, 1970. Hubert had seen our radio communications set up in operation. He had been impressed by it and by Ron Butcher, who was now concentrating on this growing requirement of modern film-making. With the possibility of getting the film if the tests went well, we agreed to help out.

The tests with our radios went successfully in the week before the race and during the race itself. I was off to Los Angeles when it was finished and Hubert arranged for me to meet Steve and his producer, Robert Relyea, while I was there. Solar Productions, Steve's company, had very smart modern offices at the CBS Studios, which reflected their prestige after the tremendous success of *Bullitt*. They liked the tests and I left them, very pleased, with the sound job for *Le Mans,* as well as communications.

It was obvious that Hubert had been right in seeing the importance of radio communications on the film. As well as the normal production requirements Steve's film was going to need totally reliable radio links to ensure everyone's safety. Eighty percent of the *Le Mans* circuit is on public roads, which are obviously closed for the race. The French authorities had agreed to make available to us five mile sections, one at a time over the six months we would be filming. There would need to be police controls at all the intersections of secondary roads into the main road race track. They would need radio links with the production units and so would the film and car crews out on the circuit.

Hubert went ahead of the main unit to set up our base and asked me to join him to go through the communications network, quite apart from the technical considerations of the sound recordings. I decided this would be the ideal opportunity to put my Lotus Plus 2 through its paces on the winding

French roads and of course the famous Mulsanne Straight. Jean decided this was one trip she was not going to miss. Thanks to the weather, we were both proved wrong. A foot of snow blanketing northern France turned our pleasant continental saunter into an endurance test. We may have arrived at Le Mans on dry roads and in bright sunshine, but we stepped out of the car feeling that we might as well have been motoring through Antarctica in search of Captain Scott.

Hubert had been in France long enough to realise that it was widely assumed that an American film company was fair game as far as prices and rents were concerned. His first intention of renting a commercial block on the outskirts of the town was shelved when he heard what people proposed charging. So he called their bluff and decided to build his own hutted complex close to the racetrack and pits to cut down unnecessary travelling. The race authorities offered a site at a peppercorn rent and when local contractors asked prohibitive prices for sectional buildings, Hubert made enquiries in Switzerland and found he could get everything he wanted for considerably less: foundations, buildings, even marquees and catering facilities. The Swiss price also included returning the site to its original state after filming and here Hubert could pride himself on having the last laugh. Once they were no longer needed, all the huts were sold locally, saving transportation costs back to Switzerland and, because they were being bought in French francs, more than off-setting the duty that had been paid when they were imported. He was rightly proud of his achievement, built in a square compound, and had its gravel watered and rolled every Sunday to keep the place tidy. Inevitably it earned the nickname 'Stalag Froelich'.

His resourcefulness did not stop at providing our accommodation. Gulf Oil were sponsoring the Porsche cars that Steve and team were going to be shown driving in the film. So Hubert suggested they might like to extend their sponsorship to the unit as a whole and provide us all with free petrol. For six months not one of us bought a single litre of petrol; whenever we needed a fill-up there was always a Gulf tanker on site ready to supply all we wanted.

Hubert also struck an incredible deal with Peugeot who agreed to lend us sixty brand new cars for the duration of the film as self-drive transport. During a two-week break in filming Keith and Ron drove one of these back home without any documentation, spent two weeks with their families, made two Channel crossings through French and British customs and drove back to Le Mans, and were not stopped once.

Back home, before filming started, I set to with the two of them to prepare the equipment and bought more radios and a second truck for Ron. In the film camp we set up one ten-channel set with an aerial mast and installed another in the second truck, complete with its forty-foot pump-up mast which gave us good aerial height around the course. After a while I installed a spare radio in the tenth floor apartment Jean and I rented in the old part of Le Mans. It came in very useful for me to radio home – 'Come in channel four – we have finished shooting. I'm just going to rushes. Put the meat in the oven. See you soon.'

During the actual twenty-four hours of the race twelve camera crews were at work, with seven extra sound crews from Paris, positioned round the course. I recorded a series of soundtracks of the massed start from a vantage point on the roof of the grandstand. From there my crew moved to the pits. The next day I had to climb back on to the roof to cover the winning car crossing the finish line to take the chequered flag.

Steve McQueen was an accredited driver, after winning a race in America earlier in the year, at Watson's Glen, at the wheel of his own Porsche. For the film the car had been modified to carry three of our film cameras, two pointing ahead with one facing back for the race proper. Steve's original intention had been to drive in the actual race, with Jackie Stewart as his co-driver. But the

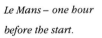

Le Mans – one hour before the start.

insurers refused to cover him and the closest he got was shooting scenes in the Porsche pit during the race, apparently making a driver change as the car was being refuelled. It was always hoped that a Porsche in the Gulf colours would win, but no final planning of the film script could be made until after the race, if for no other reason than the regular changes in the weather.

Once all the material from the camera crews filming the race had been viewed, it was possible to start plotting the pattern of the eventual film. This required very precise continuity records about the state of individual cars over the course of the race: whether they were wet or dry; how dirty the windscreens were; how many fly spots there were on the headlamps. These details were so important that one member of the crew was delegated to fly-spot screens and headlamp glasses to match a particular lap. Another had to wet the cars and muddy them down. And a third was responsible for checking the car numbers and sponsors' trim, as well as any details peculiar to that car. A number of cars had to pull out of the race because of mechanical problems. Although our camera car was not an official entry, it still crossed the line in ninth place, possibly due to its being driven well within limits.

While the picture was being checked, we in the sound department had over two hundred rolls of tape to wade through, a job that took time and made us very unpopular in camp as we played the tapes through a huge speaker for hours on end. Eventually we were banished to a caravan out in the wilds where the crackle and roar of exhausts no longer disturbed anyone.

John Sturges, the director who made *The Great Escape* with Steve McQueen, was assigned to Le Mans and approached it with some reluctance because he was not at all happy with the script. Cinemacentre and CBS, who were backing the production, had wanted the film to start with an horrendous and gory accident, which Steve held out against. In fact he refused to film, with the result that we had a clutch of writers working away at scripts for different factions: director, star and backers. All we could do to keep the production going was to shoot cars racing on different parts of the circuit while the dialogue and action scenes were being written.

We used to move out early in the morning to whichever section of the circuit had been allocated by the police. This would have been closed off to other traffic the previous evening and an armco barrier gang would have worked all night bridging the gaps across intersecting roads, bolting together the steel sections to make a continuous run of crash barrier.

We had a complex of hangar-like buildings in Arnage, a village a few miles away, in which all the cars were maintained and prepared for filming. Every day a selection of these would be driven in a snaking procession through the lanes by mechanics staying in first gear, escorted by French police 'motards' on their BMW motorcycles.

One difficulty in using these relatively small sections of circuit was that the cars would run in the correct race direction for filming, but would have to stop, turn round and return to the start position for the next take. This required a fool-proof system of control which began at the start, where the cars to be filmed would wait in correct race sequence. The number to run would be radioed to the finish control and was also monitored by control points along the length of the course. When the cameras were turning the cars would be flagged away. If there was a non-starter, a revised total of cars would by radioed to the finish control. Only when the complete total had been counted on arrival would any order be given to send them back to the start. This was the only way of ensuring there was no risk of collision from cars travelling in opposite directions. Our American first assistant director was not disposed to wait for this system at times. Also, his order 'Have the cars come' was misinterpreted by the French assistants as a question. My insistence that nothing must be allowed to jeopardise safety was upheld by the producer and the American technician was sacked.

We had the same casualty evacuation procedures to the hospital in Le

With Steve McQueen.

Mans as the race itself. They only needed to be put into operation once during the whole six months after one of the drivers mounted a barrier on a practice run; even so, we won great praise from the professional drivers for the fastest transit from accident site to hospital on record. However, Hubert realised we needed a nurse to take care of first-aid and approached the Mother Superior of the Hospice de la Charitée in Le Mans to see if she could spare one of her sisters for the period of our film schedule. She said she could and Sister Brigitte, an Irish nun and trained nurse, was seconded to the unit. She became totally dedicated to manning the crash wagon whenever the cars were racing and also set up a first-aid room in the camp where she held morning and evening surgery. She coped with cut fingers, bruises, hangovers and malingerers. She also handled Hubert with great skill, never conceding when he complained she was spending too much at the pharmacy; always ready with an answer. Sister Brigitte was one of the few people on the unit who could stand up to Hubert's Teutonic stubbornness with her own brand of Irish cussedness.

Brigitte drove a Citroën 2cv like the wind. I would see her flash across an intersection in old Le Mans in the early morning, using all the back doubles, always beating me to the camp. Once there, she would prepare for a day of standing by in the ambulance, if the cars were to run. Ron would check her radio saying, 'Give us a kiss, Brigitte,' and to her reply of, 'Oh, you're an awful man, Ron', he would say, 'Go on, I promise not to tell Mother Superior'.

I had one of my periodic bouts of malaria which she diagnosed in French as 'paludism', insisting that I should go home to bed and wait for the doctor. I was no stranger to the symptoms, first feeling a cold coming on, then a raging temperature, followed by uncontrollable shivering and splitting headache. Poor Keith had to cope with dialogue scenes in a caravan during the day or two that I was off. The 'channel four' radio link made it possible for me to keep in touch from my sick bed, to give him moral support.

John Sturgis was determined not to start serious filming without a script which was acceptable to all. One morning he and I were watching Steve McQueen running up and down the course, ostensibly to 'warm up' his brakes, when John said to me in his wonderful gravely voice, 'There he goes, eighty percent boy, twenty percent man.' (I have to admit that the real Steve was a quiet introspective person, who disappointed Jean greatly when they met, an encounter she described as 'just like shaking hands with a piece of wet fish'.)

Soon after John and I had watched Steve 'warming up' his brakes, our star flew off to Morocco in his private plane to wait for a copy of the final approved script to be sent. He never acknowledged its receipt, much to the director's disgust, and a day or so later John Sturgis announced, 'I'm too old and too rich to hang about any more. I'm going back to my boat in California', and he did.

There were more delays while a new director was found, this time nominated by CBS. From thereon the film took on a totally different aspect as the lawyers representing Steve and Solar Productions did battle with those representing the backers.

Since our temporary buildings were far from sound-proof, a tacit agreement was reached whereby one party would hold a closed meeting in the 'board-room' while the rival party played handball into a net that had been erected well out of earshot. By now rumours were spreading that the production was going to fold; local suppliers began to call for cash payments, the French extras union had meetings. I found that a pilot's throat microphone taped to

Squeezing into the Porsche with my Nagra tape recorder securely anchored

the chipboard partition wall that divided our workshop from the 'board-room' made an excellent bugging device. I wanted to be able to get all my equipment away from the compound if the rumoured arrival of French bailiffs ever materialised. The virtual takeover of the film by CBS from Steve McQueen, who ceased to be producer, kept the production going.

Although Steve did as much of the driving as he could, Derek Bell, who has won the race many times, doubled for him in the Porsche. When we needed sound effects from the interior of the cars I had to ride along too. There was just enough space inside the Porsche; however, I found that the Ferrari, driven by Mike Parkes, allowed me more room to squeeze inside with a Nagra tape recorder on my lap, both feet tucked together and braced against the side of the body just clear of Mike's left clutch foot.

Dressed in fireproof long johns, vest and hood, with outer one-piece overalls topped with a helmet into which my headphones had been fitted, I crouched beside Mike on the race start grid beside the grandstand. A green light blinked on, followed by a kick in the small of my back as we surged through the gears, passed under the famous Dunlop tyre bridge and took a right-hander into the Mulsanne Straight, which had been closed to traffic for the day. We flashed past the famous Hunadières restaurant at over 160 miles an hour and continued to accelerate towards the 200 mark before breasting the final 500-metre gradient, where at each hundred-metre marker Mike dropped down a gear until, in first gear, he took the car round a steep right-hand corner at Arnage. Now travelling at not much more than forty miles an hour, the rear of the car weaved as the giant tyres held it down on the road and with another series of kicks in my back, it surged up through the gears again.

That was the first of many such experiences. Over the following months I repeated it on each stretch of the Le Mans course. The soundtracks were then edited together to give us the complete circuit of Le Mans as heard inside the Ferrari. When Mike Parkes listened to the tapes he could tell us exactly where on the circuit the car was at any given point and in which gear. Our first run for sound past Maison Blanche to the chicane before the pits was not good enough for Mike, so we called control to get clearance to return. On the way back, just after Maison Blanche, there was a complete change of note. I asked Mike what this was when we had stopped. He answered that he had never driven in that direction, against the normal clockwise one of the race, and that all four wheels had left the ground over an unfamiliar bump in the road.

Maintaining the continuity of something as simple as the appearance of

*Me dressed for
action in the
Ferrari.*

the road surface turned out to be quite a headache. Throughout the race proper the surface had been wet at times; sometimes saturated, sometimes lightly dusted with rain drops; sometimes dry. It became obvious that we needed some way of spraying them that was efficient and speedy. Sass Bedig, our special effects man, who never did anything by half measure, hired four huge tankers. He had a steel framework welded on to the back of each chassis, where he mounted a diesel pump to squirt water through pipes fitted with roses, spanning a width of sixteen feet. Two of these monsters would move off just before shooting a 'wet' scene with the race cars, trundling the five miles of circuit to wet down the tarmac, at huge cost but most efficiently.

Another of Sass's tasks was to prepare a radio-controlled car which had to become airborne at Arnage, one of the 'S'-bends, after misjudging the corner. Sass knew all about explosions, fires and rain effect, but radio was not in his book and he did not want to be personally responsible for any new-fangled devices. Our English special effects man, Malcolm, was given the job of installing the radio receivers in a mock-up of a Lola, which was also fitted with electro-hydraulic units to operate the steering, throttle and brakes.

Malcolm took himself off to a nearby airfield where he practised manoeuvring the car on a disused runway. He needed several weeks to get the hang of it, knowing that there would almost certainly be only one take. When he felt ready, a date was fixed for filming the scene at Arnage corner.

The timing of the scene in the race called for wet roads, which did not help matters, because the car had to be started in second gear and this made the wheels spin on the wet surface. Malcolm's radio control unit was placed up in a tubular tower alongside the camera. The car was lined up in the centre of the road facing the first left-hand bend. Keith and I had settled ourselves with our equipment in a ditch on the left and Harrik Maurey, our French assistant, was hidden with his tape recorder in a bush close to where the car was meant to land.

All radios were switched off to prevent interference with the radio car controls. Another car was sent on past the cameras to take the left turn into the bend. Then there was a roar as the radio car revved up and moved off. We saw it hurtling towards our hide with tyres squealing. Keith and I were all set to make a run for it when the car suddenly turned right round and set off back the way it had come, this time charging right for the camera tower and production crew. It slammed into the tower, by which time Malcolm had actuated the throttle cut-off.

Take two was prepared. This time the car worked perfectly, roaring up the ramp to give it lift as it sailed over the corner, through an advertisement hoarding before landing with a cloud of dust in an open space. The only near casualty was our young French assistant, who saw it careering towards his bush. The car looked alarmingly close and in the film Harrik can be seen running with his Nagra recorder over his shoulder, microphone in hand, crouching down as the car sails overhead; as far as the audience are concerned, a television sound man making a run for it.

Several more radio-controlled cars were used, including a mock-up of Steve's Porsche which hurtled off the track straight into a barrier. To my mind this is the most compelling scene in the whole film. In slow motion the fibreglass body disintegrates in relentless and deliberate certainty as wheels cartwheel away in slow arcs through the air, Steve safely held fast in his harness.

More than half-a-million people flock to the Le Mans 24-hour race each year and a good half of them never see a car. They start arriving several days before the race, the majority camping in the surrounding pine woods, some in luxurious tents, others in simple bivouacs, the rest with just a sleeping bag. The car enthusiasts make for the grandstands opposite the pits where they can see the massed start and, twenty-four hours later, the winner going past the chequered flag. In our film finish the flag was held and waved by the son of Dr Porsche, who designed the first of the sports cars of which Steve's was the most recent successor.

Our final stint of filming took place in the area behind the pits where a colossal fun fair and tented village is set up each year for the race. There are all the rides and sideshows you find in every fair but there are also restaurants, snack bars, German beer tents, fortune-tellers, strip shows, ladies of the night; there is even a twenty-four-hour Mass. All of this takes place alongside the ear-shattering noise from the circuit.

After six months the filming came to an end. 'Stalag Froelich' was dismantled and the unit dispersed. We stayed longer than most to clear up a backlog of sound effects, such as wheel clanging, pneumatic wheel wrenches – even a skylark to create a sense of loneliness for the opening of the film when Steve visits the spot where his greatest pal had been killed the previous year.

Regretfully *Le Mans* was not the film it should have been. The storyline was very weak. It never merited the excellent coverage of the race scenes that has made it a classic for sports car racing buffs who never tire of seeing it over and over again each year at Le Vingt Quatre Heures du Mans.

Chapter Fifteen

SLEUTH, GOLD AND THE BIBLE

In 1972 I was given the opportunity to work on Anthony Shaffer's *Sleuth*, an unusual film in that it had only two characters, played by Laurence Olivier and Michael Caine. Jo Mankiewicz, a seasoned American scriptwriter and director, was going to direct it. *Sleuth* had all the feeling of a small but exclusive production and I was pleased to be part of it.

The setting was the spacious splendour of a country mansion. It could easily have been made on location, but Jo's preference was to work in the studio on a set that would allow walls to be 'floated' out to make it easier for the camera.

Ken Adams, famous for his sets on so many of the Bond films, was given the job of creating an enormous room with balustraded stairs going up to a gallery. It was certainly a masterpiece with solid hardwood banisters, vaulted, stained-glass windows and expensive furniture and set-dressing, all of which pushed it seriously over budget. Even before we started filming the producers asked us all to take a cut in our fees. I am glad to say we all stood out against that.

Michael had never worked with Olivier and I knew he was quite apprehensive; in fact on the first day of shooting he addressed Larry as, 'Sir, er – I mean Milord'. Olivier soon put that to rights.

Jo was the type of old time director who knew just what he wanted, but left it to the two actors to achieve the result. It was very important to stick to every word of Peter Schaffer's script, but there were times when Larry, who was still recovering from one of his many illnesses, found it very hard to memorise lines. He had already suffered the nightmare of forgetting his lines on stage and had decided not to appear again in the theatre. Frequently he asked me to his dressing-room to hear his lines, though quite often he was tired by five o'clock in the afternoon. Always the great professional, he was afraid on *Sleuth* that he might not be giving his best.

He and Michael built up a great affinity. I am sure there were instances after a take was cut several times because Olivier had fluffed, to be followed the very next time the camera turned by a mistake from Michael. With a smile

Roger Moore on location, Live and Let Die, *1972.*

he would look Larry in the eye saying, 'We can't be perfect all of the time can we, my lord?' This was just the break needed. Any tension evaporated and the next take was invariably perfect and one Jo was happy to print.

Our only location for *Sleuth* was at a house called Athlehampton, near Piddletrenthide in Dorset, where a Hampton-Court-like maze was built for the opening scene. This was constructed on wooden frames to which chicken wire was fastened to hold yew tree cuttings that were stuffed to form the hedging. The effect was so convincing that the owner of the house, who allowed in the paying public, asked for it to be left as an added attraction to his garden.

My hunch about the film was right. Audiences liked it and so did the American Academy, which nominated both Michael and Larry for best actor, the first time that two actors on the same film had received such a nomination, and also nominated Jo for best director.

Cubby, Harry Saltzman and Roger Moore.

Live and Let Die, *1972.*

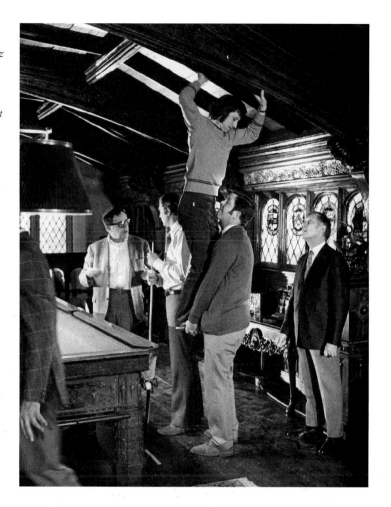

Sleuth, 1972 – Joe Mankiewitz discusses the next shot with Michael, whilst we, the sound crew, position a hidden microphone.

After a period of a few months 'resting' the offer came to work on the new Roger Moore film, based on Wilbur Smith's novel *Gold*, which presented a problem for the technicians because it was being made entirely in South Africa. Our trade union had banned its members from working there but I knew the producer Michael Klinger and the director Peter Hunt, who were both convinced that a refusal to go on our part would not do much to solve the issue of apartheid. The whole film crew agreed and within a short time we had flown to Johannesburg, which was to be our base.

Two days later Klinger called us together to say that he had received a cable from our union recalling us to London. Michael said we could have our tickets, but he would be staying on to make the film. All of us agreed to stay with him. In turn he promised to brief lawyers on our behalf if the union penalised us in any way.

The filming started in the millionaire section of north 'Joburg', which happened to be where the film's backers also had their homes. They manufactured furniture for the black population using local black labour. Later we moved to the vast gold mine at Buffelsfontein to film the mine sequences. They kitted us out like the miners, with helmets and overalls. Then we were loaded into a cage and dropped two miles in two stages down into the ground. The final trip, in an inclined trolley with the roof only inches above our heads, took us to a section where the 'rand', or rock, was being cut out with pneumatic drills. It was dusty down there, but not dirty like a coal mine. The first level, where the cages came to a halt, was a high cavern, with cool air circulating and the hum of fans and generators.

Our mining day started at eight o'clock in the morning and we worked through until four in the afternoon, when blasting started. The mine authorities were very strict about the timing. One afternoon when the assistant director tried to make us stay for one more shot, we all refused; even then the last man out to reach the safe level was only just clear when the explosive charges were detonated.

The film was made in only nine weeks, three of which we spent below ground. Down there with us were 4,000 black miners who could not wait to get out when the whistle blew at the end of their shift. There was a stampede to get to the lift cages where gangers herded them in between chain barriers. It was quite an experience to be squashed in together with ninety other bodies and whisked up the eerie shaft as water dripped down on us.

We saw the young miners under instruction, first learning how to walk in miners' boots. Round and round they went in circles, getting used to the boots and the helmets on their heads, dressed in rough shirts and trousers which got more bedraggled every day. I saw no sign of any militancy at the mine, though Jean found she was often jostled into the gutter in Johannesburg and it was certainly unwise to go into the Hillsborough area at night.

Ray Milland was in the cast and he and I spent a lot of time together. I enjoyed listening to him talking about Hollywood in the thirties, when the studios had a tight grip on their contract stars. He told me that he used to see such stars as Bette Davis, Myrna Loy and Joan Crawford being driven along Sunset Boulevard at five o'clock in the morning on their way to make-up calls.

Before Ray flew home I arranged to record some extra lines in his hotel room, but he telephoned me to say he had been in agony all night with a pain in his bladder. A local clinic was alerted and he asked me to go along with him. The waiting-room was full of elegantly dressed women. Ray and I were asked to take a seat until the consultant called him into his surgery. Some time later Ray emerged a changed man, wreathed in smiles. He flung his arms wide saying 'I love you all' to the waiting ladies, not realising he had been dealt with in a gynaecological clinic.

As we expected, the Film Technicians Union condemned our continued working in South Africa and when we got home we were ordered to appear before a kangaroo court. Michael Klinger, the producer, kept his word and arranged for a QC to act for us. He put forward a strong case that the union rules did not justify refusing us the right to earn a living. The union accepted this grudgingly and we were sent on our way with a warning. The cameraman who had previously worked in South Africa was suspended for three months.

Michael appreciated our sticking with him on *Gold* and he asked several of us to join him in Israel for a film he was setting up with director Moshe Mizrahi. This was *Rachel's Man*, based on the Old Testament story of Jacob and Esau. Mickey Rooney played Laban, Leonard Whiting was Jacob and Rita Tushingham took the part of Laban's daughter.

Moshe met me in London to outline the story and tell me about the locations he wanted to use in Southern Galilee. Keith and I then set to work packing our equipment for air-freighting to Tel Aviv by El Al. We had been warned about the airline's stringent luggage examinations. Every equipment case had to be presented unlocked; no batteries could be left in any item; and the whole consignment was placed in a decompression chamber for twenty-four hours to minimise the risk from bombs triggered by detonators set to explode in the low-pressure atmosphere of high-altitude flight.

We had to hand in our own personal baggage three hours before take-off. El Al warned passengers not to over-pack their cases because everything inside was going to be unpacked by their trained security staff. My prized travelling companion for more years than I care to mention has been a Revelation suitcase, which opens in two halves. The top half holds three suits on hangers, folded so cleverly that even after forty-eight hours a suit can be unpacked and worn without showing a single crease. Patched and battered, that case still serves me well. The El Al girl at the search counter had never seen a case like it and in spite of her assurance that she had never been caught out incorrectly repacking the thousands she must have come across, she had to admit defeat with mine. Maybe that is why Revelation no longer make it.

We spent our first, humid, night in Tel Aviv. The next day a string of cars took us to the ancient town of Safid where the director was waiting for us. I was a bit surprised to see we were heading north and not south, but did not think it was my business to ask why.

The next day Moshe wanted to show Ossie, the cameraman, and me the locations. From Safid we dropped down a winding road with hairpin bends to a town called Roshpina. We crossed a muddy river on an army Bailey bridge, the original stone one having been demolished. There were burnt-out trucks on the far bank and as we started to climb the steep winding road more derelict vehicles and wrecked tanks came into view. Our little VW Beetle kept climbing until we reached a cross-roads beside which stood the remains of shattered buildings. I felt the time had come to ask Moshe exactly where we were, to which he replied that we had crossed the River Jordan and were now on the Golan Heights where the ruins alongside us had been a Syrian forward position a few weeks earlier; the fighting had stopped now, he added in reassurance.

That still did not explain why we were at the wrong end of the country. It was all to do with the flowers, he explained. The start date for the film had been put back for various reasons. In southern Israel the flowers were all in bloom, which didn't suit the stark background he wanted for the film. Up on the heights they bloomed later, so this was where we would be filming.

The location for Laban's nomadic encampment was a few miles from the cross-roads, well away from the unsightly detritus of modern war: burnt out tanks, shelled buildings, huge rubbish dumps of empty cartons and containers, all sorts of indestructible plastic bags, bottles and sheeting, which defiled the stark beauty of the landscape unchanged since Biblical times. The only risk we faced, Moshe told us airily, was uncleared landmines. Perhaps he realised that the non-Israeli members of the unit were less easy-going about the security risks we faced. Whatever the reason, we started filming by a stream close to Safid, which opened our eyes to the mixed backgrounds of our Israeli colleagues. The electricians from Tel Aviv and the Arab Israeli property man were experienced film hands, but for most of the others *Rachel's Man* was their first film.

The hairdresser had come from a salon in Haifa. The wardrobe girl was a professional dancer. She was zealous in looking after the costumes to the point that young Jacob appeared on set to tend his flocks in a pristine white robe which would not have been out of place among the heavenly throng. She looked crushed as our make-up man set to work with mud before bashing

Rachel's Man,
Golan Heights,
Israel, 1975.
With Keith
Pamplin.

Jacob's outfit against a nearby rock to give it a bit of rapid ageing.

Most of the crew turned out to have been recruited as the friends of friends. Our truck driver was an actor from a repertory company in Tel Aviv. He was a nice fellow but he stalled the truck on every hill and did not like helping with the heavy gear we had to carry up and down the gullies where we were filming. He slipped away one night back to Tel Aviv and we never saw him again. His replacement was a complete contrast with his ancient VW combi and his devil-may-care attitude. Zevik was a graduate of Jerusalem University. He had served as a commando in the Six Day War, in which six of his pals had been shot down around him in an ambush. As one of a handful of survivors of the patrol he had had a mental breakdown and was now bumming around in his old VW, which he called 'The Queen'.

Zevik was just what we needed to make life tolerable. He was quite the best scrounger I have met and his wonderful personality and engaging cheek worked wonders. Every morning, before we left for location, he went to the hotel kitchen and filled flasks with iced tea, which was far more thirst-quenching than the caterer's lemon squash. On arrival he would set up a folding chair for me under a large garden umbrella he had somehow acquired. Only when I was comfortably installed, did he push off back to The Queen to light a suspicious looking cigarette and inhale it with a rapturous smile on his face.

Zevik, like most Israelis we met, had a complete disregard for protocol. If I put a bottle of beer by my place at the table at lunchtime, Zevik was likely to drink it while I was getting something to eat; it was there, why should he not have it? Michael Klinger got a taste of this the first day we filmed on the Golan Heights. I was sitting under my umbrella, iced tea at my elbow, keeping out of the heat which was pushing towards forty degrees Celsius, when I noticed Michael coming over the crest of the hill, on foot. Over-weight, out of condition, a large cigar sticking out of the side of his mouth, he looked close to collapsing when he reached my little oasis of shade. He called for his chair and was not pleased to find Zevik lounging in it; a terse lesson in film etiquette followed. I asked Zevik to fetch Mr Klinger some iced tea at which Michael erupted, 'How come you buggers get all the attention? I'm just the producer.'

The day was not going well. His driver had refused to drive off the main road to the film location because of the risk of landmines, so Michael had had to walk through the broiling heat. He was obsessed with the sharp practices and shady deals he was getting from the Israelis which drew the complaint, 'I wouldn't mind so much if they was gentiles who were taking me for a ride – but they are my own people.'

A lot of Mike Klinger's British team were also Jews. Bob Stern, the production manager, teamed up with the Israeli production manager, who was a doctor of philosophy from a nearby kibbutz. Our health was the responsibility of a doctor from New York who had settled in Safid with his family. He dispensed Coca-Cola from a large stock of crates at his surgery. Coca-Cola seemed to be his remedy for any ailment: stomach upsets, headaches, hangovers. He would probably have suggested rubbing it into injured joints to cure sprains and strains. His daughter, who had terrifying Zionist opinions, acted very efficiently as an assistant director.

Shooting up on the Golan heights was often interrupted by Mirage fighters streaking over us at zero height, a stark contrast to the timeless Old Testament story we were trying to capture on film. Night shooting was every bit as exciting; the army insisted on ringing us with sharp-shooters and had an armoured car standing by in case we attracted the wrong sort of attention with our arc lights. The only difficulty was the sudden drop in temperature after dark. The British contingent were prepared with quilted anoraks and warm boots. The Israelis dressed in shorts and T-shirts fared less well and the sports shops and outfitters in Safid did a brisk trade when they opened for business the following morning.

We needed large flocks of sheep and goats in the film and the responsibility for providing them at our various locations fell to a friend of Zevik's. 'The animal man', as we called him, had been in the same commando unit as Zevik and with him had been one of the few to survive the ambush. Like our driver, he had turned his back on the world and appeared to live like a hermit in a refuge overlooking the Sea of Galilee. He had a natural aptitude with animals and birds and could turn up with whatever beast of the earth or fowl of the air the script demanded. We would often see him as we were on our way home at the end of a day's shooting, making his way through the night to the next location, driving his flocks before him. He was always in place waiting for us the next morning, surrounded by his animals grazing contentedly or drinking from the small tanker that had been sent on ahead.

Keith and I had the chance to get to know him better on one of the rest days when we needed to record bird sounds and Zevik offered to take us to a good spot where there were plenty of birds. I did not realise he was taking us to the animal man's territory, but after we had clambered up a winding runnel high above Galilee, we came across a rock shelf on which stood a little stone house – the animal man's home.

Our friend appeared, beaming behind his Old Testament beard, followed by an attractive blonde lady who called off a couple of evil-looking dogs that had followed close on our heels in the last part of the climb. She was Swedish and had come to the international artists' community at Rospina where she had met our animal man. His powers of attraction obviously extended beyond the animal kingdom because she never returned to her wealthy husband in Stockholm.

Together they had built their house with the stone around their rock platform, into which we were invited. There was a large living-room with an open hearth, a kitchen and bedroom. Outside they had diverted a stream to feed a tank with fresh water. There was even a bath, built from stone and rendered smooth with sand and cement. Here they lived an idyllic life, separated from the outside world, enjoying those cigarettes that we were offered many times during our stay; Keith and I opted for cool drinks before setting off to make our recordings.

By evening we were famished and on the way back to the Queen asked Zevik if there was somewhere to eat. He suggested a restaurant on the lakeside where we could get good fish, quite close to a little church that marks the place where St Peter used to preach. On the menu was St Peter's fish, a delicacy from the Sea of Galilee, served, at some expense, all round its shore. On the plate it looks succulent and fleshy, but beneath the skin it is something of a disappointment, a large rib cage over which is stretched very little meat. How Jesus managed to feed the five thousand baffled me even more.

Zevik did not restrict his resourcefulness to the sound department. When the property man was on the look out for a pestle and mortar, Zevik offered to find them. That evening he invited Keith and me to go with him to a village where a schoolmaster friend of his might be able to help. He could only drive The Queen into the village square; from there on the alleyways were only wide enough for a passing donkey. A crowd gathered round as we pulled up and Zevik was surrounded by three laughing girls, the eldest and prettiest of whom was hugging and kissing him. He seemed to know a lot of attractive women dotted about the country.

We were introduced and then led to one of the larger houses, festooned with tobacco leaves hanging out to dry. Inside we met the schoolmaster; at least he had been a schoolmaster when Zevik had first met him. He had given up the classroom and come back to the village of his childhood to run a market garden. The pretty girl who had greeted Zevik so warmly was his wife. She had been one of his pupils and now, still only twenty-eight, she was the mother of the two teenage girls with her.

The business with the pestle and mortar was quickly accomplished. An old lady in the village agreed to lend us what was obviously a centuries-old family possession and with it safely installed in The Queen we settled down to a huge meal that was typical of the hospitality we came across during our stay.

Zevik's other preoccupation was more disruptive. It did not dawn on me that he spent most nights smoking pot until I had had trouble tracking him down several mornings and finally found him in a stupefied state one day, in no shape to drive. Keith and I bundled him into The Queen and drove out to our location which that day was half-a-mile inside an army artillery range and guarded by a manned gate on the main road. During the morning we got a radio message that two men at the gate were asking for Zevik and wanted to talk to him. When we passed on the message, Zevik took Keith to one side and asked him to look after a leather pouch he was removing from his belt. Keith refused and indicated a distinctive pile of rock, where Zevik could hide it and retrieve it on his return.

The morning passed, lunch came, but Zevik failed to return. Then a radio message came for me, to say that Zevik was being held in Rospina Police Station and that his two visitors had come from the narcotics bureau in Tel Aviv. After shooting we drove through Rospina to see the police, expecting to find Zevik behind bars. Instead the duty officer told us he had left early in the afternoon after being questioned by the men from Tel Aviv. When we returned to the hotel, Zevik was waiting for us, brushing aside my enquiry why he had not returned to work. Before taking him in for questioning, the narcotics men had been through all our rooms following a tip-off that drugs were being used by the film unit. They did not find anything, though Zevik said blithely that if they had looked outside his room they would have found a cache of pot below the window ledge.

They gave him a pretty thorough questioning at the police station until one of the policemen asked about his surname, saying he had served in the army under a brigadier of the same name. That was Zevik's uncle and from then on the tone of the enquiry changed completely. The three of them had lunch and the two narcotics men left Zevik, only asking him to report to them when he got back to Tel Aviv. The evening pot sessions quietened down for a while after that.

The Queen came into its own in a completely unexpected way later in the production. Ousama Rawi, the cameraman, and Rita Tushingham were hitting it off and I was not surprised when Ossie asked one evening if he could borrow the truck. I helped him unload it with the proviso that I wanted to be best man at the wedding. Although they did not call on my services, they did end up getting married and moved to Toronto, due in no small measure to that moonlit night on the shores of the Sea of Galilee in our sound truck. After many years together they divorced, Rita now living in London, Ousama in Toronto.

The side of Israel I had not expected was that of the huge Arab population. There were tens of thousands of them born, living and working there in complete harmony, or so it seemed. Our prop man came from an Arab village near

Nazareth and took Keith and me with him when he went back there on a property-scrounging trip. His home could have doubled as a set for the Nativity. The ancient house was perched on a hillside above a crude, open stable. There lived our prop man's father, surrounded by his family living in more recent single-storeyed houses round about, and waited on by his daughters and daughters-in-law. He quizzed us with piercing eyes and, hearing that we were English, said the only English he had ever seen before had been troops in the First World War, when he fought with the British army against the Turks. If our images of the land of Christ's birth had stayed there, it might have been preferable. Nazareth was a terrible disappointment, full of tacky shops crammed with tasteless souvenirs, as is Bethlehem.

Mickey Rooney would have got on well with the old man in Nazareth. As Laban, Mickey revelled in being waited on by his film family. He made no attempt to disguise his American accent and sat cross-legged in his hut, looking more like a grinning Buddha than an Old Testament patriarch. I enjoyed getting him talking about his Andy Hardy days when he and Judy Garland were the top earners for Metro Goldwyn Mayer; without the huge profits from their films Louis B Mayer might have had serious financial troubles. The one person on his pay-roll he could not dictate to was Mickey, who used to pull his leg mercilessly.

On his last day of filming, Mickey was determined to be off and away as soon as his last scene was in the can. Michael Klinger had other ideas. He was not releasing his star until he had confirmation from the London laboratory that everything was all right with that day's work. Mickey had forty years' experience of handling producers and won the day when he appeared that evening clean shaven. As far as he was concerned, his time on *Rachel's Man* was finished and to prove the point he had cut off his biblical beard.

Our last task was to return the pestle and mortar. Zevik bowed out for some reason, saying that we could find our own way there. The schoolmaster's family appeared with an old lady who snatched back her pestle and mortar and disappeared down an alley with them to her house.

We left Safid with fond farewells and returned to Tel Aviv to pack our equipment for the flight home. The Israeli Film Federation invited us to be their guests on our last day when they treated us to a guided tour of Jerusalem. Whatever disappointments I may have felt about other biblical sites, I flew home from Jerusalem resolved to go back one day with Jean.

Chapter Sixteen

THE DEVIL, JESUS & VALENTINO

Two years after *Gold* Michael Klinger defied the technicians' union again when he announced his intention to film a second Wilbur Smith story in South Africa, *Shout At The Devil*.

This time the shooting was taking place in Transkei, so-called independent homeland with its own government, and our base was the town of Port St John on the edge of the Indian Ocean. To get there we had flights to Johannesburg and Durban followed by a long, tiring and very dusty minibus drive at the end of which we were greeted by Michael Klinger, still wearing his familiar tropical suit and panama hat and still puffing at a huge Churchillian cigar.

We lived across the river from the town in a group of holiday bungalows strung along a hillside overlooking the sea. These were basic, but adequate and came with a maid who kept the place tidy and cooked if need be. The girl who looked after us was wonderful. She used to arrive every morning to make us breakfast at whatever ungodly hour we had been called for. After walking four miles in the dark she was never late and always had a smile. Her reward for this punishing routine would be educating her eldest daughter to the level at which she could become a nurse; though because she was earning good money, her husband seemed content to sit around their hut all day drinking home-made beer.

The first job on my list was to set up radio communications between the production office, the locations and our airstrip, perched high above the town on a rocky outcrop. The art department had moved into Port St John several months ahead of the rest of us and the carpenters and plasterers had been busy building prefabricated sets to be transported to their locations. The main one of these was an enormous bungalow which served as the home of Lee Marvin and his daughter, played in the film by Barbara Parkins. This was situated in a forest clearing a few miles from our base and was approached down a narrow winding track that had been cut through the jungle. Quite why this particular spot had been chosen, we could never work out. It was near the Oovombubu River on which we were scheduled to be filming but neither site

could be seen from the other. The production manager may have silently raised the same question on our first morning as we mustered in torrential rain to hear that the track down to the bungalow was a quagmire, only passable in four-wheel drive vehicles; luckily the VW minibus which we were using as a sound truck had been taken down the day before. A very bedraggled film unit stood around for an executive decision. It came from Michael Klinger who informed us that he had not come 'all this bleeding way just to sit around – so get off your arses and move on down.' At least we would all be there when the rain stopped, he added comfortingly.

Roger Moore with young Transkei friend.

The first Land-Rover made the trip with the director Peter Hunt and the cameraman Mike Reed and his crew. They radioed back to report a safe arrival and with that link established we decided to send each vehicle down one at a time. After a long wait for news of the camera boys' arrival and a 'negative' from the film set, we saw them clambering back towards us to say that their vehicle had spun off a corner and rolled down a steep bank.

The next to leave was the Land-Rover carrying two of the stars, Roger Moore and Barbara Parkins. Roger politely said that he was not prepared to be driven by a local driver or anyone who had not been down previously and I found myself deputed to drive the valuable 'money'. Setting off in four-wheel drive with warnings from Michael not to harm his actors, we slithered and spun our way down through the mud, clawing round sharp bends to arrive safely at the set.

The art department had done a brilliant job with the bungalow. Creepers draped the verandahs on which Roger and Lee would eventually fight themselves to exhaustion after wrecking the rooms inside. Outside was a flower and vegetable garden brimming with plants that had grown to full-maturity in a couple of months under the tropical sun. Michael Klinger's weather forecast was surprisingly accurate. By noon the clouds had rolled away and we saw little rain for the rest of our stay; a couple of days later the quagmire down to the bungalow was a dust-bowl.

While we were filming there, the art department was busy building a full-size replica of the First World War German cruiser *Blücher*, which had a prominent part in Wilbur Smith's story. The original *Blücher* had been severely damaged by fighting ships of the Royal Navy in the Indian Ocean and had taken refuge up an estuary in German East Africa, where it had been beached. In our film the river at Port St John was used, and the whole front half of the cruiser was constructed from bridge to bows, including gun turrets, from wood and plaster. The after part of the ship was just a framework of scaffolding over which camouflage nets were stretched to give the impression to the camera of a ship several hundred feet long. From across the river it was impossible not to believe that a complete ship lay there beached on the opposite bank, though from the air it was barely visible. This last detail was important, because in the story a Vickers Vimy bomber had to be shown searching for the *Blücher*. As no original Vimy was available, a flying replica was built at Durban airport and towed up to Port St John like a glider.

As we got to know Lee Marvin he became every bit the larger-than-life character we had imagined him to be. In *Shout At The Devil* he was just playing an extension of his part in *Paint Your Wagon* and talking to him one day, he told me the story behind his famous recording of 'Born Under A Wandering Star'. He had been on a bender the night before and went to the recording studio with an almighty hangover. He said that his head had been bursting so much that the orchestral backing in his headphones had to be turned down, and he sang at an almost inaudible level, his lips almost touching the microphone, to produce the marvellous gravely close-up recording to which he owed a large part of his popularity, and its success as a film.

We found that Lee was given to going on benders, on average about every two weeks, when armed with cartons of canned beer in his bungalow he would not report for work on the set for twenty-four hours or so. The day we filmed the air attack on the *Blücher* he was not on call. None of the main artists were because the special effects department had placed explosives around the upper work of the ship and in the river to simulate bomb blasts and splashes. It took until well into the afternoon to get everything ready, by which time several gun crews were in place.

The replica Vimy bomber was on the airstrip ready for the radio message from the assistant director for it to be towed into position to make its bombing approach over the cruiser, when a panic call came in from an assistant on the ship. One of the German sailors in a machine-gun crew was causing trouble. The countdown to shooting was stopped and more of the production crew were sent across the river, led by Michael Klinger, to sort things out. On board they found Lee wearing the uniform of a German sailor and insisting that he was in charge of the gun's crew. Michael managed to get him back on shore and into a Land-Rover, still clutching his six-pack, to be driven out of harm's way.

Lee Marvin and his servant played by Ian Holm.

The filming of the air attack went well. The Vimy made two runs, one in each direction, the second very low and losing height over the cruiser which was fine for the cameras. We watched it pass out of sight, its underpowered engine racing, to make a forced landing on the beach at the mouth of the river, never to fly again.

Another spectacular sequence was shot in the hills outside Port St John where hundreds of local men hauled huge ships' steel plates slung between massive eight-foot wheels. This portrayed an event that had actually taken place in the First World War. When the *Blücher* had been successfully beached, the German crew found that she had sustained heavy damage from Royal Navy gunfire and that many of her plates below the water line had been holed beyond repair. They had the idea of sending a working party led by the chief engineer overland to Dar es Salaam, 150 miles up the coast, to remove plates from German freighters laid up there and then transport them back on enormous wheeled trolleys, to be riveted onto the *Blücher* in place of the damaged ones. The art department and construction crews created totally realistic looking trolleys and steel plates entirely from plywood, and dragged over the rocky terrain to the chanting of the Transkei hauling teams. Those sequences were a vivid evocation of that historic trek.

When our stint in Transkei came to an end we packed our equipment and flew northwards, crossing the whole of Africa to our second location in Malta. After our fairly spartan life in Transkei, Michael Klinger had promised something better in Malta and had taken over part of a magnificent hotel near the silent walled city of Rabat. It was a luxury to enjoy such simple things as running hot water and flushing toilets, quite apart from our sumptuous rooms that looked down on the towns of Medina and distant Valetta.

This final phase of shooting *Shout At The Devil* involved another mock-up of the *Blücher* that had been built in the famous film tank on the island. Here we simulated the gunfire from the British ships. The wave machines started pounding, the smoke pots and explosives were detonated and our stuntmen from England flung themselves from the upper decks, ablaze with petrogel, though safely cocooned in flame-proof coverings, thirty feet into the water below. Their numbers had been swelled by a squad of young marines who set to enthusiastically, throwing themselves over the side and then clambering back up to repeat the jumps. They were each making three jumps to every one from the professionals, to the stunt supervisor's dissatisfaction. Stuntmen may stop at nothing, but they are careful to surround their work with a certain

The full scale Blücher.

The mock-up Blücher at Malta.

amount of mystique.

Our last sequence was the wedding of Roger Moore and Barbara Parkins which took place in a church near Valetta. Lee Marvin was very much in evidence, suitably attired, suitably drunk and sporting a magnificent black eye from the make-up artist's box.

The end of picture party was gate-crashed by a fresh-faced stranger, unknown to cast or crew. Only the familiar can of beer in his hand and the gravely voice blew his cover. For four months we had got used to seeing him with scrubby beard and moustache. Clean-shaven and sober, Lee Martin was unrecognisable!

From the 'Devil', I turned to 'Jesus', directed by Franco Zeffirelli. Gerry Humphreys was the sound chief and dubbing mixer at Twickenham Studios, where I was spending some post-production time briefing the sound editor on the hours of sound effects I had recorded for *Shout at the Devil.* I'd met Gerry on my way to the car park one evening. He asked what I'd been up to and what I was working on next, to which I replied with the not unfamiliar answer that I hadn't a clue. In that case, he said, how would I fancy a week of artist tests for Franco Zeffirelli, who was planning to film *Jesus of Nazareth?*

I had always regretted having had to turn down working with him on his *Taming of the Shrew* with Richard Burton and Elizabeth Taylor, after we had completed *The Spy Who Came in From the Cold*. At that time Ron Butcher, Keith and I were a team, reputedly one of the best in the business. Zeffirelli's offer had been for me alone, working with an Italian crew, and I had been loath to split up a successful partnership. The week's work on *Jesus* was a different matter and didn't compromise my working relationships; given the second chance to work with Zeffirelli, if only for five days. We started the week of intensive tests the following Monday, firstly to confirm Robert Powell's perfect casting in the title role; then to choose from a group of young actors those who would play the apostles.

I seemed to hit it off with Franco right from the start. I liked the care he took with each of the actors, taking time to put each one at his ease. Rather than dumping them in front of the camera, he liked to play a scene from the script, changing characters as he assessed each one in the role of a particular disciple. Even so it came as a surprise on the Wednesday when Franco took me to one side and offered me the film.

I had to turn him down a second time as only the week before we had signed for *It Shouldn't Happen to a Vet*, the James Herriot film, which was scheduled as the first of a four-film programme to be made over the four seasons. I did have the nerve to suggest to Franco that I would be very happy to join him as soon as we had completed the vet film. He countered by asking if I thought he would ever change crews during a film. There wasn't any answer to that.

We had a pleasant nine weeks filming in Yorkshire, though it was soon obvious that there would be no follow-up films with the same cast and director. The potential might have been there, as the BBC went on to prove with their highly successful series, but that was little comfort to us as we trooped home with no prospect of working until the New Year at the earliest; November to March has traditionally been the slack period in our business.

So the call from Zeffirelli's associate that came a few days later, via my agent, lightened my darkness considerably. Was I free to take over the sound on *Jesus of Nazareth,* complete with crew and equipment, he wanted to know? I accepted by return and immediately started to prepare the equipment that was to accompany me to Tunisia, where the bulk of the filming was taking place.

Franco's change had been forced on him by the original sound crew who had received another offer and had asked to be relieved. They had been given a date by which to pull out, which should have given us enough time to settle in. However, we hadn't allowed for the vagaries of the Tunisian customs. Only two days before the retiring crew were due to depart, our equipment was still impounded in a shed at Tunis airport, defying all attempts by our local agent to have it cleared.

A further supreme assault on the customs, helped no doubt by suitable back-handers, gained its release but still it had not arrived in Monastir from Tunis. The producer paced the hotel foyer that evening, grimly facing the following morning with no sound facility and only partially mollified by my assurance that we would work through the night to be ready for the eight o'clock shooting call. That's just what we did, though come eight o'clock we found ourselves alone on the location. By now the rest of the unit had learned to leave the hotel only when word filtered down that Franco had been wakened. Like so many men of the theatre, he never went to bed until the small hours; he also hated getting up in the morning.

Our first day's shooting was in an olive grove where Franco had set a scene between Nicodemus (Laurence Olivier) and Jesus. Franco had devised this to show a great deal of the branches, making it virtually impossible to use a conventional microphone. The stiff breeze rustling through the leaves didn't help either.

After the first rehearsal I went to Franco to say that I'd be using radio microphones. He looked surprised. My predecessor hadn't liked using them, but Larry butted in to reassure him, 'Leave it to John – he knows what he's doing.'

We went ahead with the promise that I would play back the first take for Franco's approval. He liked what he heard and always accepted my judgement after that. From then on and in spite of having to contend with the incessant blasts on the little gold whistle that hung round his neck, I enjoyed every minute I worked with him.

Franco had been very astute in gathering his stars. For a six-hour project of this sort the cost would normally have been prohibitive. He started, cleverly, with Olivier, asking him to play Nicodemus, which Larry accepted for a nominal fee because he liked the script. This opened a floodgate of famous names: Rod

Steiger, Anthony Quinn, James Mason, Peter Ustinov, Anne Bancroft, Ralph Richardson, Christopher Plummer, Michael York, Ian McShane, all of whom took their lead from Larry and agreed to appear for a fraction of their usual rate

Franco's genius extended to his attention to detail, only matched in my experience by David Lean. Before the start of production people were despatched to find primitive looms as far afield as Greece and Turkey, where cloth was still woven as it had been in biblical times. When the costumes had been made by seamstresses in Rome, they were all 'aged' by scrubbing and washing and then wire-brushed and rubbed down with sandpaper. Only then were they handed over to the cast with the instructions that they had to be worn all day and every day until we started filming. Robert Powell lived in his; by the end of production his clothes were literally falling off his back.

Some of the robes worn in the scenes in Herod's palace were quite magnificent, thanks once again to Franco's ingenuity, after he had spotted that

Robert Powell.

traditional Tunisian wedding garments are heavily embroidered with gold wire and wouldn't have looked out of place in Roman Judaea. Most of them were far too expensive to be bought for individual weddings so several firms provided a Tunisian 'Moss Bros' service hiring them out from one wedding to the next. I often wonder whether weddings in Tunisia had to be put on hold while we filmed the scenes with Peter Ustinov as Herod, for it seemed that every available wedding costume was in use on our set.

The film set for the palace was as opulent as the costumes. Italian film craftsmen had constructed an open-paved terrace leading out of the ancient fortress at Monastir. The set for Herod's throne chamber was vast, as big as a film studio set in Hollywood or London. Nearly all scenes to be shot in the palace were scripted as 'night', which presented no problem as the totally enclosed four-wall set and roof could be treated just like a film studio. For the cameraman, lighting it in the normal fashion would have presented no problem, but Franco was not to be dissuaded. The script said 'night' and therefore he would film at night. No amount of entreaty or persuasion would make him change his mind. Even the accountant's assessment of the extra payments for night-work could not budge Franco's conviction that people behave differently at night. Some of the more cynical maintained this conviction was heavily influenced by his own nocturnal disposition.

One of the most spectacular scenes was to include Salome's famous dance of the seven veils, for which agents had been approached on both sides of the Atlantic in the search of an actress who could dance in a suitably erotic way. Weeks passed without success until word reached us that just the right teenager had been found in America and was on her way to Tunisia with a chaperone. Her arrival went quite unheralded. To anyone who knew him it was obvious that Zeffirelli hadn't liked what he saw and certainly would not have her in his film.

Covert searching continued as the day drew closer for the filming of Salome's dance scene, until a Spanish girl arrived on set. No teenager, apparently no dancer either, she wore spectacles and didn't speak a word of English. We watched with amazement as she went to her costume fitting (not that Salome had much to worry about apart from the seven veils).

Franco's great friend and choreographer, Alberto Testa, arrived from Rome and struggled to teach our new Salome the rudiments of a dance that he performed with great skill and artistry and that she followed with stumbling attempts of considerably less allure. The final film of Salome's dance was a masterpiece of editing, while her voice was provided by one of the many unsung and unseen post-synchronising talents that abound in London.

Next on the schedule was the birth of Christ, not set in an inn stable, as we have been led to believe for most of the Christian era, but in a hillside cave that had been cleared of its sheep and donkey inmates. The location was even stranger, a cave hewn out of a hillside overlooking Monastir Airport, the arrival point of a myriad tourists who have only to cross the main road to start their two weeks' incarceration in one of the mammoth blocks of the Hotel Sahara.

Jean flew out to join us on our first day of shooting the nativity though it was a lonely arrival for her while I toiled away all day recording our Lord's first cries as he entered the world. She said as much to Franco when I introduced her to him in the hotel dining-room on her second evening. 'Really, Mr Zeffirelli,' she complained mockingly, 'this is too much. I have been here now for two days and have hardly seen my husband – in fact we have not even had time to make love.'

Franco sympathised with all his charm; of course she was right, of course he understood, in fact, he promised, 'Tomorrow I shall send a car for you to come to the location, where you will both make love together in front of us all!'

Jean was to be in good company on that film. Later in the schedule we heard that Princess Margaret was to visit Tunisia as President Bourgiba's guest and would be dropping in to our film set. The date fixed coincided with the shooting of a scene in the synagogue where Cyril Cusack, as a rabbi, would be reading from the scrolled scriptures.

Strict warning was given to Franco that on this morning especially he must not be late, but must be ready on set to welcome our distinguished guests. The rest of us were there on time, waiting for our director to give us the first set-up of the day, when we heard that the president's party had arrived and were starting their pre-arranged tour through the film sets of Bethlehem, guided by Vincenzo Labella, the producer. The minutes passed with no sign of Franco, while the guided tour passed on relentlessly. We were on the point of improvising some sort of show for them. However, as they stepped onto the set, right on cue Franco entered by another door, totally unruffled and charming as always.

After the introductions had been made, princess Margaret enquired, 'Tell me, Mr Zeffirelli, what exactly are you doing?'

Before Franco answered, the Cockney voice of Bobby Stilwell, our focus 'puller', called out from beside the camera, 'If you can find out, luv, don't keep it a secret, because we don't bleedin' know!'

The princess and the rest of the British contingent burst out laughing as did our director, leaving the President of Tunisia and his entourage standing with blank faces bewildered at the antics of the mad British.

Franco was a great one for getting people into costume to appear in crowd scenes. One day, while filming at Peter's house in a little fishing village nearby, we were intrigued by a small bearded member of the crowd gathered round listening to Jesus. We speculated on the identity of the newcomer; not one of the regular Tunisian crowd, but who? Much later in the afternoon the mystery was solved. Underneath the beard and hooded robe was Babs, Robert Powell's pretty blonde wife, who was another to fall for Franco's on the spot casting. It mattered not who they were or where they had come from.

Franco's charm on *Jesus of Nazareth* eased him through situations that, in biblical terms, would have tried the patience of a saint. Those situations certainly tried the patience of our poor continuity girl, Yvonne Axworthy (whose flaming red hair had earned her the nickname Copper Knob). The film was divided into thirteen half-hour script episodes for television broadcasting and poor Yvonne had to lug around all thirteen scripts, together with copious notes and

Robert Powell's wife Babs.

Filming Jesus of
Nazareth.

continuity sheets, for none of us knew what Franco might decide to do next.

One memorable morning we were driven to a distant location where Franco had decided to film a scene with Robert Powell in a natural amphitheatre formed in the hillside. The whole circus of trucks, generators, buses, cars and caravans had arrived for an eight-thirty call. The actors were in costume, made-up and waiting. The camera and sound crews were at the ready. Even the director deigned to show up more or less on time, though his visit was brief. Driving past us all to the top of a ridge, he stepped out of his car, surveyed the scene and then stepped back inside and drove off, without a word. Frantic calls in Italian came from production assistants and the circus prepared to roll off to a new location, leaving we three non-Italian speakers in the unit without a clue where we were supposed to be going.

I screamed across to Pepe, Franco's personal assistant, 'Where on earth are we going?' He shouted back that Franco had decided that he didn't want to shoot that particular scene after all, but had decided to shoot some more cover shots at our Mount of Olives location. Apart from the enormous cavalcade of vehicles having to lumber its way up the olive grove, poor Robert Powell was faced with having to prepare for a completely new scene and re-learn its dialogue at very short notice.

For the second time that morning we prepared for Franco to give us the set up. Lunch-time came and went, without any sign of the director. When he eventually emerged from his caravan it was with a small lightweight Arriflex camera, that he used to make shots of his own. Ignoring most of the unit standing waiting for instructions, he collected a small group of Tunisian extras, men with striking faces, women young and old and a gaggle of children, and led them onto a hillside where he spent the rest of the afternoon making individual close-up reactions to be cut in with Jesus's Sermon on the Mount. Apart from the camera crew, none of us were used at all that day, and an embarrassed Pepe was despatched to Robert to tell him that he would not be required after all.

If episodes like that brought some of Our Lord's trials into sharp focus for Robert, they were nothing compared with the scene of the crucifixion itself. Franco had pictured this set against the grim fortress walls at Sousse. He saw the scene in failing light and pouring rain. The light was a simple matter of timing, the presence of rain was assured by the local fire brigade who were positioned with fire-hoses to douse Robert and the two thieves beside him as they hung from their crosses.

The day we shot the scene was dull and overcast. The rain poured down on cue and Franco made several takes. At the end of the last of these Robert showed no signs of reacting to a call of 'cut'. Hanging limply from the cross it was clear that he had passed out. The crew got him down as quickly as they could. The unit doctor arrived and diagnosed that he was suffering from hypothermia. This coincided with a breathtaking sunset that spread from below the lowering clouds and shot the castle walls with magnificent light. With only minutes to work in, Robert was manhandled back into position on his cross, the cameras rolled and Franco captured yet another awe-inspiring scene to

Director Franco Zeffirelli, 1977.

which the film owes much of its fame.

Franco's total disregard of time and cost was beginning to unsettle Lew Grade and money men back in London; so much so that Bernard Kingham, Grade's accountant, was despatched from the ATV head office to have a serious talk with Mr Zeffirelli. For several days he was seen hovering uncomfortably on the set, dressed in his suit, ignored by crew and director alike.

When Franco finally agreed to grant him an audience it was in his hotel suite one morning before he left for the film set. Franco was in the habit of viewing the rushes in bed on video and by all accounts he finished watching a cassette before acknowledging Bernard's presence with the disarming greeting, 'Oh hello, Bernard, nice to see you. When did you arrive – have you been here long?'

In spite of several days in which to plan his dressing-down, Bernard was completely thrown and had barely started to spell out the financial realities to the wayward director when Franco interrupted to reassure him, 'Now, Bernard, I want you to go back to Sir Lew. Tell him everything is fine – he has nothing to worry about. It's going to be a marvellous film. Goodbye Bernard!' With that he placed the cassette into the video machine, settled back into the pillows to carry on with the rushes and waved an imperious farewell as Bernard Kingham was ushered out to make his dispirited way back to ATV and a less than thrilled Sir Lew.

Many weeks elapsed before Franco received the ultimatum that he must secretly have been anticipating; the production had to cease by a certain date, after which the camera and sound equipment would be returned to the UK. His capitulation seemed assured, but we should have known our director by this time.

The day after the official deadline, in the midst of all the packing, he managed to inveigle an Arriflex camera from Vincenzo Labella with which to re-shoot part of the scene in which Lazarus is raised from the dead. I was called on to go alone with a Nagra recorder over my shoulder, one microphone in my hand, to the tomb that had been constructed in a disused quarry some way outside Monastir.

When I arrived I found that Franco had decided to re-shoot the entire scene, having called for Robert Powell to rejoin him, even though the wardrobe people had already packed his robe and worn-out sandals. Luckily I had a walkie-talkie with me with which I could summon Keith and John with the rest of our equipment. The scene completed, we returned to Monastir; but still Franco persisted filming individual shots of the multitude eating the loaves and fishes until the camera was taken from his hands as the final magazine ran out of film.

Some ten months later Jean and I were invited to a six-hour marathon running of *Jesus of Nazareth* at the British Film Academy theatre. After the first three hours there was a break for a buffet lunch. Franco made his way among us greeting everyone affably, but this was no duty call. Catching sight of us he came across, kissed me on the cheek and turned to me accusingly to ask, 'Don't you ever buy her any new clothes? She wore that dress in Tunisia last year.'

That was the moment when my wife joined the tally of Franco Zeffirelli's conquests!

1977 gave me the opportunity to work again with celebrated director, Ken Russell. I had met Ken ten years earlier working with him on the Michael Caine film *Billion Dollar Brain*, much of which we shot in the surreal setting of the frozen waters of Helsinki harbour in the depths of a Finnish winter. That film brings back sad memories for me for the tragic death of its female lead Françoise Dorleac, sister of Catherine Deneuve. We had almost completed filming when she was involved in a car collision just outside Nice Airport. She and her little dog were burned alive Ken had always tended to query my insistence on recording dialogue immediately after the camera was cut, when unwanted noises had been obtrusive on the 'take'. 'We can post-synch her later,' he would say. He did give in to my determination, however, and on that occasion it was to pay off with poignant consequences. Ken told me that on no account would he have revoiced Françoise with another actress.

Ken had asked me to join him for *Women in Love* and *Tommy*, both of which I had had to decline because of previous commitments. But in 1977 I was able to take up his offer of *Valentino*, with Rudolf Nureyev. We met to discuss the film in Lee Brothers Studio in Kilburn at eight o'clock one morning. Up in his office I found Ken, with his bare feet on the desk, a full glass of Chardonney in his hand, giving me the 'Russell' look, as well as a glass of wine

The late Françoise Dorleac with Ken Russell.

Where Franco Zeffirelli had a flair for detail, Ken was a genius at sniffing out locations and once he had explained the technical requirements he wanted in the sound department, he launched into an enthusiastic description of his latest trawl of superb discoveries.

The Tower Ballroom at Blackpool, with all its gilded baroque splendours, was going to serve as the 1920s New York dance hall where Valentino first worked as a gigolo. The Tower Circus was going to act as the setting for the boxing match challenge that Valentino had with a New York journalist, who, it had been claimed, had slandered him. We were going to use the Russell Cotes Museum in Bournemouth as Nazimova's home, full as it is today with *art nouveau* furniture and trappings of the Twenties. A cliff-top house was going to provide the setting for a private hospital up to which Nureyev would drive in his Bugatti. Shooting was also to take place in the Great Eastern Hotel, where Nureyev was going to dance an extraordinary tango with Anthony Dowell.

His greatest coup, he informed me, had come on the train journey from Bournemouth to London, during which a well-wined and dined Ken claimed he had spotted a mosque-like building through the carriage window as they passed somewhere near Woking; it was precisely what he was looking for: a 1920s Beverley Hills mansion. The location manager grudgingly trooped off to Woking the next day, convinced that a fuddled Ken had imagined the whole thing. But in matters like this Ken Russell was rarely mistaken and the location manager returned that evening having found the very building, a mosque, and completed a deal for its use.

The tally of superb period locations was rounded off by the 1920s bungalow that he had unearthed in the Fylde near Blackpool. Ken planned to use this as Valentino's final home where he dies of a massive haemorrhage. Built in a square, with an open glazed area in the middle, this had rooms on all four sides, with a surrounding balustrade from which steps led down the enormous living area. Everything was of the very best quality: beautiful mahogany panelled doors, stained glass windows and hand-wrought iron fitments. A wealthy builder had designed it as his dream home and fifty years later he would have had reason to feel proud of his achievement.

We began filming *Valentino* in Almeira, in Spain, where we used the much-featured wild-west film set for a typical 'western' shoot-up in the saloon and main street. The next venue was the bull ring in Almeira to stage Valentino's role as the toreador in *Blood and Sand*. This was followed by days on the sand dunes near the airport which Ken used as the setting for *The Sheikh*.

While we were in Almeira, the choreographer Gillian Gregory was brought out from England to teach Nureyev to tango. She was terribly nervous at the prospect of teaching the most famous dancer in the world how to dance and her anxiety wasn't helped when Rudolf appeared for the first lesson wearing the ugliest of thick crepe-soled boots. His answer to her suggestion that some other footwear might be more appropriate was that he always wore those boots, as proved to be the case throughout the film. 'Anyway,' he added, 'I wore them when I met the Queen and she did not object.'

Boots or no boots Nureyev mastered the tango in his first lesson, but when I first saw his bare feet, quite the least appealing pair I have ever seen, I wondered whether his affection for his boots was that they were more comfortable than any other footwear. He must have put his feet through years of discomfort; they certainly showed all the signs of continual wear and tear. Even during filming he would spend each lunch-break at a portable barre going through his exercises, ready for an evening performance after a day on the set. Putting out so much energy gave him a voracious appetite. Two or three steak sandwiches was his standard fare at lunch, while the morning and afternoon breaks saw him devouring four or five Chelsea buns in succession.

Ken's then wife, Shirley, was the dress designer on the film. For Nureyev she managed to find the Saville Row tailor who had made Valentino's suits in the days when he could afford them. So Nureyev appeared in the film dressed just as Valentino had done in strikingly patterned cloths with wide-lapelled jackets and lapelled waistcoats cut straight across the waistline.

Shirley's painstaking research was applied to the rest of the costumes. Wherever possible she found actual dresses from the period, or reproduced virtually stitch for stitch, the flamboyant gowns worn by Nazimova. If ever an Oscar nomination for costume design was deserved, it was Shirley Russell's for her efforts on *Valentino*.

Leaving Almeira we stopped off in Barcelona where Ken wanted to film a scene in the zoo. This involved constructing the set of an office suite in front of the barred cage in which lived an enormous white gorilla. Apart from providing an arresting backdrop to the scene in producer Jesse Lasky's office, it was also completely in keeping with Valentino's bizarre life; for in his day Jesse Lasky had indeed owned a pet white gorilla.

Two days later we were in San Felieu which I hadn't seen since filming *The Spanish Gardener*. Here, in horrendous heat, we shot a wedding scene on the steps leading up to the church. The actors were running with sweat which saturated my little microphone transmitters, taped to their skin in cloth pouches, causing very poor reception.

Once the shooting at San Feliu was completed, we packed our equipment for air freighting to London, before being bundled into a coach that took us to Barcelona airport, hot, dirty and hungry. We had been told that this uncomfortable state of affairs was due to the tight departure time of our flight, but on arrival at the airport this was anything but the case. In fact the production associate was still haggling with Varig, the rather dubious South American carrier he was trying to persuade to fly us home. We had already had a run-in with this particular individual after the dreadful hotel he had dumped us in while we were in San Feliu. He pleaded a shortage of accommodation which was soon translated as mere penny-pinching on his part. Now it was the same at the airport where he blithely announced that he had no Spanish money to pay for our meal in the airport canteen. Our misery was compounded soon after by the elements which brought a thunderstorm of such violence and intensity that the drains overflowed and flooded the entire departure lounge.

In the midst of this Ken suddenly made his appearance, through the curtain of the baggage carousel. He was sitting astride his cases, bottle of wine in hand, moving slowly round and round with the luggage until someone waded round the back to find the control switch. In the circumstances even the decrepit aircraft that eventually lumbered into the leaden skies to carry us back to London seemed something of a refuge.

We finished filming at Elstree and at the end-of-picture party Ken presented me with a copy of his newly published biography. On the flyleaf he had scrawled, 'To John, KING OF SOUND, Ken Russell – many, many thanks.'

We never had the chance to work together again, much as I would have liked to. Working with so-called 'difficult' people was seldom a problem for me. One day during the filming of *Valentino* I went over to him with one of my 'I don't suppose you will agree with me but . . .' suggestions. Looking directly at me he answered, 'You always bloody well argue with me – and you're nearly always right!'

I took that as a compliment. There weren't many from Ken Russell and I value it highly.

Ken Russell

The Adaptor as Creator

Joseph A. Gomez

Frederick Muller Limited · London

Ken Russell with the cast and crew of Valentino.

Chapter Seventeen

FROM CANADA TO CAIRO

No one who had seen and enjoyed *A Touch of Class* could refuse an offer to work with Glenda Jackson and George Segal on Melvin Frank's next project *Lost and Found*. The film was to be made in Canada and once again I was asked to work alone, using local technicians in place of my crew. Fortunately Keith and Ron were already working, so I could accept the offer without deserting them.

Getting a permit to work in Canada is never easy and with the film industry closely controlled by the big American film unions I wasn't surprised at the grudging reception I got when I landed with my equipment at Toronto. In fact I was surprised that our unit comprised a full camera crew, including grip, production manager, stills photographer and publicity department, all of whom had been imported from the UK. Our headquarters were in an old house with spacious cellars in which I set up shop with my equipment plus battery charging facilities alongside the wardrobe department.

My first surprise came when I asked for a list of boom operators for me to interview, only to be told that one had already been allocated. According to union rules the most senior man on the availability list got the job. This did not bode well and my doubts were confirmed when I interviewed my chosen assistant down in my cellar. Despite having all my recorders, microphones and radio microphones spread out on a table, none of them prompted any interest or questions whatsoever as to my method of working. After his departure I had talks with our production manager with a plea for me to bring a boom operator from England, or at least for me to be accorded the courtesy of meeting other Canadian boom operators. But in Canada union regulations were rigidly adhered to; they were a part of IATSE, the American film technicians union.

During that first weekend I called a friend of mine from Denham days, Reg Morris, now an established lighting cameraman in Canada. He insisted on my coming round to their home for an English Sunday lunch, during the course of which Reg asked if I had brought my boom operator from England. When I answered 'no' and told him who had been allocated to me by the union system, he said just one word – 'Disaster'. This man was a cameraman's nightmare, let alone a sound mixer's.

On the Monday, I repeated my request, merely to be told that, 'It's the system.' Then a strange thing happened; I had asked the chief property man to order some carpet runners for me. These are lengths of stair-width carpet that can be put down onto hard floors, out of the camera's vision, in order to reduce the level of actors' footsteps in a dialogue scene. This prop man had a room in the attic of our HQ and the message came back that he wanted to have a word with me. Thinking that it was to check on the carpet runners, I was surprised when I sat down to hear him say, 'So you don't want the boom operator who has been allocated?' I could not understand why a prop-man was asking this, until he said that he was chairman of the union in Toronto, and that either I accepted my boom operator or the film would not start.

That did not leave me with much of a choice. All I could hope for was better luck with the third member of the team, a position that was not governed by the seniority system; though by a grim irony the first interviewee turned out to be the prop man's nephew, or could it possibly have been nepotism? Either way I retrieved some satisfaction in turning him down. The list of possible

Close Encounters of the Third Kind, *1977. Steven Spielberg persuaded his backers to allow him to film a sequence in India featuring the famous chanting crowds. It was shot in five days by a British Camera crew and a lone John Mitchell.*

candidates was running thin when finally a chap with shoulder length hair appeared. A hippie type, to my eyes, Peter Tarsish by name, he had a CV running to two pages that detailed a variety of jobs from lumberjack to oil-rigger, with a recent period working in television as an assistant floor manager. By now I was beginning to get interested – he struck me as being very bright.

As I handed back his CV, he got up and made his way to the cellar stairs and I asked where he was going.

'Well you haven't read my CV so you obviously are not interested,' he answered. I just found it hard to work out how he had achieved so much, after all, he was only twenty!

However, I had a hunch he would be a 'good un' and we struck a deal – I would take him on for the first two weeks of filming on the understanding that if either he or I did not want to continue, there would be no hard feelings either way. By week two, he had proved to be both intelligent and indispensable. Without him I would surely have handed in my resignation, for everything that Reg said about the boom operator was true. Chick Waterson, considered to be one of our top camera operators, was in a constant state of nerves coping with the microphone being dipped into the picture, or causing a shadow, purely as a result of total incompetence.

One function with which I would not normally have been concerned was to 'dress' small personal radio-microphones onto the actors. These are connected by a thin cable to a small radio transmitter, hidden either in a trouser hip pocket; or in the case of an actress, placed in a close fitting pouch which is pinned under the dress at waist height in the small of the back. Without Glenda Jackson and George Segal's co-operation I would have been hard pressed at times to cope with this additional task. Never having worked with them before, I adopted my well proven method of introducing myself as 'sound without fury', to quote Noël Coward's description on *Our Man in Havana*. The first day of shooting called for the use of radio microphones on both stars, so, with the transmitters' batteries in place, I knocked on George's motor-home door; to be told to come back later as he was busy.

Glenda was being dressed in her film costume and as I approached her with the little microphone and lead, she slipped out of her blouse. Fumbling slightly as I planted it between the cleavage of her bra, she gave me that quizzical look of hers saying, 'What's the matter, haven't you seen a pair of tits before?' From then on that more or less daily routine went well, with her even taking the transmitter off at lunch breaks in order that I could insert fresh

On the set of Lost and Found *with* George Segal.

batteries for the afternoon's work.

George was equally helpful but after several more occasions of being asked to come back later, he said to me, 'You know, I don't know why it is, but every time you come near me with that little mike – I have to go to the bathroom and dump!'

The storyline of the film concerned a university lecturer, played by George, who during a ski-ing holiday in Banff literally bumps into Glenda on the slopes. They both fall for each other in spite of George breaking a leg. It also dealt in some depth with the strange North American academic system in which college teaching staff have no job security until they have secured 'tenure'.

Many of our locations were in the university, and around town in Toronto and its suburbs. My boom operator had no interest in the morning 'line-up' routine of our equipment with its customary checks. He also had an uncanny knack of being absent during rehearsals; though I always knew where to find him – at the 'chuck wagon' stuffing away as if he hadn't eaten for days. As soon as the call 'wrap' was made we could be sure that he would stroll over to our sound truck, lodge his microphone pole against the driving mirror to shamble off to his car, leaving Peter, our driver, and me to pack the equipment into the truck.

On one occasion when his car was out of action we had taken him out to the location. That evening on the way back to the city I asked our driver to stop at a liquor store where Keith Hamshire, our stills man, and I wanted to replenish our stocks. I could not believe my ears when the great hulk announced, 'If you stop, it will put me into penalty treble time payment – my time stops when I get into Toronto.'

Filming out at Toronto airport one day, I had arranged with the announcer to record some calls over the public address system that applied specifically to our storyline. The recordings were scheduled to be timed during our lunch-break. I left the 'hulk' to feed while I took Peter with the microphone to a quiet area of the concourse. With the help of the airport liaison officer we were well under way when our production manager interrupted to ask why I was not working with the boom operator. I said I didn't need him, in answer to which came the reply that I was breaking union rules and that he would be charging penalty overtime. It was almost as if I had a habit of attracting these local difficulties.

My problems were not restricted to my own sound crew. We had a large number of limousines on the film which transported director, actors and other personnel. Very early on we were shooting at a bungalow, when 'quiet' was called and I was immediately aware of a high background noise of cars revving. On investigation I found all our unit cars with drivers muffled up inside, running their engines to heat the interiors. When I asked why they could not sit six in a car in two vehicles only and well away from our film set, I thought we might well have a strike on our hands. After all, the drivers were members of the Teamsters Union!

My antics had been watched by a visiting journalist who interviewed me

Filming on the streets of Toronto.

about what had been going on. The next day an article appeared in a Toronto paper, a copy of which I still have to this day. In it I am quoted as saying, 'In England we cannot afford the petrol.' The journalist then asked what we did to keep warm. My reply was, 'We just jump up and down.'

But for these irritations, *Lost and Found* would have been the most pleasant of films to have worked on. Fortunately, Jean came out to join me in a furnished apartment that I had rented. We made the most of our spare time in visiting Niagara and Quebec and all the amenities of Toronto. She loved the shops and I tried hard not to bore her with my tales of woe of an evening.

When shooting finished Mel Frank had laid on an end-of-picture party on a lake steamer. I shall never forget him putting his arm round me to say thanks for my efforts and those of my 'great crew.' I didn't have the heart to spoil things by giving him a run-down of what I had to put up with; he had obviously been totally unaware of my problems. That was some consolation.

Happily I was reunited with my own crew for my next production when

Lord Brabourne invited us to work on his second Hercule Poirot film *Death on the Nile*. Once again it was to star Peter Ustinov as Poirot, supported by an incredible cast: Bette Davis, Maggie Smith, Angela Lansbury, Mia Farrow, Jane Birkin, Lois Chiles, Olivia Hussey, David Niven, George Kennedy, Jack Warden, Simon MacCorkindale, Jon Finch and Harry Andrews; plus the famous Indian actor and film director J. S. Johar, who played the tour guide on the Nile Steamer the *Karnak*. The film was to be directed by John Guillermin, with whom I had worked in the sixties on *Waltz of the Toreadors*.

While English locations were being filmed, an art department with construction crew was already in Egypt, erecting a strange looking wooden structure up the side of one of the pyramids, to await our arrival. It looked like an inverted 'V' and turned out to be a track on which a large wooden box with greased runners could be hauled up (with cameraman inside), counterbalanced by a similar box running down the other leg of the 'V'. This device enabled the camera to be tracked as it followed Simon and Lois in a scene in which they climbed up the enormous stone blocks to the summit.

In the meantime we were filming at Sutton Park, the famous Surrey home of J. Paul Getty. I was amused to see public telephone boxes on the walls

Peter Ustinov in Evil Under the Sun, *1979.*

when we were shooting in the grand hall; although a multi-millionaire, Getty refused to pay for his guests' phone calls. One can only presume that regular guests always came with an ample supply of 10p pieces.

Whilst filming here, John Guillermin had his first brush with Lois Chiles; a disagreement over her climbing some stairs. This clash of personalities was to manifest itself even more so at a later location near Banbury where he criticised her inability to ride a horse across a lawn at a fast canter. In fact her horsemanship, or lack of it, was to dog her throughout the film. When we arrived in Egypt, there was a scene where she and Simon had to come at a flat-out gallop towards the Sphinx. This time Guillermin's frustration got the better of him when she blamed the horse for failing to stop in the right place. He asked her to dismount, leaped into the saddle, tore away, wheeled the horse around, and galloped towards us, stopping right on the mark. Before dismounting he reared the horse on its hind legs to illustrate a point and jumped off saying, 'Nothing wrong with this horse.'

Our main base in Egypt was at Aswan, where we stayed in the Oberoi Hotel on Elephant Island. We had been warned that because of the tourist season, we may have had to share rooms. Because of this I reluctantly decided to leave Jean at home, a decision that I have ever since regretted, for I had a duplex apartment to myself the whole time we were in Aswan; as I had later in both Luxor and Cairo. I have always been fascinated with Egypt and its history and this would have been a wonderful opportunity for us to have shared that unique 'perk' working in films sometimes affords, the chance to see the world at someone else's expense.

Work started on board the *Karnak*, a period Nile paddle steamer which we would board daily, on its mooring alongside the hotel jetty. Our electricians had gone out ahead to install a generator in the bows to supply electricity for cameraman, Jack Cardiff's, lights. And the noise from its diesel engine presented me with my first sound problem. I was assured by the gaffer that they had put a baffle around it to reduce audibility. If they had it was not quiet enough for me, so we set about making a good job of reducing the din still further. It is strange how soundmen's ears seem so much more sensitive to noise than those of an electrician!

Angela Lansbury, playing an appropriately zany authoress, was the source of another sound problem. She had been dressed by famous costume designer Anthony Powell, complete with rows of beads around her neck and jangling bangles on her wrists. This costume may have been completely in keeping

Death on the Nile, *1979.*

with her character but every time she moved, the microphone picked up a cacophony of rattles. I must say that my friend Anthony was most helpful in having the wardrobe lady painstakingly anchor the beads by hidden stitching. (The next film with Angela and Anthony was another Agatha Christie, this time the Miss Marples story *The Mirror Crack'd*. When we met up on the first day they both called out to me, 'No noisy beads this time, John.')

Olivia Hussey, with whom I had recently worked on *Jesus of Nazareth*, was playing the part of Angela's daughter, a timid retiring spinster completely overawed by her extrovert mother. She became the bane of my maintenance man, Ron's life, for she spent most of her time away from the camera playing her walkman. Hardly a day passed without her coming to Ron with a horribly tangled mess of tape spewing out of the cassette. We never did fathom how anyone could cause such havoc, nor how she depleted batteries so quickly. Ron, who is a nice chap, took it all in good part, as well as replacing batteries at Lord Brabourne's expense.

Each one of the cast was wonderful in his or her own way, but, the day was fast approaching when we were all to be put on our mettle by the appearance of Bette Davis. On that day we were well into the shooting of a scene on the upper deck some way down the Nile, when a radio message was picked up from the production office situated on the top floor of the tower at the Oberoi Hotel: 'Miss Davis has boarded her launch at the jetty, she is on her way to board the *Karnak*.'

Shooting stopped as the launch came alongside the gangway. John Guillermin looking like a wild man from the woods, wearing only a pair of trunks, no shoes, his hair an unkempt mass, was waiting for her to reach the upper deck, his favourite Dunhill pipe between clenched teeth. Almost like an officer of the watch greeting an admiral aboard a battleship, he spoke two words, 'Morning, Bett'.

There was complete hush while she fixed him with those famous staring eyes. 'I will have you know my name is Bette, pronounced Betty not Bett; preferably Miss Bette Davis or Miss Davis.' Peter Ustinov and David Niven walked away, splitting their sides with laughter.

Then in her seventieth year, Bette Davis put her stamp on the production; from the moment she stepped onto the deck of the *Karnak*, work on *Death on the Nile* was transformed. Like most, if not all, of those Hollywood pre-war

stars who had been subjected to the extreme disciplines of people like Louis B. Mayer, Harry Cohn, Samuel Goldwyn and in her case the Warner Brothers, she was a true professional. They are never late on the set. They know their lines. They even know which light is their 'key light'. In most cases they even react favourably to the soundman's comments.

Bette Davis was no exception. She never let her air of mild aloofness slip but for those with an eye to look for it, underneath she could be warm and approachable. I became friendly enough to call her Bette and to get her to tell me many stories of those early days when she was Warner Brothers' top star.

With most of our filming set on the *Karnak* we did finally get ashore to shoot the end sequence of the film alongside a jetty at Aswan, where they all took their leave after Poirot had solved the case.

As always I had been having problems recording good sound effects with the unit working all around me, so I grasped a wonderful opportunity that presented itself unexpectedly. Our next sequence was one where the whole *Karnak* party were to go ashore to visit a temple. This location was some distance downstream. A decision was made to send the steamer down overnight, with the director, actors and crew following in fast launches the next morning.

I opted to go on the *Karnak* overnight with my pal Keith so that we were able to stop engines and just drift down with the stream parallel to the river bank while I recorded the most wonderful evening backgrounds noises: distant voices, animals and poultry. Further on we gathered a collection of the steamer's own noises: the paddle-wheels at varying speeds forward and astern, the whistle, the engine-room noises and most important of all the rumble of the engines as heard below decks. These effects were crucial for the sound editors back at Pinewood, where scenes in the cabins, stateroom and dining-room were shot in studio-constructed film sets. Not only that, but such unique sound effects have a market value in sound libraries where they can earn handsome fees, charged per foot used.

Keith and I worked into the small hours, managing snatches of sleep in one of the cabins before mooring alongside the river bank where our temple stood about half-way between Aswan and Luxor. Just ahead of us was one of those strange flat-bottomed, square-sided tourist boats. With no catering facilities on the *Karnak*, except the means to make a cup of tea, we were delighted to hear an American voice call across, 'Anyone aboard? Come over for breakfast.'

On board our hosts were revealed as two former Pan-Am pilots who had put their retirement savings into strange craft in which they ferried tourists between Luxor and Aswan. It could take about twelve passengers in total air-conditioned comfort, each state room complete with en-suite bathroom. If the rest of the catering was as good as our breakfast, I am sure that there were never any complaints.

The launches from Aswan began to arrive, first bringing the crew and equipment; then the director who roughed out his set-ups. John Guillermin really did his homework. Unlike many directors he always had a desk on the studio floor, working at the next scenes. With an Agatha Christie story this is vital, for with all the twists and turns of her plots it is very easy to get lost in their complexities.

This particular sequence we were going to film involved the party coming ashore from the steamer, and assembling together, before moving off to the temple in the distance. Guillermin had accumulated a collection of camels and donkeys on which he intended various members of the cast would ride. Peter being told he would ride a camel declined and settled for a donkey. David, being the nice person he was, agreed to ride a camel. Finally all was fixed, leaving only Bette to be given her choice of mount.

'I am not riding any camel or donkey,' she informed John, 'I am gonna walk.' She had obviously been sizing up the situation during John's preparations and had worked out that if she walked behind the whole party, who would be moving away from the camera with its wide angle lens, she would be the most prominent character to the audience. These old Hollywood stars knew their stuff! So that is the way it was – she in her Edwardian style costume with wide brimmed hat, open parasol in her hand following behind through the dust and scrub.

After the first rehearsal they all returned to the start point where John made some changes. I was taking shelter with my equipment under the shade of a tree. On Bette's return I produced a stool for her to sit down.

'I don't wanna sit,' she said and I did not press the point.

After the next rehearsal, back she came, shoes full of dust.

'He will go on rehearsing this many times,' I told her, 'and then have several takes with the camera – why don't you sit down?'

She did and on each subsequent take returned to the stool and sat while I took her shoes off, emptied them of sand, put them back on and did up the straps for her to stride off again. By the time that sequence was completed, the sun was setting, so director and actors were sent back to Aswan. We, inevitably,

Bette Davis in Death
on the Nile *1979.*

Hello & thanks
for meeting J
Dit!
Hope we work
to gether again
Be...

with the camera crew, had been the first to arrive and the last to leave the location. This meant that it was nearly dark when we set off to cover part of the Nile that is notorious for its shifting sand bars, which lie hidden in the shallows. Someone had to be up in the bows looking down into the water to avoid running aground. Creeping back up river, with no lights to help us in the dark, at times almost going aground, the journey back took hours in comparison with the comparative ease with which the 'knobs' had returned to the hotel at dusk.

Next day it was time to pack, ready to move off by road for the Valley of the Kings. At Luxor we had much filming planned amongst the giant pillars of the temple of *Karnak.*

Our filming in the Valley of the Kings was a marvellous experience – a location ready-made so many thousands of years before. We shot scenes of George Kennedy chasing up a long narrow and steep flight of steps with high walls on either side, then past an enormous headless torso carved from Aswan granite, lying on its side some hundreds of miles from the quarry. How did it ever get there?

The peak of that part of our filming was in the temple of *Karnak* with its rows and rows of giant pillars connected at the top by enormous rectangular bridging blocks of stone. George Kennedy was to play a scene on the top of the columns where he levered a facsimile block to send it crashing down just to miss Lois Chiles below.

We were fortunate enough one evening in Luxor to have time to see the unique *Son et Lumière*. Like no other, it begins the evening with the arrival of the audience who are part of the show. You walk between those columns with changing lights, listening to a dramatic commentary over hidden speakers, finally to take a seat in an enormous tier overlooking a lake, for the main part of the story to unfold. Sadly by the time we reached Cairo the *Son et Lumière* season beside the Sphinx had ended. That is definitely one not to be missed. The main unit were flown to Cairo whilst a reduced crew filmed at the temple of Abu Simbel with Mia Farrow sitting on the foot of one of the four massive crouching figures that had been rescued from the rising waters of the Nile when the Aswan Dam was built after the war.

After a troublesome unchartered flight to Cairo we crashed out exhausted that night and were woken up early the next morning for a sequence at the pyramids. There had been protracted negotiations to get permission for us to climb to the top, but it is wonderful what our producer was able to achieve, he being Lord Mountbatten's son in law, as well as having the ear of the British ambassador.

Those square blocks forming the pyramids look quite small from afar. Close up they are huge, not at all easy to scale with my little legs. Fortunately the construction department had made wooden step-ups which halved the height of the stretch onto each slab. It was laborious to manhandle the equipment up each block in turn, but the view from the top made our exertions worthwhile, sweetened by the knowledge that no tourists can ever share that privilege.

I suppose I couldn't expect such a location not to be without its sound problems. We certainly had them in the form of loud music from the Mena Palace Hotel. That was easily dealt with; however, away towards Cairo, drifting across to us from the sprawling suburbs that stretch across the sands towards the pyramids, was din of the type of awful discordant music that permeates the east. John Guillermin blew his top; demanding that it be stopped. Locals and assistants were sent off in taxis in what looked like the hopeless task of tracking down the source. I was fully reconciled to coping with it as best I could, when suddenly it stopped – in the silence, we rushed to shoot the scene.

Fortunately most of the filming was without dialogue, just Simon and Lois climbing to the summit to have Mia pop up from the top of the Pyramid to spoil their visit. We only needed the one day shooting on top, thank goodness, for most of us had had more than enough by the time we were back on the desert floor.

The following days were spent filming Peter in his Poirot Palm Beach suit, tropical topee on his head, sitting in a deck chair contemplating the Sphinx, with Simon and Lois galloping past on horseback. It was also fortunate that I

Filming on the pyramids.

did not have to shoot in the streets of Cairo – the streets of Luxor had been quite enough. But on our last morning before our evening flight to London we returned with the camera crew to the pyramid area to reshoot Simon and Lois galloping; John Gullermin was not going to let her get away with her earlier attempts at riding.

For once it was beautifully quiet and I was getting some very good tracks of the galloping hooves. However, on some takes I could hear a voice. I told John, who blew his famous top, 'Who the bloody hell is talking? For Christ's sake keep quiet whoever it is.'

The next time it happened, there was the same voice again and John called out, 'Who the hell is it?'

With one voice the whole crew called out with concerted glee, 'You'.

He had been so engrossed in urging on the riders I suppose he had to be forgiven; after all, he was the director.

With the sequence successfully in the can, we returned to Pinewood Studios to find a full scale *Karnak* filling one of the stages, surrounded by an all-round backing, painted for night, with hundreds of little pea bulbs that could be made to twinkle like the stars in the tropical sky. Lighting any night scenes in the script would have been impossible on the real boat for cameraman Jack Cardiff. The open sided set that accommodated camera, lights and sound boom assured a smooth progress through what remained of the script.

The main saloon, in which Poirot spent much time questioning suspects, culminating in his summing up where he reveals all and then points a finger at the murderer, formed a separate set in another studio. Its proportions were much larger than that of the *Karnak* which we had only used for exits and entrances. Work proceeded smoothly – John Guillermin at his desk consulting his graphs in order to make sure he did not miss one of the 'Christie' twists.

Towards the end of filming we were working on a scene with David Niven in which he had some tricky dialogue, questioning certain members of the cast. It was late afternoon when John Brabourne came onto the set calling David and the director aside. Apparently one of David's young daughters had been involved in an accident when the car she was driving had slid off the icy road and crashed as she approached the Niven winter sports home in Gstaad. David went pale, telling John that he must return immediately to Switzerland. We had all but completed his scene, which he said he would finish – and finish it he did under great stress. A car was waiting to take him to the airport where John Brabourne had chartered an executive jet to get him to Geneva. After that the atmosphere on the set was very subdued, for David was so popular with everyone. Although she made a complete recovery, his daughter's injuries were very serious and his anxiety wasn't helped by the fact that she was also under age to be driving in Switzerland.

On the last day of shooting, Bette Davis came on the set and gave me a still photograph of herself, complete with parasol, on which she had written, 'Hello and thanks for insisting I sit! Hope we work together again. Bette Davis.' Then she said to me, 'I wanna tell you something. I have had four husbands. If any one of them had made me do something against my will as you did, I might have been a far better person than I am today.'

As so often in the film world, her reputation belied her true nature. The lady had humility and greatness in equal measure.

As Christmas approached, with all the cast anxious to return to their homes, there inevitably remained certain lines of dialogue that had to be recorded. An arrangement was decided upon; as each member of the cast became due to leave, they came in early on a Saturday or Sunday morning. The production department made a rota list, guided by the editors, of how much time each one would need to complete the recording. We used the steamer's set and cabins to work in, so that the new recording would match the original acoustically. The editors set up a moviola on which sections of sound and picture could be run to refresh memories of the original playing of the scene.

It was interesting to see the different approach from each actor as his or her turn came. With a possible five customers each Saturday morning, I remember George Kennedy breezing in to complete his stint in double-quick time – with a 'Goodbye and hope we work together again.' Then he was off to the airport. The same was true with Bette Davis, Jack Warden and Angela Lansbury.

It was a different story with Olivia Hussey; always diffident and unsure, her session was no doubt agony. I can't remember if she had a tangled tape cassette with a request for a battery, but I would not have put it past her.

We naturally cleared the Americans first, but then followed with Maggie Smith and Peter Ustinov, with absolutely no problem. These weekend sessions also gave me a unique opportunity to ask them all in turn to sign a group photograph taken on the upper deck of the *Karnak* by Lord Snowdon, all except for Mia Farrow who had already left for the States. That omission was to be remedied a year later during filming in Bora Bora.

The cast of Death on the Nile, *photographed by Snowdon. I once told Lord
Snowdon, who took stills of many films on which I worked, that I was not
an envious person, but that I did envy him one thing. His personal label on
luggage and camera cases bore just one word in large black capitals:
'SNOWDON'. That name no doubt helped him through crowded airports,
railway stations and hotel reception desks with minimum fuss!*

Chapter Eighteen

FROM TAHITI TO ROME

During one of my 'rest' periods in 1979, I had gone into Pinewood Studios to check over some equipment in my store room. As always on such occasions this allowed me to combine business with pleasure by looking up any old friends who might be working there. Ours is a business where showing one's face can do no harm; for quite a lot of information can be gleaned as to who is doing what, and where, and what is in the pipeline.

In this instance I met up with an old friend, Golda Offenheim, who for many years had been production secretary on the early Bond films. She had now moved on, working for the De Laurentis Corporation, having been the UK contact for his production of *Hurricane*, a remake with Mia Farrow, filmed entirely on Bora Bora, one of the Tahitian islands of French Polynesia.

The production had suffered many setbacks whilst filming; the first being that a hotel which Dino De Laurentis had planned to build for cast and unit was barely finished by the time filming was completed. This was as much a financial disaster as a social one; for Dino had intended to offset its cost by charging the film company for accommodation during the production, leaving him with a tourist hotel built for virtually no cost. Bad weather was another problem to dog the film, compounded by the stretched lines of communication that caused costs to escalate. Everybody had had to be flown by light aircraft into the wartime airstrip laid down by the Americans on a strand of coral off Bora Bora, whilst every nut and bolt was brought in by sea in an ex-Guinness ship, which Dino had purchased specifically for the purpose.

Hurricane was in the editing stage when I met up with Golda who regaled me with countless stories of the goings on during filming, such as how the ex-Guinness ship with its enormous hold was originally designed to carry casks of the 'black gold' from Dublin to Liverpool, before a brewery was built at Park Royal outside London. It now plied between Long Beach and Bora Bora with dozens of ex-US Army jeeps, and miles of steel girders for the construction of a gantry on the special effects tank in which the actors would play their scenes with tons of water cascading down shoots from tip tanks high up on the girderwork. This was just a small part of its consignment of all the many different requirements to satisfy the needs of a major feature film. There were also many stories of discontent among the crew over the accommodation, that in many cases was pretty basic in comparison with the cast's and that of Signor De Laurentis. I enjoyed catching up with Golda, comparing some of her most recent *Hurricane* stories with our wonderful treatment from Cubby Broccoli on the Bond films.

Next day at home the phone rang. Golda was on the line to ask if I would speak to Stanley Sopel, whom I had known first as the accountant on Bond productions, and who was now financial executive for the De Laurentis Corporation based in the Hague. He said that if I was not doing anything that afternoon perhaps I would care to come up to town for a viewing of a film.

As it is my habit never to say 'no' or to turn down an invitation, I accepted, to find myself a few hours later in a private review room in Audley Square watching a rough cut of *Hurricane*. It was interesting to see yet another version of a well-known story, but I suppose my professional ear began to notice that soundtrack left a lot to be desired. Nevertheless, it was an interesting afternoon's experience; and when the lights went up and I got up to go, Stanley Sopel called me over saying, 'John Mitchell, meet Mr De Laurentis'. He in turn said, 'So this is the gentleman who is going to make my sound better.'

Before I had time to realise what it was all about I was agreeing to go to Bora Bora to record natural sounds, choirs singing in church, additional lines of scripted dialogue, surf and waves, plus a forlorn hope that we might encounter high winds or even a hurricane to lend authenticity to my work.

With that mandate it was certainly not a one-man band effort, so I opted to take Keith with me, which proved to be the first stumbling block. Dino De Laurentis, who likes to think his word is law, informed me through his production executive, Bernie Williams, that I was to pick up crew and equipment in Hollywood en route to Tahiti. My reply was that I would only do it with Keith and my own equipment, particularly as much was to be recorded in stereo.

A period of impasse followed, during which I even stuck my neck out to the extent that I offered to pay Keith's return air fare to Los Angeles, so adamant was I that I wanted him with me. Eventually a call came from Bernie that Dino had said OK – make a deal and go out as soon as a flight was booked.

We flew with a load of equipment via Los Angeles to Papiette. There we were to be met by Dino's daughter, Raphaela, for the short hop to Bora Bora where she was in charge of his now completed hotel. As so often is the case, no one was there to meet us, except an agent to help with French customs facilities; a help that we really needed as the authorities were none too keen to have anything to do with *Hurricane*. Customs cleared, we then had to arrange a flight by light aircraft to Bora Bora, where we discovered that Dino's daughter had been on our flight from London in the same first-class compartment unbeknown to us, and had left Papiette for Bora Bora without bothering to contact us!

The Pacific Islands are a wonderful sight from the air, particularly when seen from a low altitude. Most of them are ringed with a coral reef creating the wonderful varied colours from blue through to green. Bora Bora is no exception, with the boat ride from the airstrip to the mainland giving a first glimpse of marine life in the crystal clear water.

Dino's hotel was quite something, built in traditional Tahitian style with an enormous palm leaf thatched main building housing a reception area with adjoining bar, lounge, kitchens and dining room. All looked out onto a bay with the coral reef as a back drop. Strangely though, the bar was sited in such a way that one sat with one's back to this idyllic view, which was even more magnificent at sunset. The accommodation was in a series of bungalows spread under waving coconut palms, each containing a lounge-cum-bedroom with shower room and loo; outside was a pleasant verandah with lounge chairs. Some of the bungalows were built out over the water on stilts, approached along catwalks with hand rails. One could see Dino's reasoning in building such a project for the filming but I doubt even if it had been ready in time whether it could have supported a large number of people. The kitchens may have been first-class and the standard of comfort more than adequate, but simple things which are taken for granted in every other hotel, such as hot water, even at times cold water, and above all a reliable sewage disposal system, seemed to have been completely overlooked. Added to these shortcomings was the electricity supply on which the whole complex relied for all its services and which depended on the efficient running of a very noisy diesel engine and alternator, both of questionable age and reliability.

I have often found that one meets up with the most unlikely people in the most unlikely places around the world; Bora Bora was no exception. Dino's disinterest in the mundane was never more apparent than in the choice of that particular power plant. If it had not been for the loving care bestowed on it to keep it running by a Pole named Helmut, who had just happened to show up

With director Don Seigal, Rough Cut, *1980.*

in Bora Bora at the time of the filming of *Hurricane*, the plant would have been useless.

Helmut had decided to leave Poland to seek a better life elsewhere, and had opted to sail round the world. The simplicity of this plan had only one major flaw – he had never seen the sea, let alone sailed a boat. Nothing daunted, he made his way to Gdansk where he bought an eighteen-foot sailing dinghy and proceeded to teach himself to sail. An extended whale-back in the bows gave him a tiny protected wedge-shaped cabin, barely two feet in height, in which he would shelter if he had bad weather or when becalmed. The art of sailing single-handed mastered, he set out from the Polish port with food and water on board for a prolonged trip. With four chickens to supply him with eggs; he was finally to eat the chickens. He eventually reached Panama, making his way from the Atlantic via the canal to the Pacific, where he lived through terrifying weather, riding out the storm in his cramped shelter in the bow. His landfall in Bora Bora coincided with big troubles with the hotel diesel; in fact the actors who were now living there were in a stage of revolt over lack of lights, shortage of hot water and an abundant mass of unsightly sewage just off the shore where their bungalows were sited. Even Dino's demonstration that there was no problem, by wading into the sea, did not mollify them. Only the heaven sent arrival of Helmut, who understood generators, stopped a mutiny; after months sailing the seven seas he in turn was delighted to have a job.

It was some six months later that Keith and I arrived in Bora Bora to find him still there, having thoroughly tamed the temperamental diesel engine and made the sewage plant work properly. The pay-off to the Helmut story was when he invited us to go aboard his 'yacht', which was moored nearby. We couldn't believe our eyes, when he crawled out of his little cabin to greet us, that it was in this that he had sailed alone from Poland – a dinghy only two feet longer than my Fairey Albacore which I thought twice about taking outside Chichester Harbour into the Solent!

Our first two days were spent recording surf out on the reef while Pepe, our Spanish assistant director, arranged crowds and choirs. A large corrugated iron warehouse building, which had been part of the main film set, was to be used by us, but the Pacific winds gusted through the roof rattling the sheets making recording impossible. During our third night the wind was blowing at gale force; by daylight it was blowing a hurricane, the palm thatch of our bungalow lifting with the gusts, as palm trees bent over showering coconuts to the ground. We noticed that Raphaela's bungalow roof received preventative treatment, planks being laid along the thatch with guy ropes holding them to the ground. Our roof was left to its own devices, but apart from heaving up with the gusts it did at least stay in position. It was an ideal opportunity for us to record some incredible sounds of waves crashing on the shore, wind howling through the huts and palms.

Radio messages were being regularly received from Dino asking for progress to date, with orders to record the choirs and voices no matter the weather conditions. This we did not, nor could comply with, for the whole population were busy barricading the windows of their houses and tying down their roofs.

The Polynesians have a wonderful sense of pitch and rhythm which they put to full effect on Sundays. As Christians they all flock to church; the women and children in their best clothes and wide brimmed hats, the men in suits with collar and tie.

Finally, with everything completed except the recordings of local musicians which were to be used as background for the film, we had to admit defeat. The ambient noises were too obstructive. Everyone on Bora Bora appeared to own a moped; that with the birds made it impossible to obtain a clean track.

Now we were getting more hurry-up calls from London, so at my suggestion we found a recording suite in Papiette, which we used and very good results were obtained. The tail end of the hurricane followed us to Papiette, giving us an even better opportunity to record mountainous waves and crashing surf, with Keith risking life and limb for 'just another film'.

When we were waiting for flight arrangements to be made for our return via Los Angeles, who should we meet but an old friend, Eddie Fowley. He and his brother had been the property men on David Lean's film *Lawrence of Arabia*, and now throughout the film business they are famous for their efforts in sweeping the desert clear of tyre marks and footprints. Since *Lawrence*, Eddie worked on every film of David's, not just as property master, but as confidante and on advance location reconnaissance.

From Eddie I heard that David was in Papiette with Robert Bolt writing two scripts of his *Bounty* project, which was to be backed by Dino De Laurentis. This was planned as a multi-million dollar back to back epic, first the voyage of the *Bounty* and then the subsequent story of Fletcher Christian and the other mutineers on Pitcairn. A full-size replica of the bounty was being built in Wangerai in New Zealand at enormous expense. Every detail above decks was correct; even the sails were being made of canvas in preference to modern synthetic materials; only the shrouds and halyards were nylon. Steering was exactly as on the original ship, by an enormous spoked wheel that needed two men to handle it. Below decks was quite a different story. Apart from the stern saloon with its curved windows, everywhere was fitted out like a modern yacht: a stateroom in which David Lean intended to live; cabins for officers and mess deck for the crew. There was a modern galley, satellite navigation, sophisticated radio telephone, two modern diesels (one to drive the ship through the water and another to supply alternating current for the film lights). There were even plans to run refrigeration pipes up the masts, to create ice on shrouds and rigging for scenes when the *Bounty* sailed in sub-zero weather. Large ballast saddle tanks were fitted which could be flooded or pumped out to make the ship heel over either to port or starboard. The whole project was to be produced under the De Laurentis banner, which was also financing the building of the *Bounty*, while David Lean and Robert Bolt wrote the two film scripts.

Our meeting in Papiette was most fortuitous, for I was offered the film by David; a two-year project based in New Zealand with locations in the Pacific, probably Samoa. Already Bora Bora was ruled out, as the *Hurricane* production had spoiled it for any future film being made there. Keith and I were delighted at the prospect of such a plum job coming our way; however, it turned out not to be, at least not with David Lean.

We returned from Papiette via LA to allow me to go to Goldwyn Studios to deliver our rolls of sound effects shot in Bora Bora. We completed a lightning tour of Hollywood, which included a tour of Todd-AO and lunch with our old friend Fred Hynes. All that remained was to deliver rolls of tape in London to the sound effects editor, an old adversary of mine who over the years had shown a marked lack of appreciation for any of our efforts, no matter how hazardous the circumstances in obtaining them. We were not to be disappointed: in this instance the surf did not surge to his liking, nor did he really like our genuine hurricane tracks, but one can't win 'em all! We certainly were pleased with our efforts which enhanced a not very successful film.

A couple of years later a not unexpected rift developed between David Lean and Dino De Laurentis resulting in David deciding not to go ahead with his films of the *Bounty*. Major Hollywood companies did not see fit to act as backers, which left Dino sitting with a full sized replica of the *Bounty* in a dock in New Zealand, a restraint order nailed to the mast. It would be another five years before her sails were unfurled on screen, but David Lean would not be at the helm.

Having worked for Lord Grade's ITC Company on *Jesus of Nazareth*, I was

The cast of The Flame Trees of Thika, *Kenya, 1977. This was one of the few productions on which I worked for television.*

pleased to be asked to work on another ITC backed film, also for television release. It was to be made entirely in Rome and its environs, and would star Gregory Peck and Christopher Plummer. The director was Jerry London, an American. Apart from myself and my team mate Keith Pamplin, there was to be an all-Italian crew.

I met Jerry with his producer Howard Alston at the Athenaeum in Piccadilly, where they outlined the plot of the film, *The Scarlet and the Black*, which was based on a true story concerning an Irish Monsignor attached to the Vatican, a Father O'Flaherty, who, during the war, had helped to hide some 4,500 allied servicemen from under the noses of the occupying German army; subsequently to be given safe passage via a highly organised under-cover system back to their homes.

With a sound man's immediate curiosity when being briefed, my first query was whether they had taken into account the incessant traffic noise in present-day Rome? Did they also realise that during the occupation there were relatively few motor vehicles, and those that were in use, belonged for the most part to the German Army? As the outline of the script unfolded, it became apparent that they had not really appreciated the problem, especially as they wanted 'direct sound' with minimal post-synchronising, as always.

I began to play down the problem as I did not want them to think I was being over fussy; especially as I knew that I was not the only production mixer they were interviewing. However, having made my point, I left with their 'Don't call us, we'll call you,' ringing in my ears.

Howard Alston did call me to say that Jerry wanted me on his film, adding that he was commencing with a camera crew only for silent shooting, during the first week.

Keith and I were preparing the necessary sound equipment together with a selection of walkie-talkies that had not been requested, but which I knew from experience would be required. Our plan was to travel by truck, driving to Rome through the Alps, allowing for two night stops on the way, so that we could report to the studio in Rome ready for night shooting with Gregory Peck on our third day.

The first night's shoot was a bit chaotic – it is always difficult to become integrated with a unit if one joins it later. However, we had a good friend in Gregory Peck with whom we had worked previously on *Arabesque*, a most enjoyable film that had some memorable moments that included an unscripted encounter with George Brown. The last night's work on *Arabesque* was shot in

Carlton Terrace, Pall Mall. Greg and Sophia Loren were rehearsing a scene when a black car drew up at the entrance to the government's grace and favour residence of the Foreign Secretary. A very drunk George Brown staggered from the car, somewhat dazzled by our lights and made straight for our stars, drooling over Sophia, as he invited them both into his flat. They declined gracefully leaving him to wend his way to his doorway supported by his wife.

Filming was completed at about four in the morning. The electricians were busy making their 'wrap' of lights, lampstands and cables when suddenly a window on the upper floors opened to reveal George Brown. He shouted down to the sparks below, 'Stop that fucking noise, you bastards.'

Harry Black, the chief electrician, or 'gaffer' as they are known, looked up and shouted, 'Don't you fucking shout at me. Come down here or I'll come up and get you.' At that Her Majesty's Foreign Secretary retreated, slamming the window shut.

Our Rome locations were wonderful, sometimes out of doors in parts of the ancient city, then in various libraries, private palaces and of course beside the Trevi Fountain for good measure. One extraordinary location was St Peter's Square on a Saturday. All the crowd barriers had been removed so that we could film the square completely empty, exactly as it would have looked in

Filming in St Peter's Square.

war-time Rome. We filmed from dawn to dusk; on completion the barriers were re-sited ready for the Pope's balcony appearance at mid-day on Sunday.

Gregory Peck, in his role as Father O'Flaherty, had had a cat and mouse relationship with Christopher Plummer's Nazi Commandant of Rome. He had become so exasperated with the comings and goings of O'Flaherty from the Vatican, that he had a two-foot wide white stripe painted across the mouth of St Peter's Square. On one side was Vatican Territory, on the other German. O'Flaherty on one occasion had crossed the line dressed as a nun accompanied by two sisters. On another he defied the ruling, dressed in the full uniform of a senior SS Officer taking the salutes of the patrolling German sentry as he strolled across the white boundary.

Greg stayed out of Rome in the hills being driven every morning to our location of the day where his caravan awaited him for make-up and wardrobe. This was the cue for Keith to go and 'dress' a radio microphone on him. Greg would emerge from the motor home complete in Monsignor's black ankle length robe surmounted by a broad-brimmed black hat. Looking over to me he would say into his microphone, 'Good morning, John – just testing. Have you heard this one about the Pope and the Rabbi . . . ?' Each day he had a new story for my daily microphone check.

One very pleasant surprise came to us on our first Friday evening when Howard Alston had said to us, 'See you on Monday.' We had not known that because the film was being made entirely within the confines of Rome, all Italian unions had an agreement that only a five-day week could be worked by government decree. We were delighted for instead of our usual location week of six days we could enjoy a two-day weekend. Keith and I certainly made use of it, not only seeing all the ancient sites of Rome, but visiting Pompeii, Sorento and Orvieto, whose wonderful dry white wine we were already enjoying with our mid-day lunch box.

John Gielgud was playing the role of the war-time Pope who favoured the Nazis. Our first scene with John was in a palace room doubling for a Vatican interior. It was now August and Rome was like a humid oven. Christopher Plummer and his henchman, played by Walter Gotell, now my friend, were wearing heavy Prussian grey uniforms with close fitting collars, legs encased in jack boots, often wearing ankle length greatcoats. The two of them were to have an audience with the Pope. Having been kept waiting, when they did meet him, they were bathed in sweat. After each take they would strip off their uniform jackets to have their faces mopped with damp chamois leathers.

Meanwhile, John would saunter back to his production chair. In his case he was clothed in a long embroidered robe, little skull cap on the back of his head, but not a bead of perspiration in sight.

I remember remarking how I had noticed in working with him over the years, his imperturbability. His reply was that he had realised that displays of temperament were to no effect and could only be detrimental to himself. He added that old actors like himself were extremely fortunate. After years of long runs in theatre and long weeks of filming, to be offered cameo parts like this one was indeed a bonus. For this six-day engagement, for instance, he had been flown to Rome first-class and housed in the very best hotel. Every day he was collected by a Mercedes, taken to location, given minimum make-up, helped into his costume and taken on the set to a chair with his name on it. In due course an assistant director would call him to the camera for a few words with the director, before toeing a white line to say his words. When the director was satisfied he would return to his chair until they called for him again. There was no point in getting flustered – so many other folk around him were doing that! With his six days' work completed he returned to his home near Amersham; the recipient of a handsome cheque which allowed him to purchase yet another artefact or two for his house.

We had an impressive collection of German army transport whose noise I did not object to when we filmed them tearing through the deserted streets of Rome – they made good sound effects. The dreadful level of Rome's present-day traffic was far worse than even I had anticipated; however, Keith and I did the best we could, putting up baffles and introducing the director to our method of 'wild tracking' dialogue without the camera, where noise had obliterated the voices.

It was interesting to be stopped at times, mainly by women who would say that they had known Monsignor O'Flaherty and how like him in stature Gregory Peck was. Apparently he had been one for the ladies, as well as a keen golfer. His duties mostly comprised managing the Vatican office and were more clerical than spiritual, which might account for his ability to adapt and manipulate the ways of the world to his advantage.

Gregory Peck is such a nice man, very quiet but with a good sense of humour. I just regret that I only worked with him on those two occasions. When we parted in Rome he did say he would like me to work on a production he was planning to remake one of the thirties' classics from the black and white days. Perhaps he was wary of getting his fingers burned, for I remember talking about his film *The Big Country* in which he invested. Much to my surprise he had never seen any return from it in spite of its world-wide success.

His son and daughter both came to Rome during filming and I was very impressed by both of them, for, like their father, they were extremely pleasant, intelligent youngsters. Out of their earshot I had said this to Greg; I was curious to know how he had avoided the problems which frequently beset children of famous Hollywood film stars. He replied that he and his wife protected them in their formative years as best they could, until they were old enough to be sent to Switzerland for further study and finishing schools.

Towards the end of the location we worked at night in the Coloseum, a privilege that apparently no other film had been granted before. It was an extraordinary scene between O'Flaherty and the German Commandant. By now the British and Americans had landed at Anzio and were making their way north. The Germans were in retreat with Rome due to fall to Allied hands.

Christopher Plummer's character had his wife and young family living with him in the lap of luxury in Rome. He had asked O'Flaherty to meet him, where he pleaded for help in getting them out of Italy; for he had known full well of his successes with allied escapees. It was an incredible scene with both of them filmed by moonlight, two solitary figures framed against that timeless back-drop. Finally confronting each other, the plea was refused, and O' Flaherty turned on his heel, leaving the German devastated. In fact he did help the Commandant's wife with her two children. Later after the Commandant was captured and given life imprisonment, O'Flaherty paid him monthly visits in prison for many years, even converting the German to the Catholic faith.

In spite of all our problems with unwanted noise during filming, *The Scarlet and the Black* was nominated for an 'Emmy' award for 'Outstanding Film Sound'; better still, I received the 'Emmy' in 1983 and the golden winged lady has place of honour in my den.

It was a great shame that I was unable to accept the invitation from the Television Academy of Arts and Sciences to go to the States with Jean to receive the award. At the time I was in Kashmir on the final days' filming of *A Passage to India*. I had to make do with a photograph of the 'Emmy' while Jean received the boxed award. However, she had to pay duty to customs at Heathrow before they would release it to her! I never worked out how they could put a value on a guilded statuette with a base filled with lead to make it feel heavy when it was handed over at the ceremony.

Chapter Nineteen

THE BOUNTY

It took two years for Dino De Laurentis to get his *Bounty* project underway but in 1984 I was called up to London to meet the New Zealand director, Roger Donaldson, who had been chosen by Dino to transfer his script to the screen. Anthony Hopkins, who years earlier had been introduced to David Lean as a possible Bligh by Katharine Hepburn, had indeed been cast in the role. He was to give a masterly performance, as indeed were all the stars; the only piece of miscasting to my way of thinking was Fletcher Christian. The American distributors had held out for Mel Gibson to play the part; he was 'the money' as film stars of his stature are known. Fine actor as he is, *The Bounty* does not rate among his most memorable performances.

While we started shooting exteriors at Greenwich Hospital, in a stately home near Southampton for Bligh's court martial and on a mock up of the *Bounty* built on rockers in the studio, the actual ship set sail from New Zealand bound for Moorea, under the command of a ship master who had overseen its construction from the laying of the keel through to sea trials. At long last *Bounty* was being sailed across the Pacific by a multinational crew of enthusiastic youngsters aged from nineteen to mid-twenties, the average age of Bligh's own crew.

Meanwhile the mock-up ship on its tubular framework was being pre-lit at Wembley studios by Ernie Day, the lighting cameraman, ready for the first week of shooting, at the beautiful period house in Twickenham which had been chosen as Captain Bligh's home.

Monday morning saw the usual collection of trucks, caravans and generators lined up on the roadway outside location while inside the house a surprise awaited us. There was no sign of Ernie Day, instead in his place was an equally well-known cameraman, Arthur Ibbetson, complete with his crew. By all accounts Ernie had not seen eye to eye with our New Zealand director, whose ideas were unusual to say the least, and had handed in his resignation before filming actually commenced. This was the prelude to an uneasy atmosphere that quickly made itself felt as the first few weeks went on. Tension and discontent, it seemed, would not be confined to the *Bounty's* crew in the script. Each department received their share of criticism. In our case Keith was accused of being slow on cues in placing his microphone in a particular scene in Bligh's cabin. The director was to call me onto the set with a comment that he wanted me to kick my boom operator's arse. Taken aback, but presuming it was a light-hearted comment, I refused, saying that Keith was a big lad; anyway, we didn't work that way. An invitation to view the offending scene in the theatre with Donaldson was not taken up, but it served as a warning to watch out for trouble in future.

Bligh's court martial sequence, which had been painstakingly researched by Robert Bolt and brilliantly scripted, was equally well cast with Laurence Olivier playing Admiral Hood, president of the court, and Edward Fox as prosecuting officer. With a quite magnificent setting we all looked forward to a very successful sequence, but it started off badly with a delay in make-up and wardrobe for Edward Fox. Lord Olivier, true to form, was ready, made up, dressed in his uniform complete with full wig and cocked hat, and patiently sitting in his place at the centre of the courts table. The director, obviously overawed by the presence of a lord, called me over to be introduced as John Mitchell, his soundman, only to hear Larry say: 'Hello, John, dear boy, I didn't know you were on this film.' His performance was a typical Olivier *tour de force* with his querulous but searching questioning of Bligh. Anthony Hopkins was to say to me later that playing opposite was an experience he would not forget.

By the time we were due to fly to Tahiti we all knew that we were in for a rough trip; if not from the *Bounty*, most certainly from our director. However, the excitement of setting off for parts unknown on a film has always given me a thrill when the plane heads down the runway for take-off at Heathrow.

Our journey was a long one with a stop in Los Angeles, then on to Papiette, our destination. From there it was the familiar hop in light aircraft which Keith and I had experienced on our *Hurricane* jaunt. Soon we were on our way in minibuses to the various hotels; ours not being where the main body of the unit was staying but at a delightful small establishment. It consisted of some twenty palm-leafed bungalows scattered around a main building which was the reception, bar and dining-room, plus kitchen. This was built out on piles over the coral reef of a delightful bay. It was idyllic, but, what was more important, quite new, and not as we were to hear from the rest of the unit, like theirs, which had seen better days and now housed much unpleasant insect

*Anthony Hopkins
in* Bounty.

life and a colony of energetic rats.

A very large art department and construction team had been on Moorea for some months building sets and a complete Dutch style harbour for Bligh's arrival in the Dutch East Indies after his epic voyage in the open boat. Also, a complete Tahitian village had been built in a fold of the hills, along with the bread fruit plantation where Fletcher Christian sowed further seeds of mutiny. During those months disaster struck not once, but twice, with hurricanes which made Dino's previous film storms look like a windy day. The sets were flattened, roads were washed away and bungalows wrecked. For a week or so the whole advance party lived in the only concrete building at their hotel, which was the kitchen. Phone wires were down, no aircraft could fly in or out of Moorea and food supplies were starting to run low. *Bounty*, still on passage, was also subjected to this extreme weather, which was not expected at that time of year. How often have we heard the comment by local people all over the world, 'Goodness knows why you have come here at this time of the year, it is quite the wrong season, you should have been here three months ago.'

The crew of the *Bounty* had been itching to get to sea. By the time they finally reached the haven of our Botany Bay in May, quite a few were ready to quit. They had ridden out two gales and the main engine, which had been keeping the ship with sails furled on course, had spluttered to a stop and had refused to restart in spite of vain attempts by the engine-room crew. Closer inspection showed that sea water had somehow become mixed with the diesel fuel, which meant a complete strip-down of the engine, which was not completed until Bounty had arrived in Papiette under full sail. One of the main spars which carry the rig mainsails had also broken under the strain of the gales. By this time the relatively novice crew were seasoned seamen.

We were to have our first glimpse of *Bounty* lying quietly at anchor in a bay we were to call 'Bounty Bay' – a long, very deep inlet surrounded by jagged tooth-like stumps from an ancient volcano crater which forms the island of Moorea. So deep is this bay that at its entrance the QE2 can safely drop anchor, whilst calling in on world cruises.

Our first task before filming commenced was to set up a radio communications network with a main station in the production office, using a convenient towering cocoa palm as a radio mast. A small boy climbed up its trunk to fasten a rope and pulley with which to haul up our dipole aerial; a similar set and aerial was installed on the ship, with the aerial concealed and camouflaged against *Bounty's* mast, the transmitter-receiver being housed below decks out of sight in the radio office.

Dozens of hand-held walkie talkies were issued each day to assistant directors and helpers who manned check-points on the public roads that skirted the bay. Traffic had to be held up when we were shooting towards the shore. It would not have done for the local bus to pass in the background as Captain Bligh was being rowed ashore in his cutter, to be greeted by the king of the island!

Our very first scenes filmed dozens of canoes striking out from the shore, paddled by fierce looking Polynesians who surrounded Bligh's ship on all sides. The first assistant, David Tringham's, handling of these crowds, who speak French as their native language, as he does fluently, was quite brilliant.

It was obvious that our director spoke not a word of French, nor apparently had he ever handled large crowds, let alone a flotilla of canoes. He was more than content to stand back and leave it to David's voice of experience. The locals entered into the spirit of the scene, egged on by David's exhortations over the Tannoy system, to paddle faster and pass the beautiful Polynesian girls with their waist-long black tresses up into the eager arms of the Bounty's crew. The latter lined the ship's side to have flowered garlands placed around their necks from the first members of the fair sex they had set eyes on since leaving Portsmouth.

With these arrival scenes completed, we were some weeks working on board the ship at sea, moving off by eight in the morning from the quay-side at Coupang. The logistics of getting a film crew with all its equipment on board each morning, stowing everything below decks out of sight of the camera's all-seeing eye, was quite a feat. As the days rolled by, we all laid claim to our favourite hideaway, be it under one of the two long-boats sitting in their chocks on the upper deck, or in the stern cabin below. One of the wardrobe men, poor chap, was always seasick before we had even cast off from the jetty. He

Liam Neeson,
Anthony Hopkins
and Mel Gibson.

had a cache of all of his costumes under a large folded sail beneath one of the long-boats and he would lie there throughout the day enduring the agony of sea sickness.

During our time at sea a choreographer was putting dozens of men and women dancers, who had been recruited in Papiette, through the paces of a traditional tribal dance in the King's village. Here we had scenes of Bligh, his officers and crew, being welcomed with an exchange of gifts, together with speeches of loyalty for 'Kingi Georgie'.

Fortunately in that latitude there is not a large rise and fall of tide, but it did help if we were able to ease away from the quayside with the benefit of high water. Our passage through an opening in the reef was always under power, but once clear, the crew would be sent aloft to set sail, pushing *Bounty* along at a good pace, to take us out of sight of land. During this time we would have expected to be busy rehearsing the day's work, but our director never seemed inclined to do so, not until we had reached the shooting area. Once ready to shoot, the engine had to be shut down so that we could record the dialogue without the background throb from the exhausts which gurgled on the waterline as the ship rolled. Our days at sea were most enjoyable, a unique experience. How many people have actually sailed in a square rigged

Filming with Anthony Hopkins in the Polynesian Islands.

Mel Gibson and
Anthony Hopkins,
The Bounty, *1983.*

ship, especially one faithfully reproduced down to the smallest detail of Bligh's original *Bounty*?

Like many facilities on the film our catering was American-inspired and quite disastrous, being run by a gentleman from California who apparently did not believe that fresh food was available in Tahiti, or if it was would be unsafe for human consumption. As a result we were subjected to a monotonous diet of canned and frozen food, brought all the way from California, in spite of the most wonderful fruit and vegetables growing on Moorea and a sea alive with fish. Things improved a little when he was joined by a man who turned up one day on a bicycle asking if there were any jobs going. This newcomer proved to be our saviour, for he volunteered to buy fresh meat and other supplies in Papiette, which made an instant improvement to the menu. The American caterer, so completely out of his depth, opted to return to California leaving our cyclist friend to take over. It was not for some time that we found out that he had no connection with catering; he was a French geologist who, with his wife, was cycling around the world. They had been forced to stop for a while so that she could have a baby.

Another instance of the hundreds of people who are roaming the world, was the owner of a small yacht who approached our producer with a request for a job. He was made one of the *Bounty's* crew, for with his artificial leg removed and a wooden one made by our stand-by carpenter, he stomped around on the upper deck adding a touch of realism to the scenes. The acting crew had been told that they would not be expected to go aloft, but it was not long before some of the more adventurous were climbing onto the gunwales to take a first few steps in the ratlines. Soon they were climbing higher and higher until they joined the crew proper up on the cross trees furling and unfurling the heavy canvas sails. This added greatly to the authenticity in many scenes, although as an ex-navy man, I was always disappointed that one never saw them performing many realistic shipboard tasks on deck.

It had been decided that the onboard scenes during the stormy passage out from England would be filmed in New Zealand, with the *Bounty* moored alongside an enormous pontoon from which wind machines and water shoots would produce the required weather effects. A famous English special effects man, John Stears, was given the task of preparing for our arrival in New Zealand. John, who had been responsible for many of the earlier Bond films, was well versed in producing the impossible and set about preparing to give our producer all he required. It was decided to shoot the scenes in Gisborne where the large harbour could accommodate the pontoon which John had found three hundred miles north in Wangerai. This was towed to Gisborne where steel girder frames were built on its flat deck, on top of which large tip tanks were secured, fed with thousands of gallons of water by two giant pumps.

Normally wind machines powered by electric motors are available for film work, but as there were no such devices available in New Zealand, John persuaded the owners of four aircraft from the local airfield to remove the engines from their planes and have them bolted onto steel frames to drive the four-bladed propellers. Each engine was operated by a mechanic who revved them up following light cues given from John's control console. The deal with the owners was that the engines would be dismantled and totally overhauled before being put back into their respective aircraft. I have often wondered whether they ever flew again, considering the tons of salt water spray they had been subjected to.

Bounty set sail for New Zealand to rendezvous in Gisborne with John Stears' pontoon to await our arrival. In the meantime we filmed the Tahitian King's reception for Bligh and crew, together with the dancers. The scenes up in the hills above Bounty Bay went quite well, leaving us only the filming of the bread fruit nursery, plus Fletcher Christian's love affair with the chief's daughter.

By now Jean was preparing to join me for the last two weeks of our location on Moorea from where we would both go on to New Zealand, where we had been invited by Yorkey, my *Four Feathers* RAF pal, to stay after filming for a three week holiday before returning home. There were only two telephone boxes on Moorea and to telephone home to confirm the travel arrangements I used to take one of the film unit mini-mokes, and, armed with a pocket full of ten franc coins, drive to the post office by the airfield. Standing under a southern sky ablaze with twinkling stars and the blinding Southern Cross, I was able to dial our number in Cheltenham and get through quicker than it used to take with a trunk call on British Telecom. Apart from the disturbing delay in speech due to the microwave link to Papiette, then through numerous repeaters, it was always a thrill to realise that one was standing on a remote Pacific island feeding coins into a slot and able to talk to someone thousands of miles away.

Jean was to fly to Los Angeles with a rest in a hotel in Papiette, before making the flight to Moorea. I had told her it was quite a short trip by bus, being careful not to tell her the 'bus' was in fact a four-seat light aircraft. I returned from location that evening and found her resting in my bungalow, to be told she had not appreciated my 'bus' ride!

One of the real pleasures of the film was to work once more with Anthony Hopkins, the first time having been on the island of Mull in 1971 during the location work on *When Eight Bells Toll*, followed by his Quasimodo in *The Hunchback of Notre Dame*. Tony kept very much to himself with his present wife, whom he had met on that earlier film in her capacity as production secretary; on occasions, however, he did come out of an evening to eat with us. He is a shy person, quite unlike some of the characters he has portrayed in the theatre or in films, so that it was with an embarrassed query, head on one side, that he asked me one day if Ron, my maintenance engineer, could make him some copies from a cassette. When I asked him 'how many?' his reply of 'thirty-five' came as a bit of a surprise, but I was sure that Ron would fit the transfers in with his evening stint of checking radios and charging batteries. We ordered two packs of tapes from Papiette, chargeable of course to De Laurentis Productions.

The first time Ron played back Tony's original cassette he came running across to my bungalow calling me to hear it. It was a masterpiece of Anthony Hopkin's amazing mimicry, entitled Christmas Eve in the Old Vic. He had

recorded it during our rest day on the previous Sunday. Set in the cellars of the famous Old Vic Theatre, supposedly derelict and now a hostel for aged actors, it had a commentary by Richard Burton whose voice Tony has often been accused of copying, their both being Welsh. It depicts Laurence Olivier sharing an enormous four-poster bed with John Gielgud and, between them, Ralph Richardson. In adjoining dressing-rooms Burton visits, in turn: Alec Guinness, Robert Morley, Peter O'Toole, Alan Badel and Nicol Williamson; he not only has their separate voices off pat, but the vocal mannerisms by which they are so universally known. It is a great shame that Tony has not made a professional recording for a wider public to enjoy – perhaps one day he might be persuaded to do so. Ron's stint at making all the copies took several days; when they were ready we were due to eat with Tony and his wife Jenni again. It was not our turn for a mini-moke for the evening, so Tony offered to collect us in his car into which we crammed, with Ron clutching the precious cassette copies. We had a very pleasant evening chatting over old times together, after which Tony took us back to our hotel. Next morning was an early call to leave harbour at eight o'clock sharp for a day's filming on *Bounty*, shooting scenes of the mutineers arguing whether Bligh and his few loyal crew members should be killed and thrown overboard or cast adrift in a ship's boat. During a lull in shooting Tony came over to me, at my favourite spot on deck, looking his most embarrassed. With his head characteristically on one side he told me that while we had been eating the previous evening all the thirty-five cassettes had been stolen from the unlocked glove compartment; he did not know how to

confront Ron with the news. Anyway, his original copy had been taken. I was quick to assure him that we three sound crew had made copies for ourselves; sound men always do make copies. After all, what were thirty more cassettes to Dino De Laurentis and Ron, I was sure, would slog through the re-transfers for his pal Anthony.

Our leaving Moorea was celebrated with a dinner party given to us by the young French couple who ran our hotel, the Kaveka. It was quite an evening, with presents for the ladies and garlands of conch shells for everyone.

Next day we hopped across to Papiette to await our onward flight to Auckland, giving us two days to see the sights of the French capital island of Polynesia. On my previous visit I had bought a string of black pearls for Jean but had misjudged the size, in spite of trying them on the very pretty girl assistant. They were much admired but not wearable. As I never thought I would visit Papiette again, they had just sat in a drawer. Very fortunately Jean had them with her, which prompted me to seek out the shop in a little arcade complex. I had not much hope but felt it was worth trying to change them. The shop people were charming, offering to re-string them by adding extra matching pearls. It was no trouble, and they even brought in the lady who strung the necklaces to remake the necklace while we waited. After going to all that trouble, they only wanted to charge us for the extra pearls. Only by buying other things could we express our grateful thanks. Next day the six-hour flight to Auckland passed quite quickly and was soon followed by a short transfer into a Fokker Friendship aircraft for a one-hour trip to Gisborne, where we were met by Maori school children dancing to greet us with more garlands in the freezing weather.

All the unit were housed around the town in motels which are mainly small units of bungalows privately owned and very popular in New Zealand. We were given a homely welcome by the proprietor and his wife; and shown our new home, which had been well provisioned by the New Zealand production team even down to the very thoughtful gesture of a 'Bounty' bar on each pillow to greet us. Production headquarters were in a disused supermarket which gave ample space for our equipment, make-up, hairdressing and dressing rooms plus a very excellent canteen. A copy of Bligh's cabin which we had last seen at Wembley studios had been rebuilt for some scenes with a Polynesian princess, who was only cast whilst we were in Moorea, and an embarrassed Bligh.

On the first morning, we soon realised that we had left the warmth of Tahiti; and were much further south, with iced-up windscreens to prove it. I could not understand the reply at a filling station when I asked to purchase an ice scraper; I was told that they did not stock them as there was no call for them!

Our scenes on *Bounty* were also in sharp contrast to those off Moorea but as we needed rough seas for the rounding of Cape Horn sequence, it certainly suited Bernie Williams, our producer, and the director to make full use of the weather. It was a relief though for all concerned when we filmed the closer shots of actors with *Bounty* moored alongside our special effects barge inside Gisborne harbour – except for the actors or cameraman who were subjected to tons of sea water cascading down the chutes on top of them, to be whiplashed by the spray from four aircraft propellers.

One evening back in our motel bungalow I received a call from London, only to hear the voice of Richard Goodwin, partner of John, Lord Brabourne.

Rumour had it when we were completing shooting of their film *Evil Under The Sun* that John Brabourne had acquired the film rights of a book entitled *A Passage to India*. Its title immediately had us all speculating on a shipboard location on a P & O liner. Little did we know that it was in fact E. M. Forster's famous novel set in the days of the British Raj. Richard called me to find out when we were due to complete *Bounty*. He asked for my radio frequencies for use in India, and said that the film was mine if we could meet a start date in late October. With a six-week break between films and ample time to check out our equipment I didn't hesitate in accepting, especially as I heard that David Lean was the director.

Some months later David explained how the picture had been offered to him by Lord Brabourne. For years Lean had tried to obtain the film rights for *A Passage to India* without success. Forster had refused any attempts to film his books, the rights of which had been bequeathed to his old college in Cambridge, King's. Now, many years later, the trustees had been convinced by John Brabourne that he would produce a film of integrity by persuading David Lean to direct. At this point Lean and Brabourne had never met, but with the unfailing efficiency of the film business grape-vine, the news had reached David. A call from John Brabourne had produced the unexpected reply from David Lean, 'What did happen in the caves?' – the teasingly unanswered question in the book and now the film. The script was written by David during the summer of 1983 while locations were searched for and chosen in India, Kashmir and London by Eddie Fowley.

Our stint on *Bounty* finally came to a grinding halt with Dino De Laurentis 'pulling the breakers,' in film parlance, which means cutting off the money supply. My only work remaining on the film was in Auckland to run and listen to the soundtracks shot during the *Bounty's* voyage to Tahiti which might provide useful material for our sound editors. I also made a live radio interview in Auckland which went quite well until the not unexpected question was put, 'How did the British film crew get on with our very own New Zealand director?'

In the interests of Commonwealth solidarity and my friendship with Yorkie I answered, 'No comment.'

A PASSAGE TO INDIA

Six weeks in which to prepare the ravages suffered by our equipment on *Bounty*, in spite of the rough handling of our walkie talkies, seemed at the onset to be ample time. As the weeks passed we realised that the deadline date for us to hand over some sixty cases, each with its detailed list of contents, complete with manufacturer, country of origin, serial number, value and weight, would be very tight. We were well aware that the consignment was being air-freighted in company with cameras, lamps and cables, plus hundreds of costumes; even a couple of period carriages, all to be in Bangalore well ahead of the actual film crew, in order that the Indian customs could have plenty of time to make their painstaking examination of each item against its customs list.

Our flight from the UK to start filming *A Passage to India*, in the October of 1983, was the usual uneventful experience until the stop-over at Dubai, where at least two hundred Indians with family poured on board for a flight home to Bombay. We were not to know until touching down at Bombay that four more similarly laden 747s had also landed, making the baggage hall one mound of suitcases, parcels, bedrolls and rugs, over which a mob clambered to find their belongings. We decided to sit back and bide our time, so it was a couple of hours later that we were transported to our hotel past the shanty towns which housed millions of people, many with jobs in Bombay who are grateful just to have some form of roof over their heads. At least they manage to earn a living, unlike the millions more sleeping rough under the stars.

Flying the few hours to Bangalore was pleasant; our first impression of the 'Garden of the South' very favourable. We saw the administration area with its elegant British-inspired Ministry buildings set off in wide tree lined streets, a statue of Queen Victoria and lesser dignitaries still standing unmolested and free of graffiti, and everywhere evidence of the British Army's bequest of barracks and parade grounds.

As was often the case, Jean was going to join me a week before Christmas, which allowed me enough time to settle into the routine of filming. While we both enjoyed being together, I could sense that on this location she was far from happy. Wherever we went in India, she was constantly upset by the awful poverty that so many people endured. In the end she cut her stay to only six weeks.

Our hotel, the West End, was situated opposite the race-course and had been the guards officers' mess under British rule. Elegant, quintessentially colonial and set in spacious grounds, it was a much used location when we started. The hotel provided ample accommodation for all the crew and cast and still had space for the production office, camera and sound rooms, wardrobe and art department.

Three months before the main unit arrived, the art department had been hard at work making drawings from production designer John Box's sketches, which in turn had been handed over to a considerable force of carpenters, plasterers and painters from England, backed up by dozens of technicians from the Bombay Studios. Apart from some existing locations such as the Bangalore club, David Lean had decided not to risk the hassle of filming in actual settings but to have sets built in the grounds of the Maharajah of Mysore's palace in Bangalore.

My first task was to visit these sets, which were near completion and I was amazed to find a whole street in which was situated the bungalow for the character Nigel Havers was to play. Nearby, rising up on the site of the old polo ground was a complete ship's side of the P & O Liner which brings Mrs Moore and Adela to India. Farther away, but still in the palace grounds, was the framework of Dr Aziz's bungalow, which to my utter dismay was sited some forty yards from the Hyderabad-Madras highway. The constant noise of trucks and buses was a soundman's nightmare, but no amount of protesting could change the minds of the powers that be from putting it there. Thanks to David Lean's professional attitude in all aspects of film making, we struggled against the odds, but much production time, which means money, was wasted whilst I recorded remedial 'wild tracks' of dialogue which had been blotted out by traffic and trains. Sometimes David would query, 'Do we really have to?' which I would counter by saying he would regret not having them when he was back in his cutting room in Pinewood Studios.

Further location reconnoitres were made – in particular to the 'caves', as that site was to be known, situated halfway between Bangalore and Mysore, a prehistoric outcrop of rock, striped with coloured fissures, rearing upwards out of a flat plain. Here it was quiet, apart from the occasional train in the

The journey to the caves.

distance or shrill shouts from women and children in a nearby village. Co-operation with the villagers had been negotiated very early on when Eddie Fowley, the property supervisor, had been faced with filling a pool where an elephant was to bathe. Eddie's first thought had been to hire a motorised pump from Bangalore, but knowing that labour is easily available in India, he hit on the alternative of using the women from the village instead. In this way the swimming-pool sized hole was filled by each woman carrying on her head a brass pot overflowing with water from a tanker some sixty feet below, climbing eighty steps before emptying out her gallon or so. The village was happy, Eddie's budget figure for a pump was far more than he paid them and we had their goodwill for the whole period of filming there.

The actual caves in Forster's novel are farther north and by no means as photogenic as those that Eddie Fowley had found during his search for suitable locations. Also, they were conveniently situated only one hour's trip away for the film crew. They are supposedly some of the oldest rocks in the world; certainly their smooth rounded curves are unique. There was, however, a snag – there were no natural caves or entrances. David Lean and the script demanded three openings, a compromise was made by only blasting out the centre one to a depth of six feet. This allowed the two main characters in the film to move out of camera into the cave entrance. The two openings on either side were just hardboard shapes painted black and stuck to the rock face. The rock is a type of granite, very hard, which even with modern drills took days to cut away. With cunning camera angles the effect was perfectly convincing. Scenes filmed from inside the caves with Dr Aziz silhouetted in the entrance with the blue sky behind him, were actually shot in a set at Shepperton Studios.

What was not anticipated was the reaction after we had returned home from India. The Archaeological Heritage people in Delhi accused David Lean of desecrating the rocks that had survived hundreds of millions of years untouched by nature, only to be spoiled by modern man and his tools in a matter of days. One should go only so far in one's pursuit of excellence.

The rocks were also expected to pose a problem for our elephant, who was thought likely to object to clambering up the sloping rock face to reach the bathing pool; so a complicated system of wooden tracks was constructed in a winding route from the road. When the elephant arrived from the Mysore forests, where it normally worked, it took one step on the wooden path, backed off with a snort and proceeded to march up over the rocks totally ignoring its man-made path.

A good twenty years earlier our co-producer, Richard Goodwin, had worked in Mysore on the film *Harry Black* with our present producer Lord Brabourne. At the time Richard had made great friends with one of the many elephants used in the filming of a tiger hunt scene. To his amazement 'our' elephant

The 'caves' – situated half way between Bangalore and Mysore.

caressed him with his trunk and would not leave him alone. Checking with its minder Richard discovered that it was his friend from years gone by.

I quite enjoy problems being thrown in my lap but I had not been prepared for one tricky little teaser that Richard produced. In the script there was a scene in which the British Residents Dramatic Society performed a *Boy Friend*-type vocal number. I had presumed that the pre-recording would have been made in a London recording studio whilst I was in New Zealand. So it came as a blow when I found that this was not the case and that we were to record a piano and vocal solo with a chorus mixed track for playback purposes. Under normal circumstances this would have been a simple routine; but for us it meant, firstly, finding a piano on which to record the rhythm; then, to play that back through headphones to the solo voices and in turn play piano plus solo to the chorus. With our limited resources this became quite an issue; even down to finding somewhere quiet enough for the recordings to be made. All the pianos we tracked down were hopelessly out of tune. It was only a chance remark from me, when we were almost in despair, that I was given the address of the sister of the Maharajah of Mysore in the belief that she had a grand piano. A visit to her bungalow home on the edge of the palace grounds confirmed this; not only had she one piano, but in her lounge were two Steinway concert grand pianos. On one sat a signed photograph of Rachmaninov, for Princess Rani was a concert pianist in her own right. During a very British afternoon tea, our charming hostess said she would be delighted to help; a date was fixed.

We recorded our backing soundtrack in the quiet of her lounge, but not before she insisted that her piano tuner came from Bombay to tune the instrument. The solo and chorus vocals were made at the German Institute with a Heath Robinson collection of headphones. In spite of the unorthodox nature of the piece, I am happy to say that apart from the addition of an instrumental back-up, our efforts did not have to be re-recorded again in London.

Our first day of shooting drew nigh; a scene in Nigel Havers' bungalow with the arrival of Judy Davis and Peggy Ashcroft. Many of the film crew had never worked with David Lean, which was quite understandable, for fourteen years had passed since his last film *Ryan's Daughter*. For some of those years he had travelled India planning a film on Gandhi with Alec Guinness in the title role, but he was never satisfied with the script. We had met up in Japan, while I was busy filming the sumo wrestling sequence on the Bond film *You Only Live Twice*. He joined me at my vantage point in the massive stadium and offered me *Gandhi* as a future project; neither of us knowing then that he would drop the idea and that Richard Attenborough would eventually make the film.

In the intervening years he became a world traveller, still smarting from the dreadful reception that *Ryan's Daughter* had received in America from the critics. Then he had the idea of making his two *Bounty* films, which sent him off to the Pacific writing, with Robert Bolt, scripts for *The Voyage of the Bounty* and *The Pitcairn Island Story* – another project that was not to be.

That morning in India, when we started shooting *Passage*, was the first time in fourteen years he had said 'action' to actors on a film set. Many of the crew felt sure that the David Lean reputation had been built on the shooting of take after take of a scene; that this would give them time to settle in to a leisurely mode of working. We were ready with equipment checked by eight o'clock. At eight-thirty David arrived in his Mercedes estate car, driven by his young wife Sandy. The three actors were called from make-up onto the set;

A Passage to India – David Lean being blessed. Before filming in India, all the stars, crew, equipment – even the transport – had to be blessed.

and we started a rehearsal and line-up of the first scene. In fact, David took more time setting the props on the dining table, the plants in the pots, than with his actors. He had an incredible eye for detail, finalising the position of the set dressing, always through the eye piece of the camera. I had the theory that he preferred that part of his job to working with the actors! Handing over to Ernie Day, his cameraman, he waited patiently until the lamps were set. With Ernie satisfied with his lighting, the actors were called for a final rehearsal. David then called for a take, with camera and sound switched on, but he forgot to say 'action'. No one responded and he quickly added, 'Oh – begin.' About two thirds of the way through, David rose from his chair under the camera, calling 'Cut-cut', with everyone on the set quite sure that we were to shoot many more takes. To everyone's surprise he said, 'I don't think we can do better than that – print it.'

We were all taken aback that David was printing from the first take, even with only part of the scene covered. But he had such a complete picture in his head of how he would edit, that to have carried on to the end of the scripted scene would only have meant it ending up on the cutting-room floor. He was so totally in command of the situation that only he knew what he needed, which is the reason he has always edited his films with a nominee editor, in most cases to satisfy the union.

That first day's shooting set the scene for the rest of the filming of *Passage*. It was a warning that none of us should presume that the first take would not be the only one; that the actors must be word perfect, technicians on their toes. We settled down to a very pleasant daily routine of an average span of ten hours, apart from travelling to and from some of the locations away from Bangalore. Working with David was a far cry from present-day filming with ridiculously long hours. The whole process, from the writing of the script, the actual filming, until the day when he was in his cutting-room surrounded by hundreds of cans of film and his moviola doing the job he liked best, editing, was a display of sheer professionalism.

With the pattern set, we slipped into the quiet routine of David's well-proven method of working. This is not to say that there were not moments of tension when he became exasperated by things not being ready on time or by a query which so often prompted him to comment 'It's in the script – read the script.' His shooting script was a masterpiece of information, giving precise details of requirement for camera, sound, wardrobe, props or any other facet of the film. I remember well in an early scene where Turton, the 'Collector of

Chandrapore', played by Richard Wilson, was being driven through the market streets to his residence accompanied by Mrs Turton. The car, an open Rolls-Royce tourer, tore past the crowded stalls, horn blaring, just missing the bicycle ridden by Dr Aziz, to disappear through an arch. After the first rehearsal David shouted 'cut', and called for wardrobe to ask why Mrs Turton's veil wasn't streaming out in the car's slipstream. A bemused wardrobe lady said she supposed that the material was too heavy, to which David replied, 'Why don't you read the script, where you will find that there is a note detailing that the voile veil streams out behind her?' A slight delay ensued while a gossamer light veil was produced which streamed out to perfection on the next rehearsal.

Some people find these precise instructions and requirements excessive. I love them, for they are the result of much deliberation during the script-writing process. How satisfying it is to find that tree whose dried leaves rustle outside the courthouse before Adela's trial. Or to read in the script that James Fox's carriage starts off on gravel, onto a smooth surface on such and such a line to pass onto a cobbled road, each change of sound punctuating a progression in the drama of the scene.

The little mountain railway which snakes up fifteen miles of steep track to Ootacamund, with its cog wheel biting into the centre rack rail to stop it running back, was a soundman's dream. So too was the engine itself, with its fussy chuff-chuff, steam escaping from the cylinders and its whistle which the driver played almost like a musical instrument. We recorded every facet of that railway in detail: the microphone close to the driving wheels, then favouring the carriage wheels and clanking couplings, the rattle of windows slack in their frames, over the viaduct and up through the narrow gorges hewn from solid rock to enter a tunnel and emerge from the other side into the station at Ootacamund, or 'Ooty' as it is affectionately known. There the everyday noises of patient passengers with all the baggage and belongings which Indians seem incapable of travelling without, gave us further material for the sound editor. Even then, some sounds are missed, or it is presumed that they were not recorded. It gave me quite a kick when David, in his cutting-room months later at Pinewood Studios, said, 'Ah, just the chap I want; did you record the train whistle at Ooty as it came into the station?' My notebook lay on the sound editor's bench; there was a soundtrack number with the number of the roll of tape, FX 104, and the note 'Train entering Ooty station with whistle blowing, engine stops past microphone.' David called for the roll, ran it on his moviola, marked off about three feet of film, tore it off between his teeth to have it

Location filming on A Passage to India.

joined into his cutting copy, remarking, 'I knew you would have recorded it.'

He could be equally dogged in his persistence with the cameraman in obtaining a result that matched a description in the script; sometimes waiting patiently for a cloud to position in his camera's frame, but never for three months for the right waves as he has been accused of doing on *Ryan's Daughter*.

One outstanding requirement in those early days was to find a military band which would play for the arrival of the Collector and his wife at Chandrapore station, and even more importantly for the garden party scenes in the palace grounds in Bangalore. After turning down a band from the local garrison in Bangalore we travelled to Mysore one Sunday to audition what had been the palace band of the Maharajah, but in recent years was re-designated the Mysore Police Band. Their playing was much better; not so polished as to sound like a performance of the band of the Royal Marines, just sufficiently discordant to be credible. Arrangements were made for the crew and I to travel to Mysore over the next few Sundays to record the various numbers required for the playbacks used during the filming of the scenes.

Our first trip on that audition day should have been a warning that each time one travelled the sixty miles between Bangalore and Mysore one was taking a huge gamble on not arriving in one piece. These main artery roads in India have to be seen to be believed: crowded with people on foot, others on bicycles, some with impossible loads. I have seen a dozen or more cases of eggs tied up with string to the rear carrier of a bike which completely obscured the cyclist from behind. Along the verges on either side of the road would be people driving sheep or oxen, with overloaded trucks belching out clouds of diesel fumes from badly tuned and worn-out engines, enough to make a present day 'green' turn greener. Our mode of travel was in one of India's Hindustan cars, better known in Britain as a Morris Oxford of the 1950s; the original production line had been sold by Cowley to India when the model became obsolete in the UK.

Certainly it had transformed road travel on that continent with its simple side-valve engine, cart type semi-elliptic springs and easily repaired body. We soon found it expedient always to walk around a taxi inspecting the tyres for bulging slits in the walls or for signs of canvas through bald patches on the treads. Any further inspection of brakes and what lurked under the bonnet had to be taken as read, but it was always advisable to check that the tank was full of petrol. Such things as side lights and headlights could only be proved efficient when darkness fell. In any case we always made sure that our return journey from Mysore was in daylight, for travelling on Indian roads at night is a dangerous business. An ox wagon with no lights, or a pedestrian with a bale of straw on his head, followed by his wife with a brass urn full of water on hers, can loom out of the murk, quite oblivious to the frantic hooting of a taxi's horn, the only component of any car in India which always worked unfailingly.

We became quite attached to our Mysore band and its conductor who enjoyed our Sunday recording sessions. One ended with their abandoning their brass instruments, and setting up a sort of palm court ensemble so that we could record the *Boy Friend*-type number for use as playback in the amateur dramatic sequence. The band were even more delighted when they found out they were to be filmed playing at the garden party, decked out in resplendent green uniforms topped by splendid red headgear.

The location in Ooty for the mountain railway scenes was quite an expedition in its own right. It entailed a hundred and fifty mile trip, passing Mysore through teak forests to climb ever upwards to the hill station, where the British spent summer months in the cool, away from the stifling heat of the plains. They had left their mark everywhere; the church had gravestones and English and Scottish names. The club was still clinging to its past glories of

The Mysore band playing for David Lean.

Chatting with David Lean whilst filming in Bangalore. I knew him from my early days at Associated Talking Pictures, Ealing Studios, in 1934.

days of the Raj, with its billiard tables and bar still presided over by a steward who had known those former days. We were accommodated in what had been the English school, now a hotel, with rooms that had not changed for over half a century and a dining-room run by a manager who still watched over the waiters with an eagle eye. The menu was just as it had always been: steak and kidney pudding followed by spotted dick or treacle tart.

Our first room was in an annexe, small, cold and filthy, the carpet a dirty grey colour from congealed dust that had accumulated from the twig switches wielded by sweeper ladies; in India the universal tool used in streets, gardens and houses. Hot water was non-existent, so by the second day we opted for a suite in the main building, redolent of even more period elegance, but with a bathroom that worked. All was well until our last night when Jean, who always heard the slightest sound, woke me to say that something was moving in the room. I turned over telling her it was nothing to worry about, but she was adamant, and when I took a closer look discovered a rat about as big as a cat. I spent the night heaving fire logs at it. It finally vanished probably just as exhausted as I was.

Fortunately we were going to return to Bangalore that next morning, setting off on the one hundred and fifty miles which lay ahead, down the winding roads with hairpin bends before reaching Mysore and the plains. After a break for lunch we started on the second half of our journey and had barely left Mysore when we were stopped by gangs squatting across the roads. This was an organised picketing by farmers who were dissatisfied with the price of cereals set by the government. The bodies on the road were rent-a-mob, nothing to do with farming, just earning a few rupees a day for blocking traffic between eight in the morning and six at night. Unfortunately for us the first picket let us through, but at the second, several miles on, it was a different story. They refused to let us pass. Sitting in a steel car body in that heat was no joke, so we decided to return to the first friendly picket, go back to Mysore and wait until evening. In the meantime the attitude of the first picket had changed. They refused to let us go back, some clustering round the car rocking it violently until the ignition was switched off. Near to midnight we finally rolled into the West End Hotel weary and stiff. That ghastly day reached rock bottom when we discovered that our room was occupied! It wasn't long afterwards that Jean decided the time had come to return home.

David's first encounter with Victor Bannerjee who played the main lead, Dr Aziz, did not suggest an immediate affinity between them. Firstly, Victor was quite naturally very nervous of his director, who complained after the first rehearsal that his voice was too English. True enough Victor had attended a school in Calcutta based on English public school lines; his voice had none of the lilt that David wanted, Victor refusing to speak like Peter Sellers. Eventually a compromise was reached, but Victor would never give that little roll of the head on a loose neck which to Westerners seems to typify Indian men. The lilt in the voice and the head roll became an obsession with David, who would plead with small part actors, saying, 'Why can't you do it? I see all India do it except you.' It was not until he was reminded that most of the actors concerned were born in Bradford or London, never having seen India before, that it registered. They had been flown in because Actors Equity insisted that most small parts be played by members of the union.

Most of the Indian feature players also refused to co-operate in spite of David's entreaties; ironically Alec Guinness went to great pains to adopt these mannerisms. He even stopped off in Delhi to learn a mystic song with a bare-footed dance, while playing finger cymbals; his tutor was a Brahmin who also instructed him on how to deport himself. Alec was always thorough in researching his part. The chant was to be sung as Alec was paddling in the pool at James Fox's home. The script also called for him to perform a strange dance in the final scene of the film, taking little steps bare-footed around the perimeter of an enormous cart wheel lying flat on the ground, with occasional traverses across the spokes, punctuated by the sound of his finger cymbals.

David Lean's decision to cast Alec in the part of the Brahmin mystic Godbole, made many Indians wonder why the part was not to be played by an Indian actor. Some people thought that it was a natural extension of the long Lean-Guinness relationship stemming from their first film in 1946, *Great Expectations*. It is a matter of opinion whether this final coming together was to be another triumph between director and actor. We were already well into our filming before Alec joined us in Southern India, where he had scenes to play with James Fox, Judy Davis and Victor Bannerjee.

Our producer, John Brabourne, approached me on our 'caves' location one day, saying that he would like me to arrange to record Godbole's vocal chant on the following Sunday, which was scheduled as a rest day. However, he asked me not to tell David as Alec was most emphatic that he shouldn't hear it until the day we filmed the scene. This was typical of a soundman's lot, pitchforked into the dilemma of trying to placate one party and keep the other in ignorance. I knew and feared that sooner or later David would ask to hear it.

Finding a place quiet enough to make the recording was not easy. In the end I decided to use the projection room where we viewed our 'rushes'. This was situated deep in the interior of the Maharajah's palace, but it was quite reverberate, so I resorted to my standard practice of assembling a booth, draping it with heavy layers of underfelt to produce a 'dead' effect, in which we could sit Alec and microphone.

Sunday came and we assembled in our recording studio. I was quite heartened when Alec said, 'This is just like old times'; I had used the same method with him in Havana when recording dialogue wild tracks. The session went well, with him making several takes. Finally he chose one which pleased him as being suitable for playing back in that final scene in the film.

Not long after I had committed the chant to tape, we had been shooting scenes in James Fox's home film set. The following day was scheduled to be spent on a scene where Godbole, lifting his dhoti above his waist, would paddle in the pool. It was David's intention to film the Brahmin's reflection in the surface of the shimmering water. He called for us all to remain for a rehearsal at the end of shooting, using Godbole's stand-in; Alec having been dismissed for the day. Typically, David tried many ways to get the reflection effect he wanted. Nothing satisfied him until he found he could achieve a much better result with the camera upside down. At that moment Alec strolled by, showered and changed into his shirt and slacks ready for dinner. Seeing David apparently struggling, he volunteered to get into the pool, saying that he had a much better idea. Taking off his slacks, he slipped into the pool in his Y-fronts with water up to his thighs, to show our director his version. To my horror, as Alec

Cast and crew of
A Passage to India,
photographed by
Snowdon.

was towelling off on the pool side, David turned to me asking if I had a playback of Godbole's chant. Alec looked across at me, realising that I had not spilled the beans and volunteered to sing it there and then. David listened with his usual intensity, not a sign of appreciation or dislike on his face; nor did he make any comment to Alec. I had read the signs by that silence before, nor was I wrong, for as we packed our equipment in the darkness of the evening he turned to me saying, 'I shall not be using Godbole's song in the film.'

However, a scene where the old Lean-Guinness magic really worked was Mrs Moore's departure by train at night from Chandrapore on her way back to England. Mrs Moore had built up a rapport with the Brahmin Godbole – they had an uncanny understanding of each other. As the train pulled out of the station she looked from her open carriage window to see the figure of Godbole framed in the doorway of a track side warehouse opposite. Alec, almost silhouetted in his white robe, made a tiny gesture of the hand, which with the following close-up of his face framed with his gold rimmed spectacles told more to the audience of Mrs Moore's impending death at sea, than any words could have done. David's delight at Alec's performance produced the comment, almost under his breath of, 'Clever old bugger'. From David that was praise enough.

Alec Guinness was due to finish filming with us in Srinagar, the capital of Kashmir, where he had a scene with Dr Aziz, who in the story left his former home in India to open a surgery, far from the memories of his terrible experiences at the hands of Anglo-Indian justice. On the evening of Alec's final day, I was chatting to him at our hotel when he told me, 'These past few weeks have been the most unhappy of my whole career.'

There is no doubt he gave of his best, but I honestly felt that he knew he should not have played the part of the Brahmin. Some of the critics were not too kind at his portrayal, but never forget it was also David's intention to cast him as Gandhi in his film, which was planned and scripted long before Attenborough's version. David had spent several years on research and location-hunting in India finally to decide that his script did not do justice to that piece of Indian history.

The plan in Kashmir was for us to work in the old town of Srinagar in a wonderful set built down on the river bank, then move up to the snow-line for the final scenes of the film. I had always imagined that Kashmir with its houseboats moored alongside the lake would be quite idyllic; I was to be disappointed. In the first place the drive from the airport was strewn with hoardings exhorting the purchase of rugs and knick-knacks. The houseboats were moored stern onto the bank with scarcely six feet between them, easy prey for the waterborne sellers of tourist junk.

The people, quite different from Southern Indians, are taciturn, with Persian features. Men, women and children all appear enveloped in long heavy cloaks beneath which show alarmingly distended stomachs. The reason for this striking disfigurement soon becomes apparent, for under their cloaks they clutch a round earthenware pot full of glowing charcoal – a wonderfully cheap, portable central heating system, but also responsible for a high incidence of lung cancer.

Work progressed quite well, though we missed the discipline of our Indian crowds. The Kashmiri do not react to pleas or threats like 'clear camera' or 'quiet please.' Final scenes with Victor, James Fox and Sandy Lean, as his film wife, were completed at 10,000 feet in the rapidly thawing snow, before we returned to Shepperton Studios. It was there that we filmed the famous court scene, where Dr Aziz is arraigned for rape, before Adela dramatically refutes the charges following a searching grilling from the defence counsel.

John Brabourne and Richard Goodwin had given us all a New Year party at the West End Hotel, Bangalore, complete with entertainment under the trees which were festooned with thousands of light bulbs. Nearing the end of our stint in India, David and Sandy decided to give a unit party and farewell to our Indian friends on the film. Sandy decided not to hold it at the hotel, but had very cleverly found what had been the Maharajah's stable compound situated in the middle of the palace grounds. This was by no means derelict, but its original white walls sadly needed a lick of paint. The whole complex was a four-walled building with a large square in the centre around which ran a balcony. As our painters were virtually finished working on the sets (only the Mosque was left to shoot on) she had all the walls painted white. Across the width from wall to wall were hung the strings of lights which are so popular for any occasion in India. Chairs and tables were placed in the square and the catering was provided by kind permission of Location Caterers mobile kitchen presided over by Roger Jones. It was unfortunate that Jean had returned to London, for I know she would have loved the setting, which might have helped her like India more.

Apart from Peggy Ashcroft's misfortune to miss her footing and fall as she came down the balcony steps, which necessitated a hospital X-ray, though fortunately no further treatment, the party was enjoyed by everyone. At the end of the evening I was thanking Sandy and David for a wonderful time when he said, 'Out of one hundred and seventy people that silly woman had to be the only one to fall and hurt her ankle!' His exasperation was understandable; our very next scene scheduled was in the mosque, where Mrs Moore wanders into the moonlit building to be confronted by Dr Aziz, who admonishes her for coming into a holy place with her shoes on. 'Oh but I took them off,' she says – cementing from that moment their friendship between east and west.

There was no doubt Peggy was in considerable pain, but as an old pro she worked through the several nights as scheduled. David had not struck up an affinity with her from the start. He was impatient with the way she sometimes appeared slow to grasp his instructions. To our eyes she was giving a performance worthy of her usual wonderful talent and reputation. Indeed, she was to be awarded an Oscar as Best Supporting Actress, one of the only two that *Passage* received from its ten nominations; the other being for Maurice Jarre who was awarded his for Best Original Music Score, adding another Oscar to his collection for best musical scores on David Lean films. *Passage* should have won more Oscars; unfortunately for us the Americans found Mozart that year with *Amadeus*, which meant that for the second time I missed receiving an Oscar for Best Sound.

David could have strong likes or dislikes for actors. Richard Wilson, now well known by TV audiences for his portrayal of Victor Meldrew in *One Foot in the Grave,* could do no wrong. This was not the case with poor Clive Swift, who played the doctor in the British colony. He had a terrible time with David from his very first scene at Nigel Havers' gate, in which he delivered only one short line of dialogue that brought down David's wrath on his head. He again has made his name with great acclaim on television, most notably in the series *Keeping Up Appearances*, in which he plays Patricia Routledge's hen pecked husband.

David did not get on with Judy Davis, but conversely thought the world of Nigel Havers, who years later told me that David had put his name forward to Stephen Spielberg for a part in *Empire of the Sun*, the first of many such recommendations.

Judy Davis and David never built up an affinity, in fact, many times they were at daggers drawn to the point of impasse, but that particular court scene in the film is a masterpiece which her Oscar nomination duly acknowledged.

As soon as we completed shooting back at Shepperton Studios the pressure was on David to deliver the completed film in time for possible nominations for Academy Awards. The Academy ruling is that a film must have been shown on release by paying audiences in America by a certain date. *A Passage To India* made this date but the film did not qualify for BAFTA awards as it had not been seen by cinema audiences by the British closing date for nominations. This was a great pity in my opinion, though it only received two Oscars – I am sure it would have received more BAFTA awards.

Jean and I had already received our invitation to go to Los Angeles for that annual jamboree of the Oscar ceremony, at the Dorothy Chandler Centre. Before that was the Royal Premiere at the Odeon Leicester Square in the presence of HRH Queen Elizabeth the Queen Mother, The Prince and Princess of Wales and Princess Anne. Again we were invited to attend this, to be followed by a dinner at the Savoy.

A few days before the occasion I received a call to say that I was to appear in the royal line-up. The stars, David Lean, big wigs from Columbia Pictures and a host of people not involved in the making of the film were to be presented before the showing of the film. We from the film's crew were to be presented after the performance. This I found to be much more satisfactory for the Royal party, who having just seen the film were able to ask far more pertinent

With the Queen Mother at the Royal premiere A Passage to India, *Odeon Leicester Square, 1985.*

With Princess Anne.

questions. Certainly Prince Charles and Princess Diana were quite searching and I remember that she was not the shy young woman with downcast eyes I had expected, but one who looked straight at me when asking about the film. Princess Anne asked about the magnificent colourful saris and was interested in the little conductor of the band.

It was the Queen Mother who surprised me the most. She said, 'I understand that you have been many years in the film business.' It was in fact then my fifty-second year and I was aged sixty-eight.

'Yes, Ma'am,' I replied, 'fifty-two years, but I do not like it to be made public.'

'Why not?' she asked, to which I replied that Lord Brabourne, if he knew that I was of such advanced years, would probably never employ me again. The Queen Mother roared with laughter, saying that my secret was safe with her!

Back in Shepperton Studios there were scenes in a train sleeping compartment between Peggy and Judy and of course the final and most important trial scene. At work I wore, as is my wont, a jacket and tie; Sandy, spying this, called David over pointing out my tie. David looked me straight in the eye, saying, 'I suppose they all wear ties in Cheltenham.' Although David was invariably immaculately dressed in a collarless navy blue jacket, his white shirt was always buttoned up at the collar, with never a tie in sight. My reply was that I would wear a different tie every day until filming was completed.

People frequently commented on the size of David Lean's ears. They were huge, like human parabolic satellite dishes and equally effective. During this time at Shepperton he would often call me to join him in his mid-morning viewing of the previous day's 'rushes', before the unit as a whole saw them at lunch-time. His comments about the image on the screen or the performance of an actor could be quite cruel, often prefaced with, 'You are about to see quite the worst ever . . . !'

On one such occasion he had gone to the theatre leaving me a message to follow on. He had already started the rushes, so I went up into the projection room intending to go down into the theatre on a change of reel. Making some aside to the projectionist as I stood looking through the porthole at the screen, I was surprised when a young cutting-room assistant came in to tell me, 'Mr Lean says to come down now.'

There was proof enough that no one should ever question the efficiency of those famous ears!

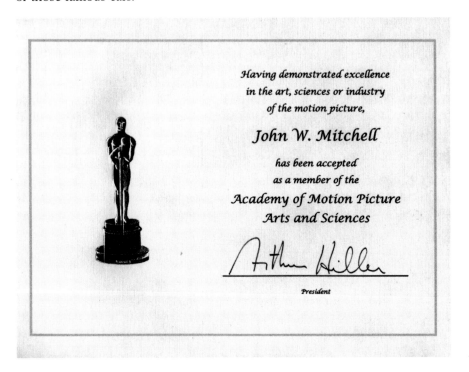

Having demonstrated excellence
in the art, sciences or industry
of the motion picture,

John W. Mitchell

has been accepted
as a member of the
**Academy of Motion Picture
Arts and Sciences**

President

Chapter Twenty

Closing Credits

Towards the end of filming *Passage* I passed the remark that I thought I might 'pack in' work – after all, I was sixty-eight.

'Don't be ridiculous,' David Lean replied, 'If you do that you will keel over.' Of course I hadn't really meant it.

In the course of editing *Passage* David was looking for his next project, helped by his personal assistant Maggie Unsworth. He finally decided on *Empire of the Sun*, but a visit to China convinced him that it was not for him, leaving it to Steven Spielberg, who had already purchased the film rights for David.

Joseph Conrad's *Nostromo* had always been a favoured possibility, particularly by Robert Bolt, David's long-standing scriptwriter and partner. A first script was written in co-operation with Christopher Hampton, but did not meet with the approval of Warner Brothers. This was followed by second and third scripts and by 1990 there was a stronger possibility that the film may have been made later that year.

I wonder if fate had been kind to me. Three years previously Jean had developed a heart problem – I most certainly would not have been able even to contemplate working on the film while she was unwell. But she made incredible progress from those early days of my looking after her, thanks to the miracle of Beta drugs. I too had been hospitalised twice; the first time with a renal collapse, followed by surgery for the removal of a malignant tumour from which I made a remarkable recovery to my former rude health.

In December 1990 I received a call from Nice to say that *Nostromo* was to start filming in the spring of the following year; sets were already being built at the Victorine Studios. Ulrich Picard, the French producer's production supervisor, had already discussed a deal with me two years earlier when it was planned to base the film in Madrid. In fact I was sent out to Madrid to look at two sites for a complete town film set, to give my opinion on the most suitable one for sound. This was obviously at the instigation of John Box, the production designer, with whom I had previously had a difference of opinion on *Passage* over his placing Dr Aziz's bungalow alongside the Hydrabad-Madras highway.

On this occasion, one site was on the flight path to Madrid airport, the other nearer to the city but alongside a motorway. By using the high walls of the film set as a baffle, the second site was obviously the best option, with less travelling time daily.

Picard tried to tie me down to working with a foreign crew, in reply to which I asked if he had ever worked with David Lean. Of course he had not, so I asked him to thank Sir David for inviting me to work with him, which I much appreciated, but that I was sure that he would only want me with the crew both he and I knew! At eight o'clock the next morning my phone rang and on the line came 'Ully' from Nice, asking for the names and addresses of my two crew members. That was 'round one' to us; followed by a protracted 'round two' as we haggled over money and the small print of the contract.

With that all settled, we began at Pinewood Studios in my store-cum-workshop, preparing a list of equipment which I deemed necessary after a careful reading of the script. From then on we followed the usual routine of checking each piece of equipment, packing it into its own transit case and making up detailed lists complete with serial numbers, country of origin, values, etc., for Customs yet again.

By mid-January all was packed and ready for freighting. Then a bombshell dropped – David Lean was unwell. He was returning to London for tests, as far as we knew, to remedy a throat infection. This turned out to be far more serious. I telephoned him when he was back at his fantastic converted warehouse home in Wapping. He would soon be better, he assured me; it would not be long before we would all be together to make *Nostromo*.

It was not to be; David died in March. *Nostromo* was cancelled. The sets at Victorine were 'pack struck'. In Almeira, where other sets were being built, all work was stopped. We received a curt letter advising us that our services would not be required.

In a way I have a great debt of gratitude to David, for I should never have contemplated leaving Jean. She had urged me to accept the film, saying that she would be fine with Anne and her husband Peter and our wonderful doctor, Pat Healy, to look after her. I had selfishly wanted to work with David again, for I would have been in my seventy-fifth year when the filming was completed. At the time, I was not to know that Jean and I were to have only nine more months together.

In May of 1991, I received an invitation for us both to attend a memorial service at St Paul's Cathedral for David Lean, planned for the October. Jean said she must buy a hat for the occasion. In spite of my protesting that it was some six months ahead, her reply was that she did not want to leave things to the last moment! Without delay, 'the hat' was purchased after much deliberation; of course it was one of the most expensive, around eighty-five pounds.

As the day of the memorial service approached I decided that we would stay at the Tower Hotel, only ten minutes from St Paul's, so that we could return there after the ceremony before taking a cab to David's home at Wapping. Then my daughter called to ask if I had remembered the steps into the cathedral, for Jean found steps a problem. I had completely forgotten, in spite of having sat on them many times on location with my equipment. Anne told me not to worry; her husband, who worked in the City, had noticed a side-door off the street. On checking with the verger he was told it serviced a lift which went up into the body of St Paul's. This solved our problem.

The Cathedral was packed; some 2,500 people were there to pay their respects. We were honoured by being in the second row. In front sat David's new wife Sandra (widowed after only three months). Robert Bolt was there with his wife Sarah Miles, so were Peter O'Toole, Omar Sharif, cameraman Ernie Day and Oscar winning art director John Box. There was the Royal Philharmonic Orchestra, conducted by Maurice Jarre, who had been awarded four Oscars for best music on Lean's films. A solo lady pianist played the Rachmaninov piano concerto that had permeated the atmosphere of *Brief Encounter.*

Maggie Unsworth, David's continuity girl from *In Which We Serve to A Passage to India,* and first assistant director David Tringham, carried two velvet cushions on which lay David's decorations, together with the numerous awards, almost too many to count when they were placed on a table before the service commenced. (Later Maggie told me that as she was walking the full length of the nave, she had noticed Alec Guinness sitting unobtrusively at the back near the big main doors.)

Tributes followed from O'Toole, Sharif and Sarah Miles; matched by an extraordinary demonstration of will power by Robert Bolt, who spoke movingly of his long association with David, in spite of the severe speech impediment he had incurred from a massive stroke suffered in Tahiti, when they had been collaborating on the *Bounty* scripts.

Melvin Bragg spoke from the pulpit of his friendship with David over the years. Fortunately for posterity, he had spent a lot of time with our film crew in India during the making of *Passage,* followed by a long interview in Wapping with both David and Robert during the writing of the final *Nostromo* script; this formed invaluable archive material in the history of British cinema.

I am sure that David would have looked down to say 'Jolly good show' – particularly at the finale, when the congregation were leaving to the sound of the Bands of the Household Cavalry, The Royals and Blues, playing 'Colonel Bogey' on the steps, as permission had been refused for them to play it in the cathedral. That tune had contributed so much to the success of *The Bridge On The River Kwai*, it was not surprising that it became his 'anthem' and that 'Bogey' would haunt him and be played wherever he appeared. Not surprisingly I had asked our Mysore band to play it whenever they were with us. Generally, David emerged from his car first thing in the morning to find us all standing to attention and saluting.

I was so happy that we had been part of that great day. Even more that 'the hat' had been worn. Jean had looked really stunning; she had great dress sense and colour co-ordination. Within two months I would lose her, and one of the most heart-rending aspects of my bereavement was the disposing of her wardrobe. Anne helped tremendously; but I was still faced with the task of

Opposite.
Plenty – Meryl Streep, Sir John Gielgud and Charles Dance.

Meryl Streep, Plenty, *1984.*

actually taking her clothes to charity shops. The last few bags that I took to the Imperial Cancer Research shop in Windsor included the famous hat. Quite by chance it coincided with Royal Ascot – I was assured that it would find a ready purchaser who would happily pay generously for it.

One thought saddened me, and continues to bring pangs of grief; Jean must have been lonely so often when she was on her own and I was away – working, to be sure, but always in the company of others. Our reunions were always wonderful – she would meet me at the airport, sometimes after months of separation. Only when she had gone did I know what it feels like to be alone. I missed her so very much – and always will.

I was to be asked continually if I would return to films. For several reasons I decided that the answer was 'No'. There is very little work available; the industry is in a sad state. And I doubt that I would fit in with today's whizz-kids, nor would I expect them to want an old-timer like me. Also, the ridiculous hours that film people are now expected to work, often for a six-day week, is something that I experienced in the bad old days and have no wish to repeat.

Over a period of fifty-three years I had worked on 156 films. Three films

Plenty. *Director Fred Schepsi seated under camera (centre).*

followed *A Passage to India* – *Family Ties* with Michael J. Fox, *Plenty* with Meryl Streep and Charles Dance, and *Manhunter* with Brian Cox – but after David Lean died I realised that last film with him had marked the summit of my career. I had known David since my early days at Ealing Studios, back in 1934, when I had been a junior projectionist and he had a cutting-room next to my projection room. Through the swing-door with its wire-mesh window I had watched him at work on his moviola. Even then he had an air of authority that radiated his complete grasp of the art of film making. We had worked together on *Great Expectations* in 1946 and then spent the next thirty-seven years managing just to miss each other as films came and went. *A Passage to India* reunited us. Half-a-century separated our first encounter at Ealing and that reunion in the grounds of the West End Hotel in Bangalore.

'Flickering Shadows' they may be, but individually we had worked hard over the years to bring them to Roger Jones's 'silver screen' and we were proud of our achievement.

David's Passage marked the end of my own 'passage'. 'The Kid' was settling into retirement, with a story to tell – and a book to write.

In my den,
Cheltenham, 1997.

Appendix – A Tribute to Cubby Broccoli

On the 17th November 1996, I was invited to the Odeon Leicester Square where a celebration of the life of the late, great Cubby Broccoli was attended by over two thousand of his colleagues and friends. It must have been unique in cinema history that one person could fill that 'temple of art', as I once heard Edward G. Robinson describe it.

It was a very happy occasion, a meeting together of old and new faces who thronged the Odeon foyer resisting the pleas of management to leave in order that the paying customers standing outside in pouring rain could take their seats nearly half an hour late. I am indebted to Donald Zec for allowing me to include his wonderful testimony to Cubby in my book:

'Cubby Broccoli died June 27, 1996. He was eighty-seven and had fought a valiant and characteristically good-humoured battle until the end.

Much of a man's worth in life can be measured by the quality of the reaction to his passing. The global tributes to the man born Albert Romolo Broccoli were unanimous in their recognition of his triumphs as a film-maker. Not least his good taste, his flair, and his intuitive rapport with millions of cinemagoers.

On television, radio and headlines around the world, the eulogies confirmed the universal truth; Cubby's contribution to motion pictures, James Bond in particular, was manifestly unique. If 007 had become a legend so too had Cubby. As the London *Times* noted:

"The founder (with the late Harry Saltzman) of the James Bond films, Cubby Broccoli, was one of the most successful producers in Hollywood. An American, it was his genius to perceive that the adventures of a British secret service agent could make the stuff of international box-office."

Further admiration was accorded to Cubby's film, *The Trials of Oscar Wilde,* now a much-repeated film classic.

It was for this, as much as for the staggering success of 007 that Cubby Broccoli received the Irving Thalberg award, the jewel in the crown of motion picture achievement. Rarely given, it is the highest award a film-maker can receive.

It would be nice to think that previous winners like Alfred Hitchcock, Walt Disney and Cecil B. de Mille were on hand up Above to congratulate their friendly, fellow recipient.

But the newspaper eulogies were unique for other reasons. They reflected universal affection for the man. The familiar producer stereotype of Cubby's day scarcely radiated sweetness and light. As old campaigners in the trade will remember, many of Hollywood's leading film-makers were more like predators than producers.

But to stars and studio hands as well as Maitre D's and parking valets the world over, Cubby Broccoli was the one, glowing exception. Despite all his successes, international awards, and distinguished friends in many countries, Cubby remained the gentle and unaffected character everybody liked and most of us loved.

He may have been designated as "Albert Romolo Broccoli" for his Order of the British Empire and similar distinctions elsewhere. But he was always "Cubby" to intimates and subordinates alike; to Ronald Reagan, George Bush and Prince Charles, and to his friend, the late Howard Hughes long ago.

We understand the incalculable sadness of Dana Broccoli and the family. But it is their wish that we celebrate, not mourn.

Today, appropriately in the cinema where 007 was born, we can salute the man who nurtured it into legend. And remembering becomes a joy.'

DONALD ZEC

Publisher's Note

Flickering Shadows was intended partly as an entertaining and fascinating story of a lifetime in film and partly as a tribute to a much loved genius of sound who has enjoyed a long and distinguished career in the industry and is now retired. However, literally a few days prior to printing, John Mitchell was approached and asked to come out of retirement for one last film – *The Dance of Shiva*.

Conceived by Jamie Payne of Epiphany Productions, who is also to produce and direct, it is hoped the film will be a watershed that reintroduces the once-traditional mini second feature to cinemas. The making of the film is itself to be the subject of a documentary film which will show two distinctive facets of technical and artistic expertise – the most brilliant of young newcomers to the industry working alongside the greatest of the greats: cameraman Jack Cardiff, production designer John Box and sound production man John Mitchell.

These films enjoy the wholehearted support of Sir Sidney Samuelson, British Films Commissioner, for their potential to be used in training within the film industry worldwide and as a wonderful demonstration of the skills of the British film industry past, present and future.

Index

cont: Films by John Mitchell

FILM	YEAR	DIRECTOR	STAR
The Spanish Gardener	1956	Philip Leacock	Dirk Bogarde, John Whiteley, Michael Hordon, Cyril Cussack
The Prince And The Showgirl	1956	Laurence Olivier	Laurence Olivier, Marilyn Monroe, Richard Wattis, Sybil Thorndike
The Iron Petticoat	1956	Ralph Thomas	Katharine Hepburn, Bob Hope, Robert Helpmann, Richard Wattis
Reach for the Sky	1956	Lewis Gilbert	Kenneth More, Muriel Pavlow, Lyndon Brook, Alexander Knox
These Dangerous Years	1957	Herbert Wilcox	Frankie Vuaghan, George Baker, Carole Lesley
Miracle in Soho	1957	Julian Amyes	John Gregson, Belinda Lee, Cyril Cussack
Windom's Way	1957	Ronald Neame	Peter Finch, Mary Ure, Michael Horden
Seven Thunders	1957	Hugo Fregonese	Stephen Boyd, Tony Wright, James Robertson Justice, Kathleen Harrison
Rooney	1957	George Pollock	John Gregson, Muliel Pavlow, Noel Purcell, Barry Fitzgerald
The Wind Cannot Read	1957	Ralph Thomas	Dirk Bogarde, Yoko Tani, Ronald Lewis, Anthony Bushell, John Fraser
Floods of Fear	1958	Charles Chrichton	Howard Keel, Anne Heywood, Cyril Cusack, Harry H. Corbett
Operation Amsterdam	1958	Michael McCarthy	Peter Finch, Eva Bartok, Tony Britton
The Thirty-Nine Steps	1959	Ralph Thomas	Kenneth More, Taina Elg, Barry Jones
Upstairs and Downstairs	1959	Ralph Thomas	Michael Craig, Anne Heywood, Joan Hickson

FREELANCE 1959-1985

FILM	YEAR	DIRECTOR	STAR
Our Man in Havana	1959	Carol Reed	Alec Guinness, Noel Coward, Ralph Richardson, Maureen O'Hara
The Battle of the Sexes	1960	Charles Crichton	Peter Sellers, Constance Cummings, Robert Moreley
Conspiracy of Hearts	1960	Ralph Thomas	Lilli Palmer, Sylvia Simms, Yvonne Mitchell, Ronald Lewis
The Boy Who Stole a Million	1960	Charles Crichton	Maurice Reyna, Virgilia Texera
The Grass is Greener	1960	Stanley Donan	Cary Grant, Deborah Kerr, Jean Simmons, Robert Mitchum, Moray Watson
The Man Who Couldn't Walk	1960	Henry Cass	Eric Pohlmann
The Bulldog Breed	1960	Robert Asher	Norman Wisdom, Edward Chapman, Ian Hunter
Very Important Person	1961	Ken Annakin	James Robertson Justice, Stanley Baxter, Leslie Phillips
Waltz of the Toreadors	1961	John Guillermin	Peter Sellers, Margaret Leighton, Cyril Cusack
The Fast Lady	1962	Ken Annakin	Stanley Baxter, Jmaes Robertson Justice, Leslie Phillips
Bitter Harvest	1962	Peter Graham Scott	Janet Munro, John Stride, Thora Hird, Alan Badel
Call Me Bwana	1962	Gordon Douglas	Bob Hope, Anita Ekberg, Lionel Jeffries
The Sporting Life	1963	Lindsay Anderson	Richard Harris, Rachel Roberts, Colin Blakely, Alan Badel, William Hartnell
Human Jungle (TV Series)	1963	(Various)	Herbert Lom
From Russia With Love	1963	Terence Young	Sean Connery, Robert Shaw, Bernard Lee, Lois Maxwell, Pedro Armendariz, Lottie Lenya
Hot Enough For June	1963	Ralph Thomas	Dirk Bogarde, Sylva Koscina, Robert Morley
Mister Moses	1965	Ronald Neame	Robert Mitchum, Caroll Baker, Ian Bannen
Those Magnificent Men in Their Flying Machines	1965	Ken Annakin	Terry Thomas, Sarah Miles, Eric Skyes, James Fox, Gert Frobe, Tony Hancock, Benny Hill
The Spy Who Came in From The Cold	1965	Martin Ritt	Richard Burton, Claire Bloom, Bernard Lee, Oskar Werner
Arabesque	1965	Stanley Donan	Sophia Loren, Gregory Peck, Alan Badel
Drop Dead Darling	1965	Ken Hughes	Tony Curtis, Zsa Zsa Gabor, Lionel Jeffries
The Pleasure Girls	1965	Gerry O'Hara	Ian McShane, Francesca Annis, Klaus Kinski
Casino Royale	1966	John Huston & Others	David Niven, Peter Sellers, Ursula Andress, Orson Welles
You Only Live Twice	1966	Lewis Gilbert	Sean Connery, Donald Pleasence, Charles Gray
Billion Dollar Brain	1967	Ken Russell	Michael Caine, Karl Malden, Oscar Homolka, Francoise Dorleac
Chitty Chitty Bang Bang	1768	Ken Hughes	Dick Van Dyke, Sally Ann Howes, Lionel Jeffries, Gert Frobe
On Her Majesty's Secret Service	1969	Peter Hunt	George Lazenby, Dianna Rigg, Telly Savalas
When Eight Bells Toll	1969	Etienne Perier	Anthony Hopokins, Jack Hawkins, Robert Morley
Le Mans	1971	Lee H Katzin/John Sturgis	Steve McQueen, Ronald Leigh-Hunt, Elga Anderson